THE GAME
My 40 Years in Tennis

THE GAME
My 40 Years
in Tennis

by
Jack Kramer

with
Frank Deford

G. P. PUTNAM'S SONS
New York

Copyright © 1979 by Jack Kramer with Frank Deford

Library of Congress Cataloging in Publication Data

Kramer, John Albert, date.
  The game: my 40 years in tennis.

  1. Kramer, John Albert, date. 2. Tennis players
—United States—Biography. I. Deford, Frank, joint
author. II. Title.
GV994.K7A34 1979   796.34′2′0924 [B]   78-31299
ISBN 0-399-12336-9

To Mom and Dad who gave me the chance and to Gloria and the kids who kept me going.

Contents

Foreword

I was interested in working with Jack Kramer on his memoirs because I always found him so fascinating on the subject of tennis and so unique to his sport. Jack has been at the center of things since the 1930s. He not only knows where all the bodies are buried; often enough he has been the body himself.

He has been successively, amateur contender, amateur champion, professional challenger, professional champion, professional tour promoter, amateur junior tennis official, television commentator, Davis Cup coach, professional tennis official, amateur tennis official, professional tennis tournament director, amateur tennis tournament director, players' union director, international tennis council executive. And probably there are a couple of other positions that have slipped my mind for the moment.

But the list should be sufficient. Every sport has its grand old men—coaches or administrators who have been on the scene for years. But invariably these fellows have held the same job, usually in the same place, for most of their tenure. What is so special about Kramer's knowledge and attitudes is that they have been obtained from such various perspectives. He was a player first, and it is ever obvious that his greatest affection—his bias if you will—lies with the athlete. But just as true: he has so often had to deal with (against) players in his other capacities that he can be as harsh on them as any critic who never lifted a racket.

I really can't think of anyone like Kramer in any other sport. It is the true measure of his command of the whole game that his recall—which is prodigious—includes as much detail for gate receipts and the rate of exchange as it does for the scores of sets.

Jack is nearing sixty now, but he is nostalgic only in the most agreeable of ways. He is never misty about the past, but he is always loyal to it—especially to his contemporaries, who had a much tougher road to hoe than the fellows making fortunes at the game today. Tennis has had such a sudden growth of popularity that there is a tendency to believe that nothing of consequence happened in the sport until Tracy Austin and Bjorn Borg reached puberty. Having been along every step of the way, Jack is able to keep history on an even keel. He has a wonderful idiosyncracy of keeping everybody eternally, equally young: everyone, even present octogenarians and those old-timers laid in their graves years ago, is referred to as "kid." Add to this his vivid memory, and sometimes it seems that tennis time has stood still, that a kid like Tilden and a kid like Connors might very well be playing this afternoon at the Merion Cricket Club.

In a sense, I think that Jack has been too involved in the game for the good of his own legend. Because he has been such a controversial figure—he has the singular distinction of being fired from ABC and the BBC, of being sued by Pancho Gonzales and Jimmy Connors alike, of being excoriated equally by the mossbacks of the United States Lawn Tennis Association and by the rebellious Billie Jean King—it has sometimes distracted people in tennis from remembering how great a player he was. However good Kramer was (he himself says Budge was the best) we'll never know, because the one thing Jack was never given in tennis was the proper foil. He never had any unforgettable matches. He beat everybody to pieces. Bobby Riggs was the champion Kramer dethroned, but Riggs didn't act or look like what the public considered to be the correct champion, so the feat was diminished. Kramer then routed Pancho Gonzales when he was too young to extend Jack. So Kramer never had a proper challenger, as Big Bill had his Little Bill and the Musketeers, as Vines had Perry, as Budge had von Cramm, as Gonzales had a succession of Australians, as Borg and Connors have one another now. And this is more a pity because Kramer was such a superb match player that there is no telling to what heights he might have risen had he had someone to push him. I don't know if Jack Kramer is the best player ever; on the other hand, I have to wonder whether he could be beaten.

Of course how very good Kramer was as a player is not crucial to his memoirs, except in the sense that excellence is likely to indicate a superior knowledge of the game. And he didn't miss much. He can be as candid about players' abilities as about their personalities.

I think you'll find in reading what follows, which is Jack's book, that he is a very shrewd and a very warm fellow, and tennis has benefited most by his odd confluence of traits because the kid has worked very hard at improving what he loves so much.

—Frank Deford

1

The Kid

While I have spent a great deal of my life traveling—and still do, to my wife's annoyance—I live a very settled life in many respects. We have been in the same house in Los Angeles for thirty years, and most of both our families are nearby. I have had the same wonderful secretary, Cile Kreisberg, for twenty-five years. Gloria and I have been married since 1944 and we have five boys, the youngest of whom is in college now. All have played tennis, and one has even taught it down at Vic Braden's tennis college, but none has ever pursued it seriously. The boys were brought up by their mother, for I was traveling, and I can never thank Gloria enough for what she did with the kids. I feel especially guilty that I was never able to give my boys what my father gave me.

You see if you want to know anything about Jack Kramer, you must start with my father, because he's the guy who made me. In a nutshell, what is good about me is a gift from my father, and what is bad is my own doing. It is a great comfort in life to grow up secure in the knowledge that your father is the finest man in the world.

Learning to play tennis was easy after my father got through teaching me ethics, integrity and fairness. He told me to be a standup guy, with no alibis; shake hands firmly and look people in the eye. That's corny and old-fashioned, but there's plenty of time to get to the forehands and volleys.

My father's name is David Christian Kramer, he was born in 1899, and he is still alive and sharp. He retired many years ago from the only job he ever had, with the Union Pacific Railroad. At the end, he was a senior engineer, Los Angeles section. He worked hard all his life—let me tell you, *any* tennis money is easy money, because I saw a man earn hard money in hard times—and Dad never asked for a thing. When he found out they had raised his pension payments a few years ago, he looked into it, because he didn't think it was right.

My mom's name was Daisy. She made the dough go a long way, and she was the one who kept the family together, always organizing get-togethers and outings. Gloria and I have continued this. I was an only child myself, but my aunt, Betty, who was only twenty-two months older than me, came to live with us when I was a little kid, so she was just like a sister. We had a wonderfully happy home, the four of us—my mother was such a comforting person—but I was only eight when the Depression hit. My father always had his job with the Union Pacific, but like a lot of my contemporaries, I know I am still affected by having grown up during those times. I know it is foolish, and I know it must have something to do with my Depression insecurity, but I carry a great deal of cash on me. I always have a couple thousand bucks in my pockets.

I live a comfortable life now. I stuck with tennis when it was a relatively small sport and it paid off. I can't even play social tennis anymore, however, because my right hip joint has deteriorated. This has been getting progressively worse, and eventually the joint will be replaced, but the doctors say it is best to hold off from an operation for as long as possible. Now I can't even play golf without a cart. I can still hit the ball. What the hell, I can hit the ball. I could hit baseballs, ping-pong balls, tennis balls, golf balls. It's a gift. I played in Bing Crosby's tournament up at Pebble Beach for many years, making the cut seven out of thirteen times, but I had to write Bing a few months before he died and pull out for 1978 because I just couldn't walk around the course.

But I don't want to sound like I'm an invalid. I'm not. I was skinny as hell as a kid. I never had to worry about my weight, and I always ate all the wrong things. Now I'm a few pounds overweight because I can't move around as well, but I still eat all the wrong things. I ought to get out everyday and swim but I don't do it, even though my doctor, Omar Fareed, screams at me to do it. I smoke cigars (when I'm out of the house), but I gave up whiskey because I contracted hepatitis in 1977. Now I drink that new low-calorie beer. I've always got many things to do, most of them involving tennis somewhere in the world. It's been a terrific life, and I should get in five sets because my grandfather Kramer lived to one hundred and two, my grandmother to ninety-six, and my father is a kid of eighty. Of course, none of them had to play Pancho Gonzales, bet Bobby Riggs, argue with Billie Jean King or compete in the marketplace with Lamar Hunt.

The fact that I played tennis so much of my life probably made me a narrow person in some ways. I didn't go past my freshman year of college, which broke my father's heart because no Kramer had ever gone to college before, much less graduated from one. (My son Bobby finally broke that record, so Dad feels a little better about me now.) Of course playing tennis all over the world must have had a positive effect on me, which I probably wouldn't have attained with a more conventional education and experience. You would have to be a dimwit to travel all over the world and not pick up street smarts. The trouble with the kids playing today is that everything is done for them. Their agents or managers or coaches or somebody takes care of the works, and they've become so dependent on others for the simplest decisions that I don't think they're going to be prepared to make the really important decisions that will face them once they're outside of the sport.

Donald Dell, my friend the agent (The Lip, I call him) says the kids need nursemaids to free their minds so that they can concentrate completely on playing tennis. But I think it works the other way. When all that is unpleasant is removed from your everyday existence, you're not worth a damn on the court in a pinch. You don't know how to be resourceful and work something out. Nothing makes me sicker than watching Vilas look over to his coach, Tiriac, to find out what he's supposed to do.

I didn't just travel. I was a travel agent as well as a tennis player most of the time. I promoted, I organized, I publicized, I chased down deadbeats, I signed, I dealt, I smuggled. If there was one impression I gained early on it was that the American dollar was the one great constant in the world. I have never forgotten that. It scares me to see what has happened. Very few Americans know what I mean because they never saw the dollar in other places, where it was the only thing that really counted. I can't tell you how many days of my life I spent scuffling around black markets all over the world trying to trade whatever currency I had for U.S. dollars. One of the most vivid memories of my life came with the news of Pearl Harbor. I was an amateur playing in Santiago, Chile, with a group of American players who were part of a Rockefeller exchange program, and the first thing all the Chileans did when they heard the news was go downtown and start buying up dollars. And we were the ones who had been bombed. I can still see the lines stretching down the block. The value of the dollar doubled right away.

So these things stay with me. Maybe that's why I carry so much cash. All things considered, I've always been a conservative person in most things, while I have always been listed as a revolutionary in tennis. I had the so-called big game, which was a flashy knockout style, but in fact I played house odds. Then as a promoter, I was accused of wanting to turn tennis upside down, but all I was really trying was to pattern it after golf, which was more successful and popular than tennis. Good or bad, I've been very consistent through the years, especially if you take into account my upbringing in tennis and my upbringing in life. It all follows naturally.

I was christened John Albert Kramer, but I was always a Jack. It's funny but on my first professional contract my name is typed out John A. Kramer, but you can see where I started to sign Jack Kramer from instinct and then felt I had to stop and go back over it and write the formal John A. Kramer. I'm also known as Jake to a lot of people—Big Jake. That is not merely a variation of Jack, but it comes from playing cards, where a lot of gamblers call the jacks in the deck "jakes." I can't remember exactly where I picked up the Jake, but it must have been quite early, because I can recall being known as Little Jake. Then Riggs called me Kid. But then, Riggs has always called everybody Kid.

And eventually, Riggs aside, I started to become Big Jake.

Card playing came naturally because I was born in Las Vegas on August 1, 1921. Gambling was not legalized in Nevada until 1931, but Vegas was a tough railroad juncture in the '20s, and no one would have mistaken it for Boys Town. There were a whole lot of people passing through, and there was a great deal of action. One of my earliest recollections is sitting in a gambling joint with my dad, listening to the World Series on the radio.

Dad had sworn off gambling the day I was born, but we still lived near the heart of things. We lived on Fourth Street, and Fifth Street is what became The Strip. There weren't many places to stay in Vegas then, and we would take in dealers as boarders. I would have to give up my bed and sleep on the porch. It was probably one of the dealers who tagged me as Little Jake. The dealers taught me a card game named Coon Can—it was something on the order of gin rummy—and even as a kid I was a damned good card player. But more important, the dealers taught me odds, so that I don't think it is a coincidence that I ended up as a percentage tennis player. A lot of the very best players—Hoad, Connors, Ashe, Goolagong—haven't learned when to play it close to the vest, when to raise, when to go for the whole pot. Connors draws for

17

an inside-straight every time. I don't think anybody in tennis ever played the odds better than I did.

Dad began as a railroad man on the Union Pacific when he was only eleven. He did what was known as "calling crews," which meant going down to the bunkhouse at dawn and waking the men up. My grandfather, John David Kramer, was a barber. The Kramers came west from the little mountain town of Cumberland, Maryland, sometime in the late 1800s. It's funny, but the only time I was ever in Cumberland was the first time I ever got any under-the-table money for playing amateur tennis. On the other side, my mother was born in Prescott, Arizona, back when it was still a territory. I am a Westerner, there is no doubt about that.

Since Dad had never had any chance to play childhood games he wanted me to have every opportunity for fun. He was a brakeman when I was growing up, and his schedule was built for me; he was on call for thirty-six hours, then off for forty. We had a lot of time together. We'd play ping-pong on the dining room table. He helped me build a pole-vault pit in the yard. I ran races. I was a basketball nut. The first trip I ever made was on the sixth-grade basketball team. We played a team in Caliente, Nevada, and I roomed with a teammate named Popeye Powell who was a black kid. Things were more open out where we lived. I played football too and broke my nose tackling a bigger kid at the age of seven. But baseball was my best sport. I could catch anything as well as hit, and I honestly believe I could have made the big leagues as a first baseman if I hadn't gotten into tennis.

Union Pacific had a tennis court—actually it was a basketball court with tennis lines painted over it and an old net that could be hung up—and Dad, who was game for anything, scrounged up a couple of old rackets, and we went out there together and batted the ball around. It was just another way to spend time with my father. I didn't take it seriously. I never suffered the prejudice that tennis was a sissy game either, which was a common rap at this time. For one thing I played all the other tough sports, and for another, out West all the major kid's tournaments were held on public courts. So tennis really didn't have the reputation of a country-club game.

We moved to San Bernardino just west of L.A. in 1934 when I was in the seventh grade. The Pittsburgh Pirates took their spring training there, and I got to be one of the batboys. But San Bernardino is primarily important because that was the first place I ever even *saw* a good player. His name was Robin Hippinsteil, and I used to watch him play on the public courts. Soon I was getting up at six to play with Robin's younger brother Glenn. By now Dad had been required to take a voluntary Depression pay cut, from $240 to $180 a month, but somehow he always found a way to divert a few bucks to me for sports.

After Dad's year of special railroad training, we moved back to Las Vegas. By then gambling was in, legally, and there were more tourists. We'd made a few extra bucks escorting them out to see the Hoover Dam being constructed. But for the fall, for the eighth grade, Dad was called back to San Bernardino for another year's work, and it was this time when my tennis really took. You can never be sure of the moment you decide on something, but I'm sure that what won me to tennis was an exhibition I saw at the Pomona County Fair—probably the spring of 1935. Robin Hippinsteil was still about the best I'd ever seen on a court, but at Pomona on a clay court set up for the racetrack grandstand, Ellsworth Vines played Les Stoefen and Big Bill Tilden himself played. He would have been past forty then, and he went up against Bruce Barnes or George Lott, I can't remember which one. It doesn't matter. Even Tilden did not affect me that much. He was the name everyone knew, but Vines was the champion. Vines was tall and thin, at the height of his powers, and I had never conceived of anything so glamorous. If you never saw tennis players in their long white flannels, I cannot begin to explain to you how majestic they appeared. Nowadays everybody walks around supermarkets wearing tennis outfits, but then tennis clothes were a rare elegance that could transform a man. Don Budge, for example. Don is many wonderful things none of which is

19

handsome, but in tennis whites he looked like a matinee idol. And Fred Perry. Fred Perry in a linen shirt, matching pants, everything tailored: there was never a champion in any sport who looked more like a champion than Fred Perry. I know very well that you can't stop progress and that fashions change—after all I was the first Wimbledon champion ever to wear shorts—but in my reverie I don't believe there has really ever been another champion who really looked like a champion since Vines and Budge and Perry. Kramer and Gonzales and all those guys in short pants must have been pretenders.

In any event there I was at Pomona that day in 1935: thirteen years old, a poor kid from the desert. And here is Ellsworth Vines, 6'2½" tall, 155 pounds, dressed like Fred Astaire and hitting shots like Babe Ruth. From that moment on I never again considered concentrating on any sport but tennis. When it was time for my father to return to his job in Las Vegas, he decided that it would be better to risk taking a lesser position in Los Angeles and to stay where I could better develop my tennis.

Now understand, Dad wasn't taking out any tennis annuity on me that he figured to cash in on a few years later. At that time there was no reasonable expectation that anyone could make a good living from tennis, and apart from the fact that I did well at all sports, there certainly was no evidence to suggest that I would reach the top. In my first tournament, the Dudley Cup in Santa Monica in April of 1935, I was eliminated in the first round. No, Dad just decided it would be best for all of us to stay in Los Angeles because I loved tennis and because he loved me, and because Mom wanted to get us into a different world from Vegas.

Up until that point I knew nothing about tennis. I played with one grip for all shots, so I just swatted at the ball and ran all day. My racket was a Tilden Topflight, an old-fashioned model with an open throat, and I showed up at that first tournament in a brown mohair sweater. It was like another world. The other kids all had on perfect tennis whites, Tilden V-neck sweaters, and they all carried two or three shiny new rackets. It was quite a gathering. Little Bobby Riggs was there, little Joe Hunt, little Ted Schroeder. Throw in the unknown little Jack Kramer, and there were present at this one junior tournament four boys who would win six U.S. Nationals titles within the next dozen years.

Before I left Santa Monica, stunned and beaten, someone kind suggested that I see a man named Perry Jones at the Los Angeles Tennis Club and pick up a schedule of area tournaments. Jones, of course, ran the Southern California Association. He was Mister Jones if you wanted to go anywhere. Mister Jones wasn't a snob the way a lot of people pegged him, but he was very prim and proper. At one time or another he turned against Riggs for being a kid hustler and against Gonzales for quitting school to play tennis. But I was a conscientious kid, and Mister Jones especially liked the way my father handled me, so he kept his eye on me from the first. He certainly didn't go overboard until I came through some, but Mister Jones wanted a nice-mannered boy.

And I began to get my bearings. We had moved to the town of Montebello—still east of L.A.—and I'd take the Number 3 streetcar several miles to Southgate for tournaments. Or I'd take two buses and a streetcar to get to La Cienega Park. I also played a lot at a park closer to my home named Boyle Heights. The competition might not have been so good, but it was a very competitive situation: loser paid for the balls—no exceptions.

Then my father found me a pro. His name was Dick Skeen, and he was a tremendous help to me. Skeen was not some kindly uncle type, though. As a matter of fact he could be a sour kind of guy—and I'm not kidding you; here it is almost fifty years later, and if I mention somewhere the people who coached me, if I don't give him enough credit he'll write my father a letter. Well, Dick Skeen does deserve to be mentioned and to be given a great deal of credit for my early success. Dad gave him $5 a month, and out of that Skeen furnished the balls and provided good competition. He was a terrific player himself (we had some great practice matches as I grew older) and he attracted a lot of good kids. He was especially good for

21

me because he was so tough that I worked hard to please him and learned to concentrate.

Skeen taught me and his other pupils on a private court he used up in Altadena, north of Pasadena. It was thirty-six miles round-trip for my mom and me. She was my transportation and my toughest critic. (As a working man my father seldom got to see me, and then he picked all the wrong times. In 1936 I won seven of ten tournaments and he managed to get to the three finals I lost.) The court where Skeen taught belonged to the family of a kid named Jimmy Wade, who was then the Number 1 ranked boy and a helluva prospect.

But these things can turn around in a hurry at that age. Wade was all chops and slices, but when he shot up he lost all his coordination, and that was the end of him as a contender. I grew into my body, Skeen changed my grip, and he taught me to control the ball with spin. I improved so quickly under Skeen that that winter my father made me choose between basketball and tennis. He told me I was too tired and irritable to play both and I had to pick one. Of course I picked tennis. Basketball is very good for tennis footwork and stamina, and I did come back and play first string my senior year in high school; but at the time, I chose to concentrate on tennis, and when I went back to the Dudley Cup in Santa Monica the next spring (1936), I was unseeded but I won it. And now all of a sudden I was everybody's sweetheart.

By coincidence too, it was about this time when I broke with Skeen. He wanted me to play doubles in tournaments with one of his students whose main attribute was that he was a wealthy pupil, while my father and Perry Jones wanted me to partner another kid who was a much better player. So Skeen got mad and dropped me from his squad. But Jones began to take care of me. He paid my entrance fee of $25 and enrolled me as a junior member in the Los Angeles Tennis Club. He also put me on the Spalding Free List, which meant that I didn't have to buy my rackets, and he gave me $50 and sent me off to Culver, Indiana to play in the National Boys' fifteen-and-under (it's now the sixteen-and-under). My father scraped up $100 in cash, and he also gave me a blank check, signed, in case I needed it. I came back with $7 and the check, uncashed, plus the national singles and doubles championships. In one year I had come completely out of the blue to become the best boy player in America.

Actually the way it worked was that the best boy player in Southern California was almost automatically the best in the country. In the years leading up to the war, there was hardly a major boys' championship that a Southern Californian didn't win. We had more tournaments than other parts of the country, we had better competition, we had one central place—the L.A. Tennis Club—where all the best players congregated, and perhaps more than anything else, we had concrete courts. I'm going to get into this in a lot more detail later because I think the whole world is now entering the era of the concrete court, but I've always thought that the kid who learned to play on concrete had the edge over the player who learned on grass (too slick) or clay (too slow).

Once I shot to the top I had only a few more defeats as a kid player. The one that hurt the most was when Arthur Marx, Groucho's son, beat me in the semi's of the California Interscholastic Championships—at a match played at eight o'clock in the morning. That cost me the chance to duplicate Riggs' feat of winning that title three years in a row. When Bobby won the three it had given him permanent possession of a fascinating cup that dated back to 1896. But you know what he did? He gave the cup back because he didn't think it was right for him to own something that had such symbolic value. Even as a boy there were these curious contradictions in Riggs.

Thanks mostly to my father, I was an easy reliable kid for Mr. Jones or anyone else to handle. The minute I started to show any kind of big head Dad would call me "Cocky" and stick me right back in my place. One time when I was just starting to win, I began to think I was a big shot, and I carried on a running argument with an umpire. When he called me for a foot fault, I blew my stack altogether and threw my racket over the fence. I looked up then and saw my father approaching the umpire's chair. I felt like a million dollars: my old man was going to show this guy that his boy couldn't be pushed around. Yes sir!

After a few seconds of conferring with Dad, the referee suddenly stood up, waved his arms, and announced that the match was over, the win going to my opponent by default. My father had called it off. Our discussion was very brief. "Cocky," he said, "you ever do that again, you'll never go back on a tennis court as long as you live in my house."

I never lost my temper that badly again. Oh sure, I had a breaking point. I played thousands of matches in my lifetime, and there were a few times when I was fatigued—cross and irritable like a kid—when I exploded. But generally I was well behaved, which is no big deal, because in my time so were virtually all the champions.

I never got that worked up over tennis officiating. To this day I think that the players and the press and the fans make too much of a fuss about the quality of the officiating. In football they're breaking the rules, holding illegally, on every play, and nobody gets nearly so worked up about that as they do when some poor linesman blows one call in the third set. A lot of the kids playing forget, too, that the linesmen are volunteers who are donating their services so that the players can make more money. The players are always screaming that they want a traveling corps of professional officials, but that suggestion always dies when the players are asked to fund such a corps out of their own purse money.

The thing I've noticed about almost all bad calls is that they are made before the ball lands. Even the most incompetent linesman should be able to tell whether a ball is in or out—and they do. The trouble is, the bad ones get in a groove and start assuming before the ball hits. That's why I think the let—play the point over—is a good idea, so long as it is called by the chair. I know the argument that you don't throw a pitch in baseball over again if there is a dispute, but tennis is different in that everyone in the stands can see where a ball lands more clearly than they can tell how it crossed the plate. There is something intrinsically wrong about letting a bad call stand just because it was called that way first. If we can repair damage then let's do it.

On the other hand, the existing situation where the umpire in the chair can autocratically overrule a linesman is wrong, because that undercuts the guy on the line. If in the umpire's judgment there is a genuine question, okay, play the point over—but don't reverse it arbitrarily. If you allow that, you might as well get rid of linesmen.

Spectators of course can be used to a player's advantage. The crowd always loves the kid who, in a grand gesture of sportsmanship, throws away a point after his opponent has apparently been cheated out of the previous point. In fact that's a sham that is not sporting on two counts. Number one, it is a slap in the face to the linesman. And second, practically speaking, if a kid is really going to be so noble, he must throw two points to make up for the one unjust call. And of course nobody ever does that.

Another thing some modern players do, which I find inexcusable, is to "remove" a linesman they don't like. It's a bad system to start with—should Tom LaSorda have the right to throw out a home-plate umpire who called a close one against the Dodgers?—but it is made even worse by the way the players rant and rave at the poor official. There were a few times when I felt a linesman was incompetent, but there is a polite way of having him cleared off the premises.

First of all you've got to assume that everybody is going to blow a couple of beauties sometime. So before you blow your top, give the man a chance. But if he throws in a couple more dubious calls, then very quietly, I would question him: "Are you sure about that?" "Gee, it looked out to me." That kind of stuff—just to let him know what's in your mind. If he gave me another bad call then, I would finally confront him. But I would do it as privately as possible, and during a break in the action—say after an even game. I would say: "Look, I'm sure your calls are correct, but I'm on edge tonight, and I've got it lodged in my mind that you're missing. And I'm thinking about that now, and that's hurting my game. So if you'd do me a favor, when you get a chance let somebody else come out and call this line."

And nine times out of ten, at the next odd game the linesman would casually walk off, his replacement would come out, and hardly anyone would even notice. We'd both retain our respect, nobody was hurt, and I could get back to tennis.

2

Playing the Percentages

The two things that turned me into a men's champion from a boys' champion were good competition and a club player named Cliff Roche. Specifically, Roche taught me the percentages in tennis. He showed me that the odds on a court could be the same as with a deck of fifty-two. Put the ball in a certain spot, and then put yourself in a certain spot, and the chance of the other player getting out of that spot would be the same as drawing a third king or to a straight or whatever.

I met Cliff Roche at the Los Angeles Tennis Club, where he was a member. He loved to play for fun, but he was around forty-five or so when I met him, and he'd never been any kind of a championship player. But Roche knew the game better than 99 percent of the guys who have ever made the top ten. Hell, we all called him "Coach" Roche—he helped a lot of kids besides me. He was a hydraulic engineer and had invented some special automotive device and made a fortune from it. He was a very blithe sort of guy to start with. "Young fellow," he used to tell me, "you never really get smart until you've gone broke twice." Apparently Coach had. He really knew the percentages.

The L.A. Tennis Club was like a laboratory. It would have been one thing for Roche to tell me how to do something, but he could sit with me and show me the best players doing what he said—or not doing it and losing. In the 1930s and then again after the war up until around 1950 or so, the L.A. Tennis Club was the one place to play the game in this country. If you wanted competition, you had to play there—especially since there were many fewer tournaments then and practice was the vogue.

Before the L.A. Tennis Club achieved this significance, there had been two other centers that had filled that role in the U.S. First, before World War I there was Golden Gate Park in San Francisco, where Maurice McLoughlin and Little Bill Johnston developed. Then a few years later the power shifted across the bay to the Berkeley Tennis Club, which gave us Budge, Frankie Kovacs, Helen Wills, Helen Jacobs and Margaret Osborne Dupont.

We should have some central tennis site in the U.S. The boom has been great for tennis of course, and we have such a large population and good weather (for much of the nation) that we can't help throwing up a number of champions, but we would do even better if we had one main tennis center. Competition is crucial to the player, because no matter how good you are technically, you cannot improve unless you play against somebody better.

When I was a teen-ager at the L.A. Tennis Club, I could get matches against Vines, Tilden, Riggs, Gene Mako, Joe Hunt, Ted Schroeder, Jack Tidball, Frank Shields, and—often as not—the players on the UCLA and Southern Cal teams. Sidney Wood would come in for long periods from the East, and Kovacs from Northern California. My parents arranged it with Montebello High School to adjust my schedule so that I could have all of my classes in the mornings and thus be able to commute to the club afternoons. It wasn't easy, and it was an hour and a half each way. But once I got there I played till dark. It was paradise.

When Big Bill Tilden was in town, I'd sometimes ditch school and play with him in the mornings. Bill played bridge afternoons, so people had to fit into his schedule if they wanted to get on the court with him. He was a strange guy, but he couldn't have been nicer to me. This was almost a decade before he got arrested for going after little boys, but he certainly never acted improperly with me—and I never heard of that at the time either. Whatever was wrong with Bill, he had it in check then.

He could still play. When I compare all the best players of the past forty or forty-five years, I feel I have a real license to do it because I've seen them all at their prime and played against most of them. Tilden predates my era, and since I never saw him play when he was even near his best, I'm not going to get into any arguments about how good he was. But I saw enough of the way Big Bill played when he was over the hill to believe all the great things ever said about him.

He was in his mid-forties when I started playing with him around the winter of '37. We played about even, but it never bothered him in the slightest that a kid could keep up with him. He just loved to play tennis. He never tried to coach me. Tilden was an advocate of the all-court game, and by the time I started working out with him I was already following Roche's percentage schemes, attacking regularly, and so philosophically Bill and I were somewhat apart. Maybe that's why he never tried to take me under his wing as a protégé the way he did with a lot of kids who had less potential than I. If Tilden was going to coach a kid, he had to rule the kid completely on the court. Obviously I was too independent for that.

Even then Big Bill had the great forehand. He could hit it hard and anywhere he wanted. But his drive backhand had wilted. A backhand is harder to manage as you get older, possibly because you're slower getting to the ball and so you're a little late starting your backswing. So Bill was late on the backhand, and he had to chip it. When I beat him, I beat him by attacking the backhand and his second serve, which had also lost a lot.

Still, old as he was, Tilden was only a few years removed from the very top of the sport. In 1934 he toured with Vines. Big Bill clobbered Elly in the opener at Madison Square Garden, and he won eleven of the first twenty—and he was forty-one then. Since he always had the name and always stayed in shape, they even had Tilden tour with Budge when he was almost fifty—and if Bill didn't win many matches, he could stay in them all for a set or more. But he was the exception. Tilden wasn't married, and he didn't have any family ties. He was content just to play tennis and travel. I think that the reason Vines left tennis when he was still so young—not even thirty—was because he had seen that specter of Big Bill as himself a few years later, and he didn't want to end up that way. Hell, in those days anything past the age of thirty was uncharted territory for a player.

But I never thought that it was primarily a matter of aging— and Gonzales and Rosewall proved me right about that later on. Above all, the older player lacked competition to keep himself match-tough. Once Budge was dethroned he had nobody to play, even though he was barely thirty. But in fact Don was so good that when he toured with Sedgman, Gonzales, and Segura in 1954 at the age of thirty-eight, none of those guys could get to the net consistently off his serve— and Sedgman, as quick a man who ever played the game, was in his absolute prime then. Don could keep them pinned to the baseline with his backhand too. But without competition his consistency had fallen off.

Of course some bodies are going to wear out before others. Rosewall, for example, is several years older than Laver, and they're both about the same size and build, but Rosewall passed Laver when The Rocket was still comparatively young, in his mid-thirties. Everybody marvels that guys like Rosewall and

Gonzales could play with the best at the age of forty, but Al Bunis, who runs the Grand Masters where the minimum age is forty-five, has made it a point to study these matters, and it is his judgment that forty-two or forty-three—not forty—is the biological age when a top player declines significantly.

But always you need the competition. At the L.A. Tennis Club there was not only pride on the line, but often as not, a lot of money too. The wealthier members would come out and back players, and if you won for them, they'd reward you. There was always a lot of betting there, even on the rainy days when we'd go inside and play ping-pong (Kovacs was the best; Riggs a close second). But the big money aside, if you hung around enough you'd eventually pick up straight practice matches. I played Riggs a lot then. He liked me personally too, but he'd never give me a break. For as long as he possibly could, he would beat me at love. He'd never give a kid a game here and there to perk him up. Bobby was always looking down the road. "I want you to know who's the boss, for the rest of your life, Kid," he told me. Bobby Riggs was always candid.

My big break came in the fall of 1937 when I got to work out regularly with Vines. For about four months we played two long sessions a week at the Beverly Hills Tennis Club, which was partly owned by Vines and Perry.

It was at the Beverly Hills Tennis Club one day when it all came together. I remember it perfectly—I was playing with Vines one October afternoon, 1937. I suddenly saw how to be a forehand player. What I saw was how Elly used weight transfer. And he was the best at that, although kids like Newcombe, Roche, Connors, and Borg have been very good at it recently.

So playing with Vines and the other top players was crucial to me. It speeded up my development by several years, I'm sure. And let's forget me for the moment. As soon as the L.A. Tennis Club began to decline in power, so did ▸merican tennis. As Casey Stengel used to say, you can look it up. We did keep on producing women's champions in Southern Califor-

31

nia—Maureen Connolly, Karen Hantze, Billie Jean, now possibly Tracy Austin—but the male line ran out as soon as the L.A.T.C. stopped attracting the best players. Since Gonzales, the only male champion to come out of Southern California has been Stan Smith, and he had a short run. There are so many more kids playing in Southern California—they have better coaching, all the advantages, but they get cut down short of the top. I can only imagine that it's because they lack competition, that they are not hardened enough. Besides Smith, look at the only other three Americans to win at Wimbledon or Forest Hills in more than the last two decades: Chuck McKinley, a limited little scuffler from St. Louis who gutted his way to the top of the amateurs (and then only because all the best players had turned pro); Ashe, a black kid, from Richmond; and Connors, from the other side of the river in St. Louis.

But tough competition is a double-edged sword. Get beat too much, it will destroy a kid's confidence. It was fine for me to get whipped by some older guy like Riggs or Mako at the club, but only so long as I could spend some of my time beating up on other kids my age. The classic example of this was when Alex Olmedo joined the pros. The Chief was then the toast of tennis—not only was he the Wimbledon champion in 1959, but he was also an extra-special Davis Cup hero. He was from Peru, but he had been allowed on the U.S. team because he went to college in the states and Peru didn't have a Davis Cup team. And in 1958 he went out and practically single-handedly whipped the Aussies in the Challenge Round on their own turf.

Then Olmedo signed with me, and he could hardly win a set. All of a sudden, from the top of the world to being a stiff— number nine or ten out of twelve players on tour. And you say, well Olmedo must have known that it would be tough moving up to the pros, and couldn't he have prepared himself for the battle and hung in there and improved his game in the long run. And the answer is, sure, The Chief knew it would be tough, but nothing in the world prepares you for losing day in and day out, and surely it is a hundred times worse to be losing every time when just last week you were the champion. It tears you apart. It did Olmedo: Alex will tell you himself. He wasn't that good to start with; he never could have played regularly with guys like Gonzales or Rosewall or Laver, but the beatings he took when he first came on made it impossible for him ever to improve.

As a matter of fact all the years we had the tour, the only three kids who turned out to be better pros than they were amateurs were Segura, Gonzales and Rosewall. And think about it: Segura was never a big name in the amateurs, Gonzales was still a baby when he signed, and Rosewall was never a big name by himself. He was always the second-horse in the entry with Hoad, and he never won Wimbledon. Segura and Rosewall could come in and take the early defeats and come back because they were potentially top players, but they hadn't been at the top. Gonzales was just beginning to develop when he left the amateurs.

Nowadays you see a lot of these kids who smell a few thousand bucks and turn pro when they're too young. They're fools. All you have to do is look at a kid like John Alexander. Before he played doubles in the 1968 Davis Cup against the U.S., I was the youngest player ever to participate in a Challenge Round. But Alexander turned pro soon after that, and he's hardly improved his game since then. If I'd turned pro as a teen-ager, you'd never have heard of Jack Kramer again either. Kids like Billy Martin and Bill Scanlon: they quit college and maybe they'll make forty or fifty thousand for a couple of years, but all they're buying with that money is journeyman status for the rest of their careers. You can't learn anything, and you can't improve getting beaten in the first round week after week.

I think John McEnroe, the 1978 U.S. Davis Cup hero, played it right. He could have ruined his career had he turned pro right after he got to the Wimbledon finals in 1977 when he was

33

only eighteen. But he went to Stanford, learned to pace himself, picked up a lot of self-esteem by winning the NCAAs, and he is obviously more confident because he took that extra amateur year.

Myself, I had a strange kind of transformation into the big-time game. Usually as you move up, you beat kids your own age, while losing to the older men. But Coach Roche taught me a grown-up game, and I caught on so quickly that I started beating men, while at the same time I would still occasionally get caught by much lesser players in the boys' game. I was the national boys' champion in '36, and while I did win the Interscholastics in '38, I never did win a formal USLTA junior title.

In 1939 I might have had some excuse—a pulled muscle—when Schroeder won the juniors. Maybe. But in 1938 I had no alibi whatsoever when a kid named Bobby Curtis from Texas upset me. But here was the kicker. Just a couple of weeks after Curtis beat me in the juniors at Culver, Indiana, I played at one of the major men's grass championships in Rye, New York, and went all the way to the semi's before Riggs beat me. In the quarters, I whipped Elwood Cooke, who was ranked seventh in the nation at the time, prompting Allison Danzig to write this (my first national notice) in *The New York Times:*

"The lad's name is John (Jackie) Kramer, and it is well to remember it, for it may be mentioned in the same breath with Don Budge and Ellsworth Vines by 1940. . . . If any youngster of his age has played any better tennis in these parts during the past 15 years this observer must have been looking the other way and grossly derelict of his duty."

To keep Al from being embarrassed, I went all the way to the quarters at Newport the next week before Bitsy Grant, Number 6 that year, beat me. Still I would have had trouble with any good junior player. There is a tremendous difference in style between a boy's game and a man's game, which is why so often there are great kid champions who never amount to anything past the juniors. One of the most amazing things about the best U.S. players today is that a whole bunch of them of the same age—Connors, Stockton, Tanner, Gottfried, Sandy Mayer, Solomon, Dibbs—have been competing with each other for national titles virtually since they were babies. Usually in any group of kid champions, you get a bunch whose games have no capacity to grow.

The difference between a man's game and a boy's game is, to start with, that a man plays about three feet closer to the net. A boy serves, merely putting the ball into play, and then he steps back to rally. He hits the ball on its descent. A man serves, leaning into the ball so that even as he hits his serve he is in front of the baseline. (I never saw a guy who hit a serve by jumping into it turn out very good. Ashe was the closest to breaking that rule. He hopped into his serve.) So a man leans in, moves in, and then he hits the ball on the rise—after its bounce, before it reaches its apex.

Now that's all very simple, primitive to the good fan, but when Roche taught me this style, it revolutionized my game. I was a tall kid who happened to be built well for a serve, especially playing on the fast California concrete (or the grass at Rye or Newport). On the other hand, once I had committed myself to an attacking game, I was tremendously vulnerable to the slow-paced boys' game. I'd get frustrated and make the dumbest errors. A boy would hit a looping balloon ball from behind the baseline; I'd slam it back, get impatient, rush in, and then he'd hit an easy return past me. Years later when my serve-and-volley style was all the vogue, I saw little Butch Buchholz play a man's game when he was barely twelve or thirteen. He'd smash in a hard serve, charge the net, and the little fellows he was playing would dink the ball back past him. Butch was obviously much better, but he just wasn't old enough to cover the shots at the net.

What Cliff Roche taught me as a kid would be perfect advice

now too. But five or ten years ago it wouldn't have been. That's because the game I was growing up into in the 1930s was a fast-court game, mostly grass. Then tennis went through its clay-court period. Only in 1978 with the U.S. Open moving off the dirt and onto fast concrete would Roche's attack game be back in style again.

Roche's first rule of percentage tennis was to hold your serve. In those days of five sets and no tiebreakers—that's before all this Sprint Tennis they play now—you literally could not ever lose a match unless you lost your serve. (And even today with tiebreakers, it's remote that you could lose a match without losing serve.) So Roche taught me to preserve my energy for serving. It didn't make any sense to go running all over the court trying to break the other guy's serve, if this left you too tired to hold your own. Priorities. Percentages.

So what Roche taught me was to play it easy against the other player's serve until he fell behind love–30. Sometimes I wouldn't even bust myself to win a game until it was love–40. The statistics show that on a fast court, a good server will hold serve more than 50 percent of the time even after he is down love–40. So early in a set I let a guy have his serve unless he got behind love–30 or love–40 off his own mistakes. I would just try and keep him honest—go for winners off his serve, try something different—whatever I could do with the least loss of energy. Then when it got to 4–all, I played every point all out (except possibly if he got ahead 30–love or 40–love on his serve).

It isn't easy to pace yourself like that. It is especially hard to hold yourself back in the fifth set. You're up 1–0, he loses the first point on his serve, and you knock yourself out to try to win the next point and go up love–30. Before you know it you're involved in every point, the guy wins a deuce game, and you're tired and have to serve. Roche taught me to play it even safer if you were serving the odd games. The guy who serves the even games serves after the break when he is rested and has had a chance to dry his hands.

When I won my first Forest Hills against Tom Brown in

1946, Roche was in the marquee. The first set was a toughie. I won 9–7. Then I went up 5–2 in the next set. Here was a perfect time for a kid to lose his head and go for the break. You're so close to 6–2, two sets to love, you can taste it. But for what purpose: you fail to break him; he's 5–3, you're tired, your hands are sweaty, he's got a good chance to break you, and then he's got a rest and dry hands before his serve. Boom, like that: 5–5.

I let Brown have the game for 5–3 without a struggle. Then I looked up and saluted Roche, and he nodded back. It was as if I were saying: "I lost that one for you." And my energy spared, I served out the set at 6–3 and then closed out the match at love.

So that is the keystone of percentage tennis. At the other end of the court, when you are returning serve, Roche taught me that the percentages were to attack off virtually every second serve. Not only are most players vulnerable to an opponent coming in on their second serve, but even more important it works on their mind. If a kid knows that you will be attacking his second serve, he is very liable to start taking something off his first serve, making sure to get that one in. He starts playing it safe.

The most important percentage shot in tennis is the second serve. A big cannonball is wonderful to have, but it can't carry you—especially since the velocity of anybody's first serve drops off as a match wears along. But a second serve can make or break you. A kid like Newcombe became a champion only because he could hit a great second serve. The only players I ever saw worth a damn who didn't have a top second serve were Rosewall, Segura, Frankie Parker, and maybe John Bromwich.

If you can't attack on a second serve, Roche taught me to come in on the first short ball. (Remember now, I'm applying all of this to fast courts.) From Cliff I learned to slice a ball to get in, hitting it halfway between a dink and a drive. But what set me apart, what couldn't be taught, was that I could follow a ball in from the baseline with my forehand. Very few experts ever figured out what I was doing and how unusual it was. I was like a pitcher with a pitch completely different from anyone else's.

A backhand by its nature is a shot you hit leaning forward. It is a natural move to hit it, lean in, and follow it in. But a forehand is hit more open, squared off to the net. I learned to slice it going forward, and with that I busted up all the usual percentages.

Two other vital things Roche taught me: if you believe in yourself, hit with your strength even if that means going into your opponent's strength. The best match I ever played against Budge (which I'll talk about more later), I played to his backhand. And second, on every important point in a match, you get to the net and make the other guy try and hit a passing shot. (Unless—I found out the hard way—the other guy was Budge, Bromwich or Kovacs; then the percentages were different from what Cliff Roche had figured out on the sidelines.)

But overall Roche's percentages were correct. It was not just that I personally had the right temperament and style for a certain teacher. Hell, Ted Schroeder had an entirely different style of hitting the ball, and it is possible that Roche's system helped Ted even more than it did me. Gonzales never learned from Coach Roche, but he picked up the percentages from Ted and me, and he finally learned to play the game correctly. Now that tennis is swinging back to the fast surfaces where the serve counts more, percentage tennis is going to be applicable again. Very few of these kids today have the foggiest notion about pacing themselves. Newcombe—who is as smart a player in every way as you'll ever see—can do it, but he's way beyond his peak. Tommy Gorman was another one who knew the value of pacing, but he's past his prime too with a bad back. In the years ahead the kids who do learn how to save themselves are going to have a big edge.

The master of pacing was Bobby Falkenberg, a Wimbledon champion who has become all too forgotten. It's a shame, because Falky was a real hero. As a tennis player he was a physical wreck. He had trouble breathing normally. That's the truth: the man won Wimbledon and he couldn't breathe easily. But nobody ever figured tennis odds and played the game to his advantage as well as Falky did.

Let me say here quickly that his breathing problems were only those relative to an athlete. He never had serious respiratory problems in everyday life. In fact Falkenberg probably ended up making more money than any player who ever picked up a racket. When he was through with tennis, he took a trip to Brazil, and when he was down there he got the idea of selling whipped ice cream. For some reason the food experts all accepted it as truth that South Americans did not like ice cream. Didn't he know? South Americans liked Cokes, they didn't like ice cream. He started selling them whipped ice cream out of a little shack on a beach in Rio. It was just called Bob's. Pretty soon he had trucks, outlets, an ice cream plant. He sold out for millions about twenty years later and lives near me in L.A. Whenever we see each other all he wants to know is why I bother still doing so much for tennis and the players. His attitude is: why help all these ungrateful little bastards? Falkenberg's favorite part of tennis today is Wimbledon— where they used to hate him. He enjoys going over there to bet.

He was a kid who always liked the action. He was a few years younger than me, but he liked to hang around with the older hot-shots. He was precocious and not intimidated by anything. As a young boy, physically he seemed all right. He was really quite quick then, with a game similar to Gonzales'—in fact he had a good record against Pancho when they were kids. But Falky was nowhere near as good as Gonzales, and he was always vulnerable on the forehand. What he did have was a great serve; he was exceptionally tall, just as skinny, and he could uncoil aces. Falky was a streak hitter too, so when he got in rhythm, he could run games. His best play all came off his serve: good backhand volley, very good overhead. He'd close in tight at the net, towering over it, and keep the pressure on tight.

39

But all things considered, Falkenberg certainly didn't have a helluva lot of equipment. Probably the only other player to win a major title on serve alone was Johnny Doeg, who beat Tilden and took Forest Hills in 1930. But what Falkenberg had foremost was a gigantic competitive temperament. My God, if guys like Falky or Schroeder had the equipment of a Nastase or a Stockton—or the other way around—they'd never get beat. I mean there were two things Bob Falkenberg couldn't do on the court: breathe and choke.

The first time I realized there was really anything wrong with him physically was in the quarters at Forest Hills in 1947. Very early in the match when we crossed over, all of a sudden he was gasping for breath. He sat down quickly. "Hey Jack, wait a second, I can't breathe," he said. It scared the hell out of me. He never did well at Forest Hills—I personally beat him three times there, in the quarters in '43 and the semi's of '46 as well as in this '47 match—because it was invariably hot and muggy then, which made it difficult for him. (And with the bad turf at Forest Hills, it should have been a set-up for his fast serves.) But Wimbledon was just right for him because the surface was fast and the air was cool and dry. This upset the British even more because he seemed to come out of thin air every year over there.

With his big serve, Falkenberg had always been a percentage player. Then when he started to have his problems with stamina, he just accentuated this philosophy. Bobby's idea—and it was unusual but completely honorable—was that you had to win eighteen games to win a big match, not nineteen or twenty. You only had to win the *right* eighteen, and it was the player's responsibility to select those he was going to try and win. There was nothing original in the premise. It was just that Falkenberg applied it in the extreme, and the open way he went about it drove the British out of their minds. When one of the eighteen games wasn't involving him, he would try and hit impossible outright winners off serves, he would dropshot from the baseline, throw away his own serve at love—and for that matter, throw away whole sets at love. A typical Falkenberg victory read like this: 6–4, 0–6, 6–4, 0–6, 7–5.

Also he took whatever opportunities he could to lay down and rest for a while. He would find ways to pitch himself to the ground so that he could then stay down on the cool turf and catch his breath. He sprawled out that way so often, all arms and legs, that the British started calling him "The Praying Mantis." Falky would sweat like a pig too, even in the driest climates, and so he drank huge quantities of liquids and was constantly wiping his sweaty hands on his pants to dry them. Halfway through any match he looked like an absolute pigpen, half of him sooty, the other half grass-stained. Then he would start running off to dry his hands on a towel at the sideline chairs. I stopped that. I think I was always a very fair opponent, but I was also firm with the rules. The rules were that you couldn't go wandering off the court between points to dry your palms. I told Falky to get a little towel and tuck it into his waist, which he did. Vilas pulls that stuff today. Somebody should tell him the same thing: carry a towel and stay on court.

At Wimbledon the general impression was that Falkenberg was a bad sport. That is why they hated him so. Nobody is ever very keen on a big guy who gets by with booming serves—fans prefer the adorable little Rosewall types—and while Falky was only unorthodox in his strategy, everybody figured that that meant he had to be dishonest. But in fact he was never a gamesman. I never once saw him take advantage of anybody in a game. It was just that he knew how to play games.

I didn't see him win Wimbledon in '48. Our pro tour was in South America, and we all put up $100 each and picked a winner. Riggs took Parker, Segura took Drobny. I can't remember who Dinny Pails took, but it wasn't Falkenberg. I took Bromwich, and when Falky and Bromwich met in the finals I figured I was an easy $300 winner. On the scene, of course, the whole crowd was for Bromwich. Falkenberg didn't help his popularity any by winning the first set and then dumping the second one at love. After he came back to win the third at 6–2, Falkenberg made an effort to wrap it up in the fourth, so he started playing to win; but when Bromwich got a break, Falkenberg threw in the towel and let John roll it out at 6–3. Then in the final set, the British grew ecstatic when Bromwich broke Falkenberg again and went up 5–3. In fact, there he had two match points. The first one was the point that did Bromwich in. He moved up to hit a volley, which he had a real chance to put away, but instead he decided to let the ball go, figuring it was hit long. It dropped in well ahead of the baseline, however, and Falkenberg—reprieved—served his way out of the next match point, held, broke, and went on to win four straight games and the title, 7–5.

Bromwich was the last man to hold a match point at Wimbledon and not ever win the title. To me it never seemed that he was the same player after that. He doubted himself. He was a precision player to start with—he used a terribly light racket weighing less than twelve ounces, and it was strung loosely. He could put a ball on a dime, and I suppose after he misjudged that one shot, the most important in his life, he never possessed the confidence he needed.

But at least Bromwich and the British got a final measure of revenge the next year—the 1949 Wimbledon. In the round of sixteen, Falkenberg had infuriated them more than ever by beating a Hungarian named Joe Asboth. Joe was a nice clay player, skinny and blond—looked a little like Richard Widmark. He was easy to root for. And this time Falkenberg won the first two sets, and then he rested for two straight sets, twelve straight games, 0–6, 0–6. He just wanted more time. He was like a horse who took the lead off a fast first quarter and then slowed the pace till the top of the stretch, so that just as the other horses caught up, he had plenty left to pull away. He whipped Asboth in the fifth set, and the British were beside themselves; also they were scared to death Falky was going to win again.

But Bromwich got him in the quarters. Falky got up two sets to love, but he dropped his first serve in each of the next three sets, and he didn't have enough energy to break John twice. So he went to Brazil where nobody was selling ice cream and played the percentages down there.

3

Don, Elly and Fred

The two players I patterned myself after were Budge and Vines. Don is still the best player I ever saw, and Vines is next. Right away a lot of people are going to say I'm an old timer, pushing the guys of my era. Don't I know that the human body runs faster and jumps higher now than in the 1930s? And I say, yes, I know that, and will you please name me a better hitter than Ted Williams and a better singer than Caruso?

I can understand records falling when you are playing against a measurable standard, such as seconds or feet. But when you factor in the element of competition against another live rival, that changes the formula. I've noticed through the years that some of the record-holders in track and field have trouble beating *people* in the big meets. Just because athletes are swimming faster against the clock—because they have better pools, better training, better suits—does that mean competitive desire and character has increased?

I'm not hung up on the 1930s. By far the closest player to

43

Budge in terms of equipment is Connors, but Connors has a habit of losing big matches to people he should handle with ease. What am I supposed to do, say that Connors is better than Budge even though he loses, just because Houston McTear runs a hundred yards faster than Jesse Owens did and Colin Dibley serves a tennis ball faster than Tilden?

As I said, I never saw Tilden when he was at the height of his powers. But then it's difficult to compare players you did see in their prime, because rarely did two of the best have their best years at the same time. Nevertheless I feel fairly confident in saying that Budge was the best of all. He owned the most perfect set of mechanics and he was the most consistent. I also feel just as safe in saying that, on his best days, Vines played the best tennis ever. Hell, when Elly was on, you'd be lucky to get your racket on the ball once you served it. I recognize too that Elly's record in the amateurs doesn't merit such a high position in my esteem. But he became a better player in the pros before he left the game . . . much too soon. Elly was a lazy guy, a natural athlete, and he lost interest in tennis. He was a lot like Lew Hoad, who came along later and went out early because of a back injury. Elly had shoulder problems himself. But when Vines and Hoad were healthy, and when they were hot, they—and Laver too—could do more with a ball than Budge. Nothing was impossible for any of these three guys when they were on. They thought of something, and then they just went and did it.

But day in and day out, Budge played at the highest level. He was the best. Then Vines. And I put four more in the top rank: Tilden, Perry, Riggs and Gonzales. (I don't feel that I can honestly evaluate Henri Cochet and Rene Lacoste, the best two of the Four Musketeers, but from all I know second hand, I'm fairly confident they would be very close to the top if only because they were both champions on clay and grass alike.)

My second echelon would include Laver, Hoad, Rosewall, von Cramm, Schroeder, Crawford, Segura, Sedgman, Trabert, Newcombe, Ashe, Smith and Nuskse—with Borg and Connors,

44

who are capable of moving up into the first group.

Leaving Laver out of the first group is probably a surprise. I'm well aware that he is the only man ever to win two Grand Slams, and he was absolutely unbeatable for a year or two late in the 1960s. But he and Gonzales came close enough together for me to make a careful comparison of the two, and I'm positive that Gonzales could have beaten Laver regularly. Hoad owned Laver before Hoad was hurt, and Rosewall beat Laver in those two World Championship of Tennis finals—and that was a title Laver really wanted.

And of course, I don't include Rosewall in the top group either. He's a great little player, but so was Riggs, and I think Riggs would have handled Rosewall. Bobby is by far the most underrated of all the top players. He had such quickness and ball control, he could adapt to any surface, and he was a super match player. Gonzales did beat Rosewall in the pros, and he beat Hoad and all the others on every surface but slippery dirt right on into the early 1960s, but I think Riggs at his best would have beaten Gonzales at his best.

Of the others in the second group, Schroeder won with heart and stamina, but he lacked in the simple mechanics. Sedgman was as quick as anybody who ever played the game, but he couldn't keep the heat on. Segura had the best shot in the game—his two-handed forehand—and while his amateur record is of no consequence, he beat everybody in the pros but Gonzales and me. We beat him with good second serves. We do know exactly how good von Cramm was: his best years came opposite Perry and Budge, and while he couldn't beat them, he was damn close. It's easy to gauge Jack Crawford the same way against Vines and Perry. Trabert had only a few top shots— backhand, backhand volley, overhead—but what he lacked in his strokes and in his mobility, he made up in his head.

This assessment will no doubt upset all the experts who know as an absolute fact that the tennis equipment is so improved that players today *must* be better. Right? Sorry, wrong. For my money the greatest single advance in this area came thirty or forty years ago when we switched from long pants to shorts.

The beef gut they use today is not nearly so good as the lamb gut we had.

The metal rackets are a marketing advance, not a competitive one. You'll notice that most of the good players who don't have endorsement contracts with some Korean plutonium racket company use wood, just like Dwight Davis did when he gave tennis the cup. It is well known that some players have tried to paint old-fashioned wooden rackets to look like metal, so they could keep their contract and also win. The Wilson T-2000, the trampoline that Connors plays with, is more of a handicap than an aid. That he wins having to control the ball with it makes his record all the more amazing.

The ball in general now is harder to control. It's lighter and livelier. Rene LaCoste, who invented the steel racket, is working on developing a lighter, less lively ball. Now if he pulls that off, that would be the first great tennis development since we started showing knees.

And equipment aside, the kids today aren't programmed to win. They're programmed to play for money. When I was coming into the game, we were like boxers; we trained *up* for a few big tournaments. I'm sure that I and most of my contemporaries were keener mentally and more prepared physically for the important tournaments.

Part of this is that the kids today never practice to improve their weaknesses. What they call practice is really just warming up. Some of the very best of them cannot perform the most rudimentary skills. Many of them, for example, cannot change grips properly. They hit with the same grip going from backhand to forehand. I see a lot of them waiting for every serve with a backhand grip. Obviously they figure that they're going to get more serves to their backhands, and therefore it makes sense to be prepared with a backhand grip. But this is false reasoning. You should wait for serve with a forehand grip because the forehand is, altogether, backswing and stroke—a

longer exercise than is the backhand, which is more straight
back and forward. Thus you have more time to switch from a
forehand to backhand than the other way around. A lot of my
contemporaries could drive these kids nuts, confusing them by
serving to their forehand.

Or the other way around. A service grip most approximates
a backhand grip. So if a kid serves and comes in, you want to
make him hit a forehand volley. Either. he'll still have a
backhand grip or he'll be in the process of changing—anyway,
you have made him think . . . or at least you would imagine so.
But you talk to kids about this, and they don't have any idea
what you're speaking of. It never occurs to them. They don't
have time to figure these principles out and practice them.
They're too busy playing for money.

Look, I'm delighted they're getting rich. I just wish they
could also get better. It just kills me to think what Connors
could do if he'd hit a drop shot now and then. He's got these
kids pinned to the baseline expecting him to hammer another
drive. If he could make them wonder that he might cut a shot
short, he'd have them completely buffaloed. Segura, who has
helped coach Jimmy, learned to hit a drop shot at a compara-
ble point in his career. It made his two-handed drive all the
more oppressive, because you couldn't lay back for it. But with
Connors, as far as I can tell, he can't be bothered to try and
learn a drop shot.

Some of the better kids like Borg and Connors have learned
to take a considerable amount of time off. And of course they
can afford to. It's what I call The Nicklaus Method: the less
tournaments you play, the better you perform in the few. But
the trouble is the kids don't practice when they're off. They
play exhibitions, film commercials, speak to racket salesmen,
warm up. When we were playing in the '30s and '40s, the
season really ended in October (unless there was the Davis Cup
in Australia in December), and players would take the winter
to improve a weakness in their game. It was not uncommon in
the spring to encounter some top player for the first time in

47

several months and discover that he had an entirely new second serve or that he had learned to hit a backhand lob.

In 1934 Frankie Parker was ranked Number 4 in the country when he was only eighteen years old. By 1936 only Budge stood above him. And Frankie had been close to the top for years. He had won the junior title when he was only sixteen. He was small, 5'8", about Riggs' size, but even as a boy he had this wonderful slightly overspin forehand drive. Clean and hard. Then for some reason, Frankie's coach, Mercer Beasley, decided to change this stroke into a chop. It was obscene; it was like painting a mustache on the Mona Lisa. For some reason Beasley got it into his head that Parker should hit with a forehand like Leo Durocher threw the ball from shortstop to first base. That was what Beasley patterned Parker's new forehand after.

Well, it limited Frankie. Lots of guys—Riggs, Joe Hunt, Sidney Wood, Bitsy Grant, some others—started to beat him regularly. He dropped down to Number 8 in 1938. At last Frankie understood that he simply could not get his new forehand past somebody at the net. An opponent could step up to the net and slap it away. So late in 1938 Frankie came out to the Bel Air Tennis Club in L.A. He worked every day, hours a day, and developed a new overspin forehand. He could never get his beautiful original stroke back because the chop had been with him too long, and a little hitch was ingrained. But he did develop a better forehand, a whole better game, and he moved back up to Number 2 in the rankings in 1939. Eventually during the war, he won back-to-back nationals. Even with the sparse wartime fields, I don't believe Frankie could have won with his Durocher forehand.

But Frankie paid a helluva price to restyle his forehand. It was a miserable few months working up a whole new shot. I'm not so sure today that a kid ranked Number 8, making $250,000 a year from tournaments, plus endorsements and a club affiliation—I'm not so sure he would pull out of tennis for a few months to learn a new forehand. So the idea that

48

progress can be measured by the simple passage of time is a ridiculous notion. Certainly it is in tennis. I am not sure of much in this world, but I know it has been almost forty years since Don Budge reached his peak, and I know damn well we haven't seen his equal yet.

I'll tell you how good Budge was by comparing him to Connors. Don's backhand was far better than Jimmy's. Budge could return serve just as well as Connors, and his own serve was considerably better than Jimmy's. Budge had a more consistent forehand, and he had no single glaring weakness like Jimmy's forehand approach shot. Neither Budge nor Connors was a serve-and-volley type, but when Don followed a groundstroke to the net, his volleys were always sure. Look at what Budge could do in doubles playing the net. He'd carry anybody with his volleys and return of serve. Finally, Don was a much brighter player than Connors, and he was every bit as good a competitor but with a much better temperament.

And understand, I don't say any of this to put Jimmy down. I compare him as an honor, because he's potentially the only present player who could match up to Don.

The one thing Budge didn't have was luck. He won the Grand Slam, he turned pro, he beat Vines, and all of a sudden he was alone at the top, with the European war growing. Now came one of those matches which ended up having an effect on all sorts of people, far beyond the two players involved. Riggs had won the last prewar Wimbledon in '39, and Forest Hills as well. By the next year, not only was Wimbledon off, but so was Roland Garros and the Davis Cup. Everything rode on Forest Hills, and if Bobby won that, which he figured to, then he was ready to sign and tour against Budge.

Unfortunately Bobby came down with a flu during Forest Hills, and he was all out to beat Joe Hunt in the semi's. I lost to Don McNeill in another tough semi-final. McNeill was a class guy who had won the French in '39, but basically he had one great year, 1940. It all came together for him that year. He was an attacking ground stroker, with a lifted high backhand that could mix you up. As a matter of fact, McNeill's backhand was not all that different from Borg's two-hander with all the topspin.

But still Riggs was the best; he won the first set in the finals and got an early break in the second. I think if Bobby could have held that lead for the set he could have swept McNeill, but he got broken back and had to play out to 8–6 to win a set he should have won long ago. It wore him out, and weakened by the flu, Bobby lost 7–5 in the fifth.

Riggs only lost two or three big amateur matches, and this one was the biggest. It cost him a top payday against Budge, and as the world knows, Bobby likes spending money. He had a good alibi too with the flu. But it is the real measure of the man, that he never complained. Right after the match we took a train to Chicago together, and as downcast as he was, all he ever did was compliment McNeill's play.

Still, whatever the defeat did to Riggs, it cost Budge more. In desperation the promoters hauled out Big Bill for him to play, and he was forty-seven at the time. Budge would have whipped Bobby that year, I'm sure. He was at the height of his powers. He would have beaten anybody. And the ironic thing is that if he had beaten Riggs in a 1940–41 tour, it would have drawn a lot of attention, and there never would have been a Budge-Riggs tour after the war. Instead they probably would have run me in against Budge, and I don't think I was mature enough to beat him in '46. And Don could have beaten Gonzales with his head in '49. So you see, if Bobby Riggs hadn't lost to Don McNeill in that one match in 1940, I think it is very likely that Don Budge would still have been world's champion in 1950.

In any event what did happen was that Riggs stayed amateur for another year, and then after he beat Frankie Kovacs in the 1941 Forest Hills final, they both turned pro to play against Budge and Perry. Frankie never won anything, but he was a draw and everybody figured he was going to win everything tomorrow. He was a big attractive guy, 6′4″, with a great smile—sort of a Nastase type, only harmless, not mean. There was one time Kovacs was playing a match at Forest Hills against Joe Hunt, and Kovacs looked up at an airplane. Hunt mimicked him, so Kovacs lay down for a clearer view, and Hunt did the same, and they were both soon lying flat out on the turf watching an airplane fly by while the fans watched them.

Kovacs had picture strokes, but the reason he could never win anything is because he didn't have any idea how to go about winning. He never had a set plan for a match. Hell, he never had a set plan for a shot. He could sort of decide what to do with it halfway through the stroke. Hoad was another one like that, although Lew was a much better match player.

Kovacs' best shot was a hard, angled backhand crosscourt, but he could never figure out how to set it up so he could take advantage of it. He just guessed most of the time. But he was such a beauty to watch that I was in awe of him. I mentioned this to Riggs one day. "Ah, Kid, don't worry about Frankie," he replied. "He looks great, but give him long enough and he'll find some way to keep you in the match, and give him a little longer and he'll find a way to beat himself."

But Kovacs was an attraction, and so he and Riggs signed after Forest Hills '41 to tour with Budge and Perry. The whole thing was jinxed. The tour was promoted by a rich kid named Lex Thompson, who owned the Philadelphia Eagles. But he played it close, and Don was so desperate for action that he came in without a guarantee—just playing for a percentage of the profits. They started the tour the week after the Japanese bombed Pearl Harbor. Profits? Budge creamed them all, but there were almost no witnesses, and since he was on percentage it ended up costing him money to be the champion. Also, since the war diverted all interest Riggs' defeats went unnoticed, and he earned a second chance after the war.

Budge probably wasted much of his best tennis years playing exhibitions for the troops on Pacific Islands. Then shortly before the end of the war, he pulled his shoulder going over an obstacle course, and it seriously affected his serve and overhead. He shouldn't have signed to tour with Riggs until he was healed, but Don needed the money, and everybody was itchy to get onto the postwar fun. So Bobby played to Budge's shoulder, lobbed him to death, won the first twelve matches, thirteen out of the first fourteen, and then hung on to beat Budge, twenty-four matches to twenty-two. At the age of thirty Don Budge was very nearly a has-been. That was the way pro tennis worked then.

As it turned out Don was to get one more shot at getting back on top—in June of 1948 in the U.S. Professional Championships at Forest Hills. This was the one pro tournament of any prestige and tradition whatsoever, dating back to 1927 when Vinnie Richards had won it. Tilden, Perry, Vines and Budge had all won it in the '30s, and Riggs was the defending champion with victories from '46 and '47. Riggs had only beaten Don in five sets that last year in the finals, and now that I was a pro, Budge wanted to get in Riggs' half of the draw so that he would get a shot at him in the semi's. He thought he could beat Bobby, and then even if I should take him in the finals, Budge could lay claim to being my proper tour challenger the next time around.

But to manage any of this, Don had to get us on the court first. Jack Harris, the promoter of my tour with Riggs, was dead set against us playing. "The stupidest thing you boys can do is go to Forest Hills," he said. You see, if either Riggs or Kramer lost, it downgraded the tour and took away our "championship claim"—and we had a lot of dates left around the world. But the press was pressuring us to play Forest Hills, Riggs was losing badly on tour so he wanted another shot against me in New York, and I wanted Segura and Dinny Pails—the supporting players on our tour—to have a shot at a nice payday. Harris was paying them slave wages. So over Harris' dead body, we all entered the tournament, and there were Budge, Kovacs and a bunch of other top pros waiting for us.

Budge didn't get his wish and get in Riggs' half of the draw. Instead he drew me in the semi's, but I was ripe. Welby van

Horn almost beat me in the quarters. When you're on tour playing the same kid night after night, anybody new is liable to give you trouble. But no excuses: Budge was primed for me. He beats me, he is back in business. He loses, and it is too late for him to come back.

It was a great match. Although Don and I are only a few years apart, we never played in the amateurs, and the bond-drive exhibitions we played during the war (when they let amateurs and pros share the same court) were only that—exhibitions. We played later several times, but this match in June of 1948 was really the only time we ever met under tournament conditions with something on the line. All that was lacking was that only one of us, me, was in my prime.

Of course only real tennis aficionados recall the match, because pro tournaments were never part of the records. I suppose we were like the old Negro baseball leagues. We played and we kept score, but somehow it wasn't considered worth remembering. You can pick up the United States Tennis Association Yearbook, printed annually, more than five hundred pages long, and you can discover that Mrs. Ruth Prosser and Mrs. Ella Felbinger won the National Public Parks championships of women's doubles in 1933. That is dutifully printed, but it is lost forever that Don Budge played Jack Kramer five sets at Forest Hills in 1948.

It was strength to strength, my forehand to his backhand. No one could serve and attack off Budge because he would strip you bare as you rushed in—you had to work your way to the net against him—so I had to make accommodations in that part of my game, but no matter how good his backhand was, I couldn't back off it. We played our games, and it was every inch a fight.

I had a lot of opportunities in the beginning, but Don kept passing me, he got tougher, and he went up two sets to one. The fourth set was to tell the tale. Don was thirty-one at this time, which is not ancient—for a frame of reference, Arthur Ashe was thirty-one when he won Wimbledon—but Budge was not in shape for five-set tournaments because there were no tournaments for him to play. Besides, it was a hot and muggy afternoon. As it was he broke my serve twice in the fourth set (remember this; it becomes very important ten years later), but each break took so much out of him that I was able to break back. He had me 2–1 and deuce, when I saved him from getting the advantage by scoring with a forehand cross-court that I hit on the dead run. Then again he had me 4–3, needing only to hold his serve twice for the match, but that was the end. He just had no more. I broke him at 15, won the next two games at 30, and the fifth set was a pathetic formality. Don only won one point, in the fourth game. So: 6–4, 8–10, 3–6, 6–4, 6–0.

I have no idea why the National Anthem would have been played after our match, but for whatever reasons, I have the most distinct recollection of Don standing next to me, glassy-eyed and weaving, as "The Star-Spangled Banner" ran on. Somehow he didn't faint. But he was finished. There were no more reprieves, no more chances.

When I took over as promoter of the tours a few years later, I often used Budge to fill out the roster. He still had a great name, he always put out and made the younger stars work to beat him, and besides, he was the sort of fellow you just plain wanted to have around. All during the '30s, when he was an amateur, Don had been straight as an arrow. Then after he turned pro he started to drink a little beer and kick up some. He got married in 1941 to a girl from a Hollywood family and he also got a little plastic surgery done on his face, which his friends thought was a smart move. After that he seemed to have more personal confidence. At any party he'd be in the middle of things, dancing or joking. He always had a special nickname for everybody, and to this day, whenever Don Budge comes to Los Angeles, I have to give up a whole week because people stand in line night after night, waiting for their chance to throw a party for him. It's always a great time.

Don was never lucky about money. He cleared more than

$100,000 after taxes when he toured with Vines and Perry, but he went through a divorce and some bad deals, so he played a little longer just to pay bills. I don't mind saying all this now, because when the tennis boom hit, all of us old guys were suddenly discovered again. We became very valuable property, and so now Don's in good shape all around—happily married again, making a great living in tennis. And nobody deserves good things more than this man.

In all the years I was with him, I only once saw him lose his temper, and that was when he was thirty-eight years old in 1954. Typically too, the incident came about because Don was trying to be helpful. I had him touring that year in a four-man format with Gonzales, Segura and Sedgman. I had just retired, and they were playing for my title. In most first rounds Don would draw Pancho, and he was just no match for him. He had not been able to beat him a single time when the tour came into L.A. The matches were in the old Olympic Auditorium, which was not the brightest-lit arena in the world.

Gonzales served the first game, held, they switched courts, and as Budge started to serve, he noticed a bunch of photographers down by Pancho. Don knew what they wanted: a good shot of the champion that they could rush into the next edition. "You guys want a shot of Pancho hitting one back?" Don hollered down. The photographers screamed that they did, so Budge took a couple of steps into the court and patted a serve toward Gonzales. Gorgo lined it back, the photographers had their shot and scurried off, we had some better newspaper publicity, and Budge went back to serve.

But when he took his stance and looked up, Gonzales had moved over to the ad court. He was acting as if the bit for the photographers had been the first point of the game. At first Don thought merely that Pancho didn't understand. When he realized he was serious, he appealed to the referee. He must have been asleep during the whole business, because he just told Budge to shut up and serve at love–15. Don at least appealed that he should have been called for a foot fault since he was a couple of steps inside the base line; he should have a second serve. The umpire wasn't buying, and by now Gonzales was screaming, "C'mon, Don, quit stallin' and serve." Sometimes Pancho could be at his worst in L.A., his hometown, where he wanted to put on a better show for his friends.

Incredulous, Budge shook his head, called out, "All right, if you're that desperate for a point," and went back to serve. He beat Gonzales 6–4, 6–4, his only victory over him on the tour.

In a more bittersweet way, I remember especially one other story involving Don, because it more than any other, sums up the whole sad existence of the way pro tennis used to be. Don and I were touring in Europe one summer with Segura and Gonzales, the two Panchos. I believe it was 1952. We were in Falkirk, Scotland, near Edinburgh, and our next one-night stand was in a place in England called Harrogate. Then we were scheduled to double back the next night to a little town named Kirkcaldy. Well, we were exhausted from touring, and since Kirkcaldy was very near to Falkirk, Don suggested that we drop in to see the promoter there and cancel that date.

The promoter was crestfallen when I made the suggestion. We were the biggest thing to hit Kirkcaldy in years. Why he already had sixty pounds in the till. The top ticket was going for seven shillings and six pence—about ninety cents. And so, regretfully, we promised him we'd be back to honor our commitment the next night. We drove all the way to Harrogate, played two singles and a doubles from around 7:00 P.M. to midnight, caught some sleep at a bed-and-breakfast place, and then the next day, drove the hundred and fifty miles back over the winding Scottish roads to Kirkcaldy. And we played all evening there.

When I went to settle up with the promoter, he was ecstatic. The sixty pounds advance sale had only been the start. We had drawn so well at the gate that our cut was ninety-two pounds— about $400 in those days. "But laddie," he said, as he gave me the money, "you and the boys played so well, we want to give you this." And he slipped me eight more pounds, bringing it up to an even hundred. Three figures!

I went out to the car where the other three were waiting. "How'd we do, Jack?" Budge asked.

"Great," I said. "We got a tip." And we all laughed ourselves silly and sat there like a bunch of two-bit hoods who had just robbed a gas station, divvying up a hundred pounds—minus the gas money and other general expenses that had to come off the top. Wouldn't you like to see Borg and Connors and Gerulitis and Vilas splitting up a few hundred bucks in the middle of nowhere, which they just drove a hundred miles to reach?

Elly Vines never had an experience like that one because he got out so that he wouldn't suffer such indignities. Perhaps he was too good an athlete ever to want to settle for anything off the top. He had the perfect slim body—6'2½", one hundred and fifty-five pounds—that was coordinated for anything. Elly won Forest Hills the first time when he was still only nineteen, but at the same time he was also devoting himself to basketball at the University of Southern California. He went there, on a basketball scholarship. So when he started getting bored with tennis, golf appeared as another challenge. He mastered that sport too. Of course Vines was never as good at golf as he had been at tennis, but he was good enough to get to the semi-finals of the PGA once, when that was a match-play tournament. He was twice in the top ten of golf money winnings, and he was surely the best athlete ever in the two sports.

In his last tour in 1938-39, Vines was beaten 22–17 by Budge, which is pretty close, especially considering that Elly was having trouble getting up for tennis then and that he had developed serious shoulder problems. I can remember that even a couple of years before the Budge tour, when I would work out with Vines, he would have to hang onto a pole that went across the top of the entranceway to the court. He would sort of twist there, trying to pull something loose. So after Don beat him and there was no one else to play, Elly just figured what the hell, he might as well try another game.

Vines never did say much about anything. He didn't bother to try and talk a good game for the press. His game was power oriented, featuring the great serve, and there has always been a tendency to dismiss big servers as being bullies who can't figure out how to do anything else. But Vines knew exactly how crucial his serve was to the whole game, and he planned the rest of his game too.

Elly told me that it was his strategy to play it safe off his weaker side, the backhand. He would just attempt to hit it deep; he would not go for placements with it. Then with his hard forehand drive, he would try and send the opponent from side to side. First he would hit crosscourt, then down the line, then crosscourt again. I asked him then: "What would you do if he got that shot back too?"

"Well," Elly said, "I would know that I was really up against a helluva player."

Very few players could stay with him when he was hitting his serve and forehand well. He could do so much damage from the baseline that he didn't have to come out to the net and volley, although he did come in fairly regularly on grass or fast indoor surfaces.

Vines toured four times as a pro, against an old Tilden and a young Budge, and in between, twice against Perry. I think Elly started to lose interest then. As good as Perry was—amateur champion over Budge and von Cramm—Vines was much too good for Fred. Actually Perry won the opening night match in four sets before a crowd of 17,630 at Madison Square Garden, but Elly had been in bed with the flu all that day, and even when he took the court he still had a temperature of 101½ degrees. After that, Vines was in complete command. They played, in effect, two tours, hitting the big cities twice. And Jack Harris, who promoted that deal too, always told me that Elly carried Fred to make things look close, and sell more tickets. But whenever I've asked Elly to admit that, he'd change the subject.

The terrible thing is that professional tennis should have taken over in the 1930s. There was some genuine agitation for an open game amongst the tennis federations as early as 1930—had the USLTA been on the ball and worked for open tennis, it might well have become a reality fifty years ago—but the motion failed by a hair, and so the pros began picking off the best amateur heroes. The only thing lacking in the pros, to be honest with you, was that they didn't have some dumb sonuvabitch like me around who could put an organized circuit together that could have fought the amateurs.

Look what the pros had, as the '30s wore on: Vines, Cochet, Perry and Budge—plus Tilden, who was always a draw, whatever his age. The only top champion who didn't sign was Rene Lacoste, and he left the game altogether. Rene had a touch of Howard Hughes in him—scared to death of germs, always figuring he was about to catch the flu. So he left the game when he was still in his twenties, and here he is, almost seventy-five, spry and sharp, and in shape to dance on everybody's grave. I think it is likely, too, that had the pros developed a unified format during this period, a lot of kids just off the top rank—Wilmer Allison, Sidney Wood, Frank Shields, Jack Crawford—might also have turned pro. If we'd had some organization and dignity, we might even have brought in a guy like Baron Gottfried von Cramm. He never needed the money to turn pro, but he was a helluva player, surely the best never to win either Wimbledon or Forest Hills; von Cramm just had the bad luck of getting caught in a blind switch between Perry ahead of him and Budge coming up.

So there was a great pro nucleus there in the '30s if someone had known how to take advantage of it and go after the amateur game.

Then Perry hurt the pros. Fred's a funny guy. He's extremely bright and hard-working, and in fact, I used him a lot as a booking agent when I was running tours through Europe. He was probably the one who sent us on that wild goose chase from Falkirk to Harrogate to Kirkcaldy. Fred didn't miss much as a businessman. But he's an opportunist, a selfish and egotistical person, and he never gave a damn about professional tennis. He was through as a player the instant he turned pro.

He was a great champion, and he could have helped tennis,

but it wasn't in his interest so he didn't bother. Fred was always consistent in that way. When the players boycotted Wimbledon in 1973, Perry not only sided with the officials, but he knocked the Association of Tennis Professionals in his newspaper column. He may have protected his British image by siding with the British federation, but all the players, past and present, who went through that boycott in support of a principle will not forget Fred Perry's stand.

Tilden called Perry "the world's worst good player," which is bitchy, like Bill could be, but it's also a fair enough appraisal. Until 1978, when Borg won his third straight Wimbledon and Connors won the third U.S. Open of his career, Perry had been the last man to hold both those accomplishments. He also stopped Crawford from winning the Grand Slam at Forest Hills in 1933. There are an awful lot of players who are supposed to have been better than Perry and who came nowhere near to piling up the number of important championships that he did.

Fred was extremely fast; he had a hard body with sharp reflexes, and he could hit a forehand with a snap, slamming it on the rise—and even on the fastest grass. That shot was nearly as good as Segura's two-handed forehand. Perry had a good overhead too, but his serve wasn't quite as tough as you would imagine. But, okay, it was good enough. Perry was like Nastase at the net. He couldn't put first volleys away, but then he didn't have to because he was so fast that he would recover and pick off the return of his first volley for a second volley winner. His only real weakness was his backhand. Perry hit underslice off that wing about 90 percent of the time, and eventually at the very top levels—against Vines and Budge—that was what did him in. Whenever an opponent would make an especially good shot, Perry would cry out "Very clevah." I never played Fred competitively, but I heard enough from other guys that that "Very clevah" drove a lot of opponents crazy.

The first time I ever saw Perry play was at the Pacific Southwest late in September of 1936. He was up against Budge in the final, and I had an excellent view because I had beaten Jimmy Wade in the boys' final that morning, and as a reward, Mr. Jones had let me sit right down front next to where the players changed over. Perry quit in the third set. I was only fifteen, but I was old enough to tell when somebody gave up. And Perry tanked, I could see that. Budge took the first set 6–2, and then Perry got one back 6–4. Then Fred threw in the towel and stopped trying. What did it matter, the Southwest? He'd beaten Budge two weeks before in New York, hadn't he? He lost the last two sets two and three. As a kid, that really hurt me—that a star player could do that sort of thing. But the trouble with Fred was that it never seemed to hurt him to lose, especially when he didn't think that a match was important. I always thought he was looking for ways to quit when he didn't care, and that never changed. I can remember as late as 1949, when Fred filled in as a player in a prize-money event in Scarborough, England. He drew Dinny Pails in the quarters, and Pails was playing very well during this period. Riggs was goofing off a lot, chasing the dames more than ever since we left the States, and Pails was beating Bobby badly. But damn if Perry didn't start smashing his forehand and get a lead on Pails. He was playing beautifully, but so help me, he just quit on the spot. He wanted to make sure that the crowd understood that this was all beneath him.

That's what hurt the pros so much. Especially when Perry toured with Kovacs (who could put on the same act), the pros could really pick up a bad name. After the war when we went into some places in South America, it had been almost a decade since a tour had been through, but they all remembered Perry and Kovacs clowning their way through a match. Very clevah. At each stop we had to convince everybody that we played for real, that we weren't some damn circus.

Another problem Perry caused was that he screwed up men's tennis in England, although this wasn't his fault. The way he could hit a forehand—snap it off like a ping-pong shot—Perry was a physical freak. Nobody else could be taught to hit a shot that way. But the kids over there copied Perry's style, and it ruined them. Even after Perry had faded out of the picture, the coaches must have kept using him as a model, because the British boys always came out on the court stamped like Perry—until they tried to hit like Perry.

The weather in England is so severe and school is so stern and time-consuming that they're never going to turn out a lot of champions. Still, it defies the odds that the British haven't had a single men's champion since Perry forty years ago. They've had some fairly good world-class players like Mike Sangster, Roger Taylor and Mark Cox, and they got to the Davis Cup finals against the U.S. in 1978, but they haven't developed a single really top player. On the other hand they do keep producing women's champions, because the women at least, are not being taught to try and hit forehands like Fred Perry.

4

The Shamateurs

The amateur system that I grew up into, and that thrived until open tennis finally became a reality in 1968, was a thoroughly rotten arrangement. Even at the time, everybody said that it was rotten except for the few amateur officials who perpetuated it for their own amusement. But if you said anything to those guys, if you told them it was unfair, they had one stock answer.

It was: "Can you name the winner of the U.S. amateur golf championship?"

Well, of course you couldn't—which was their way of proving that the pros dominated golf, which was true and which was also great for golf. But tennis officials only thought of hanging onto their petty power, not of the game.

Now I'm not saying that those fellows had the exclusive rights to selfishness. The agents who have gained such power in the open game can be just as self-seeking—and I've said this directly to my good friend Donald Dell, The Lip, who is the most powerful agent of them all. There is some difference.

The amateur officials were merely getting their kicks out of tennis, while the agents are trying to make a big buck. The amateur officials wanted to keep the *status quo,* while the agents always want to change things. But the selfish personal motives are the same, and tennis is what still gets hurt. Even Dell has created special events for his clients and put them up against regular tournaments. For three years in a row Connors passed up the Grand Prix Masters in order to play tinsel events for agents. One year he skipped the Masters, the potential championship of the world, in order to play a mixed doubles tournament. And Donald screams at that, but then he creates the Grand Slam four-man event for Pepsi and TV—which usually gives one or two of his clients a payday, and himself a payday, while taking four of the best players in the world out of regular tournaments.

Always keep in mind that when a star like Borg plays a tournament, none of the hacks around him are liable to make a nickel (except possibly someone who has a contract guaranteeing a percentage of prize money). On the other hand, if the star plays some kind of special that they have dreamed up, they can cut that pie up in order to benefit themselves.

So things are not pure in tennis today. But at least the players do have a voice and a piece of the action. In the shamateur days, we were only athletic gigolos—which is what Tilden called us—and the system was immoral and evil. I mean to be harsh. Tennis has changed so much in the last decade that it will not be long before the shamateur days are forgotten or looked upon fondly, all quaint nostalgia. I don't want the truth forgotten. Oh sure, we were kids: we had fun playing cards and chasing dames, it was nice hanging around country clubs and money, and a few of us like myself even moved up— but overall the system was rotten, and so were most of the people who ran it. (Of course there were exceptions. I heard that my friend Bob Kelleher, a noble, honorable man, and a former USLTA president and Davis Cup captain, cried when he first read these sentiments of mine as they appeared in *Sports Illustrated.)*

I hope the amateur officials who were guilty and who are still alive from that era feel terrible about what they continued for so long, because they have been proven wrong and they deserve rebuke. There is no reason why sports and money can't go well together, and open tennis has proved the point I started making forty years ago.

The craziest thing about shamateurism is that it was no secret, and yet it was tolerated. Everybody knew the kids were taking money under the table, and everybody agreed that the system hurt the game. The press was certainly never silent on the subject. There were periodic "exposés." I wrote one myself in 1955 for *This Week* magazine, the largest national Sunday supplement. It was entitled "I Was a Paid Amateur," and it contained no new inside information whatsoever. The result, however, was that the USLTA fired me as coach of the Junior Davis Cup squad—a position I held at their pleasure and my expense. In fact until that point, the USLTA bigwigs kept me in very high esteem, and I was ticketed for the top councils, but that article killed me.

The problem with the tennis press was that because tennis was way down the sports page totem pole—after baseball, football, boxing and usually horse racing, golf, basketball and hockey too—the best and brightest on a sports staff didn't want anything to do with it. Half the time when a tennis tournament came to town, the sports editor would drag some guy off the sports desk, say "Hey, the fruits are playing tennis out at the club—you wanna go get some sunshine for a few days?" And the old reporter would drive out to the club, go through the front door just like he was a member, and write what a wonderful tournament it was for the 125 people who came out.

It was the same all over. When the Association of Tennis Professionals boycotted Wimbledon in '73 almost all the press sided with Wimbledon. Then we found out that three or four of the top London tennis writers belonged to Wimbledon, the All-England Club, and all the other writers wanted to be invited to belong.

Of course there always were a few knowledgeable tennis

writers, especially in New York—Al Danzig of the *Times*, Al Laney of the *Herald-Tribune*, Jim Burchard of the *World-Telegram & Sun*. In the early years, before he got angry at my antiamateur positions, Danzig was a great friend of mine. Hell, we always went partners in the nightly crap games on the Eastern summer circuit. He was like an uncle to me when I first came East. There was one time at Newport, when I was playing Don McNeill in the wind, and I quit. Al came into the locker room after me, and he said: "What happened out there, kid?"

And I ducked my head and told him the truth, that it had gotten too tough in the wind, so I had packed it in. And he said: "I thought so. And I never thought you'd do that." And it made a damn big impression on me, because I never did quit again . . . and for that matter, I also became a pretty fair wind player.

So Al Danzig was a good friend, and he knew his tennis. In a way, that was the trouble with the few good tennis writers we did have. They knew tennis, they loved the game, and they didn't want to get involved with the shamateurism and the politics. Then the hotshot sports columnists would come out of the woodwork once a year, for Davis Cup or Forest Hills; they'd make a big deal out of discovering tennis bums, and then they'd go back into hibernation. Nobody ever kept at the amateur officials, so the game stayed their private preserve, which was all the more reason for the press not to bother. It was a vicious circle.

But what a shame. I would imagine—through the years from the 1920s, when the shamateur system developed, until 1968— that about three hundred or four hundred young men had their lives seriously damaged by the arrangement. They were exploited and abused so that the amateur officials could stay in power and be amused. Players would wake up at the age of thirty with no job and no business background. They were dismissed as tennis bums—and often by the very people who had kept them strait-jacketed. It was even common for the payoffs at many tournaments to be handled by the local representative of the USLTA rules committee.

Then too, I could not begin to estimate how many other kids stayed away from tennis because they could see the rotten system for themselves or were advised to take their talents into another sport. Compared to all the other major American sports, there was no incentive to draw a good young athlete onto the court.

Craziest of all, the system was set up so that it effectively inhibited the careers of the best prospects. The summer circuit—which was the only one that counted then—started at Longwood outside of Boston in July. Then it played Seabright on the Jersey coast; Southampton, Long Island; Rye at the Westchester Country Club outside New York; the Newport Casino in Rhode Island; and back to Longwood for the national doubles before finishing at Forest Hills. It was all on grass, an unfamiliar surface to most of the new players. As a consequence, a kid would come on tour and each week get whipped in the first round. Then he would be denied a chance to practice on grass since he was out of the tournament and the members didn't want losers damaging their courts. By the end of the summer, the kid would have regressed considerably.

The officials and a handful of the stars enjoyed luxury accommodations, but most players had to settle for old hotels—the Puritan in Boston, the Peninsula in Seabright—or dormitories. At Southampton the lesser players had to bunk in the squash courts. The instant you were eliminated from competition, you had to clear out and fend for yourself. A player would come back from a defeat and find his luggage out on the lawn. As a consequence we wasted a lot of valuable time playing mixed doubles to keep room and board for another day or two.

There were no payoffs on the Eastern circuit, but it led the league in hypocrisy. A player had to compete on the grass courts to establish a ranking so he could play anywhere else. They had you dead. As early as 1941 when I was barely twenty, I led a strike of players to get more kids put up in private homes for the national doubles.

The Eastern officials would pretend that it was everyone else in tennis who cheated. Schroeder in particular hated them so much that for many years he refused to play Forest Hills, even if he were already East for the Davis Cup.

However a kid who did play the summer circuit on the grass and got a ranking could then expect to make a little money elsewhere. In the winter the best a top player could make was about $400 a week in Florida. For a good Texas tournament, the Number 1 player might get $750, and for the Pacific Southwest in L.A.—which always had the best fields in the world after Wimbledon and Forest Hills—the top could draw as much as $1,200. But there was a catch here. If you were from Southern California, where an awful lot of us were from, charity was supposed to begin at home, and you shouldn't take any money from your own association.

Wimbledon was like the Eastern circuit; it didn't need to pay. Wimbledon was always known as a player's tournament, though, because they did treat the competitors (as they called us) in a classy way. The locker rooms were pretty good (they're much better now), and they sent limousines for us. Unfortunately you had to get to England on your own because the national associations would pay only for their best players.

One summer when I was supposed to win the tournament, the USLTA paid my way, but I had to sell my car in order to take my wife.

The national organization could suspend you if you didn't play where you were ordered to, and for that matter, they could suspend you if you played too much. There was a rule which prohibited a player from participating for more than eight weeks of tournaments, besides national and regional tournaments. The purpose of this was to keep outsiders from whispering about "tennis bums." Of course everybody knew what was going on. Once when a reporter persisted in asking Whitney Reed how he survived week after week, playing amateur tennis with no visible means of support, Reed finally replied: "I've got a paper route."

By that time (1961), Reed was among the top amateurs, so he was treated with kid gloves. The shamateur system wasn't merely hypocritical; it was cynical too. The best players could get away with much more than the lesser ones. The only outstanding players I ever knew who were suspended were Wayne Sabin, Gene Mako and Frankie Kovacs, and it was arranged so that their suspensions came at a time most convenient for them to be on the sidelines. The USLTA suspended The Lip (Donald Dell) once for not coming back from Wimbledon promptly enough, so you know he couldn't have been much as a player. Gene Scott once stayed and played in Europe under an assumed name.

The sporting goods companies exploited players just as effectively. They ran the game in some countries, such as Australia, taking kids out of school when they were still in junior high. In the U.S. the sporting goods companies were not as powerful, but they signed up kids at an early age to use their equipment for virtually nothing. I first went with Spalding. The payoff was that they would slip me two rackets, already strung, now and then, and I could sell them for $15 apiece. That gave me some walking-around money and looked pretty good at a time when gas was selling at 9.9¢ a gallon. Wilson treated me a little better when I switched to their racket, but by then I was, after all, the number-one amateur in the world.

Wilson had started out as a meat company, getting into sporting goods when somebody suggested they could lay off their pig skins and gut and other stuff butchers had no use for, in footballs and tennis rackets. So they got me a job in one of their subsidiaries, the Davidson Meat Company, at $75 a week, which was very good money right after the war. But I had to work in the freezer and I kept getting colds all the time, so I had to stop working, although naturally they kept paying me.

Everybody in the game knew there were under-the-table payoffs, but nobody ever took me aside and explained how it worked. The players who were getting money weren't particularly anxious for more kids to find out, because then the pie would be split into smaller pieces. The first money I ever got for playing tennis came after the 1939 Davis Cup Challenge Round, where I had played in the doubles. All of a sudden I had a name, and a great guy named Fred Small brought me down to Cumberland, Maryland, to play an exhibition. I wasn't expecting anything, but afterwards he gave me $25. Then I went up to Cleveland and played two sets against Harry Hopman, who was still a fringe player but who had just won his first Cup as Australian captain, and there I got $100.

Sometimes the promoters wouldn't even have the courtesy to pay you man-to-man. They made the players themselves scrap over a joint fee. Like at Jacksonville one time early in 1941, four of us were given $750. And just our luck, Riggs is one of the four. Right away he chirps up that he should get $300. Kovacs says that if Bobby is worth $300, so is he. Wayne Sabin, subtracting quickly, demands $100 of what is left. And what was left of the $750 after that was $50 for me.

Early in 1947, a bunch of us were touring Florida again. With postwar inflation, an offer to play Daytona came to $1,500 this time. Naturally we grabbed it and divvied it up, and since I was the champion, I got the lion's share. A few months later on my way to Wimbledon, I was notified to drop by the offices of the USLTA and meet with Holcombe Ward, who was the president. Mr. Ward had been a national champion himself around the turn of the century, when tennis was more innocent or something. We shook hands and then, gravely, he pulled out a clipping from a Daytona newspaper which said that I had been among a group of players who had taken $2,500 for playing. He handed me the clipping and said: "Is this true, Jack?"

I read it and handed it back. "No sir," I said.

"I didn't think so," Mr. Ward said.

Of course the only reason the clipping wasn't accurate was that it had us splitting $2,500 when in fact we had cut up $1,500. I'm not proud that I was just being technically honest. But the truly sad thing is that any tennis official might think that the article wasn't true. How did he imagine I managed to eat and travel and support a family? With a paper route?

A few months later I was hauled in to meet with Dr.

70

Ellsworth Davenport, who had been in the thick of things for years as the referee at Forest Hills. Now he was in charge of the committee that was presenting a new award, the William Johnston Trophy, which would be presented to the player who made the greatest contribution to the sport each year. Dr. Davenport began by saying that there was no player more deserving than I. But, he went on, there was "this problem." This problem was the rumor that Kramer was taking money under the table.

This time I answered by telling the truth in spirit as well as in simple fact. I explained that I was a man of twenty-six, that I had a wife and a baby, that I had no family money behind me, no money in the bank. I told him that I took what I could, merely to be able to play the game. "I'm doing exactly what I have to do to be the best player in the world," I said. And then: "What would you do, sir?"

Dr. Davenport listened and nodded. It was as if I were explaining to him that the world was round. Then finally, he said two things. First, that if he were in my shoes, he would do exactly what I was doing. And second, that he would make sure I won the Johnston Trophy—which I did. But of course he didn't get the USLTA to follow up. Nobody ever did anything to correct the system.

Now on the other hand, I have to admit that it was all a helluva lot of fun. The tour today does not have anywhere near the camaraderie that we enjoyed. With the wives and children on tour today, the players spend less time with each other. It is not uncommon now for a couple of players to be in the same tournament for two or three weeks in a row and never even see each other. Also, so much of the schedule is now in public arenas. We used to stay together at the country clubs where we played.

Today too there are so many more tournaments. If you were a top player in the old shamateur days, you wouldn't play every week, but your only option was to play or sit out. You didn't have a choice between Gstaad, Switzerland; Cincinnati; Newport or a new invitational at Forest Hills—which was the choice the players had the week after Wimbledon '78 . . . if they weren't playing World Team Tennis or Davis Cup. And sure as hell you weren't making commercials. In the old days too many of the best tournaments lasted two weeks. And there was a rhythm to it. You weren't in Tucson one week and Prague the next, hard court, then dirt, then indoors in Tokyo.

I'd play a pleasant little Florida tour in January, come home for the Southern California and Cal State championships in the spring, take a boat to England for Queens and Wimbledon in June, and then come back to the east for the grass summer circuit leading up to Forest Hills. Then home for the Pacific Southwest and the finale in San Francisco around October 1. That was it.

We were in better shape than the kids today. I'm not saying we were superior human beings or finer people, but we were what we had to be. Pitchers went nine innings in those days too. Most of the tournaments were best-of-five sets, and of course there was no tiebreaker. We prided ourselves on having stamina. When you were sizing up a player, that was one of the very first things you mentioned. Today stamina just isn't an issue anymore. Newcombe is the last kid to have a reputation for being strong in the fifth set.

The tiebreaker has changed the game in other ways too. You get more upsets with it. And you get more upsets with the sudden death nine-point tiebreaker than you get with the twelve-point tiebreaker (which the ATP favors), where you have to win by two. You also get more upsets playing no-ad games—best of seven points. On the other hand you can't put on a comeback as easily when you don't play deuce games and deuce sets. The lesser player can get hot and put the star away. I recognize all the marketing reasons for playing tiebreakers. I know you have to cut it short for TV so that people can get home at a reasonable hour. I also know I'd rather have Gerulitis or McEnroe playing in the finals instead of getting upset 7–6, 7–6 on Tuesday.

All the advocates of the tiebreak game talk about how exciting the added pressure makes the game. You play no-ad—

and they even do that in the colleges now—and a game is three points apiece, next point wins, and of course there is pressure. There is pressure in Russian roulette too, but I don't want to pay to see it. Do you come to see a pressure match or a tennis match? It makes a different, less interesting game, because when you play deuce rules, you can lose a point and still stay alive. At three points apiece, everybody is going to play safe. At 40–all, one player is encouraged to take chances, and it's a more interesting game.

Wimbledon and the French Open throw out tiebreakers in the fifth set and make the contestants play to a conclusion, 10–8, 13–11, whatever it takes. This means that stamina does count.

The longest set I ever played was in the pros one night in Seattle. Gonzales beat me 30–28. It was the first set, best-of-three, but I came back and won the next two to take the match. The most interesting thing is that I led 5–0 in the third set, and then Big Pancho came back to 5–4 before I served it out. You have got to be especially proud to be in a match like that, because neither man got demoralized. We always played by the rules too: a minute at the crossover didn't mean a minute, ten seconds. It was like between rounds in boxing; when the bell rang we were ready to go.

The Aussies have become recognized as the best conditioned players, but in my era they didn't have any special reputation in this regard. Hopman emphasized stamina, and I'm pretty sure that he picked that up from me when I was in Australia with the 1946 Davis Cup team. As I've mentioned, we trained more for a few big events. I looked upon big tournaments as championship fights, and I patterned my training after boxers. I skipped rope, I did sit-ups, I ran. Hopman took note of this, and in the years that followed, the Aussies became famous for rigorous training.

The Aussies as a group did bring beer to tennis. Back in the '30s when I was coming into the game, the players drank very little hard liquor and even beer was not commonplace. A kid like Frank Shields, who was probably the handsomest guy ever to play any sport—his granddaughter is that beautiful child actress, Brooke Shields—used to stay up all night drinking and chasing dames, and we marveled at it. He was a rare exception. But then the Aussies came to prominence after the war, they drank a lot of beer together. Everybody else started imitating them because they won, and it was easier to imitate their beer-drinking than their hard work.

We all gambled. Today you'll never see the players on tour playing cards, but a few do play backgammon. On the Grand Masters tour (ages forty-five and up) however there's a good chance of always finding Sedgman and some of the others in a poker game. We always had something on in the locker room. Bobby Riggs was not atypical. And of course I had been around gambling all my life, going back to Las Vegas. Even as a kid around Los Angeles I would go to Santa Anita and Hollywood Park. My mom gave me $2 once to go out and bet on Seabiscuit, but of course he didn't go until the feature late in the afternoon, and that deuce started burning a hole in my pocket, so I put it on a nag named Blue Suit—I still remember the name—in an early race, and old Blue Suit ran up the track. And of course Seabiscuit won.

When I got into the pros, the card games were pretty stiff: $20 ante, $20 high spade. The second time I toured with Segura (with Riggs, Gonzales and Parker) Segoo had lost more at poker than he had won in tennis salary—and that was nine weeks along. But in the amateurs it was the action more than the stakes: a two-bit ante for seven-card most of the time. Remember, none of us had any money. Every now and then it could heat up, however, if some of the wealthy club members got in. I remember once at Southampton when Pete Davis, the son of the man who donated the Davis Cup, came into a game and lost $400 and was out before he even got the deck.

There were a lot of craps as well, especially when Bitsy Grant was around. And then often as not, Riggs would move into that. I remember watching one night in Rye, when a movie producer was rolling with some of the players on a ping-pong table. It was much too steep for me, but Bobby took $5,000 off the guy, Grant won $3,000, and another player, Champ Reese, $800. They finished around three in the morning, and then the producer just whipped out his checkbook and wrote the three checks for $8,800. Riggs wanted to sleep in, so he got me to drive his wife Kay into Manhattan the next morning so she could go to the loser's bank. But the check carried. No problem.

I don't gamble that much anymore. I decided to bet the California colt, J.O. Tobin, when he went in the Derby in '77, and it suddenly occurred to me that I didn't know any bookies (which was just as well, since Seattle Slew beat him). But certainly the last thing I ever wanted to see was tennis gambling. We just don't need it. Of course they always have odds on the players at Wimbledon, but the books are all away from the courts. What got me upset was the one year, 1974, when they brought the bookies onto the premises and set them up right next to the strawberries and cream.

But first they tried out on-the-spot gambling the week before in the tournament at Nottingham, and the players almost broke the bank. There's an old expression at the race track that if you could make book, the two most profitable places to do it would be in the jockey's room and in the press box. In other words: a little knowledge, etc. But this time at Nottingham, the bookies were new to tennis and they hadn't done their homework. The tour was coming from dirt to grass, and the books were reading the past performances without taking this into consideration. Aussies were going in as underdogs against dirt kids from the Continent, who had no chance on grass. The players were literally standing in line at the betting tent to get these overlays. It was one time when the bookies got beaten.

But anyway, we bet against each other in the locker room, we played each other on the court, we met a few pretty girls, we had a lot of laughs. I remember one time when Shields held Grant by his feet out of a high-story window at the Westchester Country Club. But generally we were good kids. We minded our manners, and certainly we didn't dress like all those midnight cowboys who are on tour today. As a matter of fact we were graciously accepted by many of the country club members, who were supposed to be snobbish, while we were treated much shabbier by the tennis officials, who should have been looking out for our well-being. A player who took advantage of the social opportunities—say a kid like Talbert—could use his tennis to make business connections. But you had to work fast since there was no prize money, it was a very expensive proposition, and you had to win quickly or have a nice bankroll behind you. Besides, if you did hang around for too long, then your reward was to be called a tennis bum, and who wanted to hire a tennis bum?

But I made it on top right out of the gate. Frankly my goal was to succeed in the line of Vines and Budge, and I was encouraged enough in this ambition not to let anything else, like education, stand in my way. After I graduated from Montebello High I was given a full scholarship to the University of Southern California. Tennis players didn't usually get the full ride, but I was a comer—I played Davis Cup that summer, and USC gave me a prestige "job," right along with the football and basketball stars. My student-athlete occupation was to guard a field; that is, not let anybody take it.

I was terrific at this work too, but not as good at the rest of school, and after a few months, with the Florida season coming up, I got itchy and quit. My father was furious. "All right, Cocky," he said. "If you're smart enough to quit school, then you're smart enough to take care of yourself." He made a hard living all his life working his ass off, and I guess he figured I would get the cruel world thrown in my face and retreat back to the comfort of college.

But of course Dad didn't know about the silly world of amateur tennis. I could make enough to live off with the rackets from Spalding, expenses here and there, and playing money matches out at the L.A. Tennis Club. The rich members would back you, and cut you in if you won. Tennis kept me out of school. There was just enough for a kid. Riggs and Kovacs, McNeill, Hunt and Parker were still ahead of me in the country, but I was younger than all of them; I wasn't out of my teens until just before Forest Hills, 1941. That was a bad year for me, though. I had a lot of bad draws, Kovacs beat me in the quarters of the Nationals, and I dropped in the rankings from fifth to ninth. And Dad was right: I was a cocky sonuvabitch.

But my path was cleared when Riggs and Kovacs turned pro, and I had a right to be cocky. On that Rockefeller tour to South America in '41, when Pearl Harbor was bombed, we had a nice cruise to Rio, we played a lot of golf, and I damn near beat McNeill in five great sets in a major tournament at Buenos Aires.

I was still only twenty, but hell, Elly Vines had won the Nationals at nineteen. Somehow I found my way to Florida after South America and rediscovered higher education as the star of the Rollins College tennis team. For homework I played roulette at a lot of illegal gambling joints in the area. I got over a thousand dollars ahead, and my plan was to get a little further in front and then, on my way back to California, detour through Michigan and pick up one of the last new cars. But then one night I got greedy and lost my whole bankroll to a wired wheel in a backroom place called the Flamingo Room. All I was playing was red-and-black, even money, and they cleaned me out.

Back home that spring, I beat Parker in the finals of the Southern California. Except possibly for my pal Schroeder, there was nobody else to beat. All I had to do was stay out of the draft for a few more months and the Nationals were mine. I wasn't dreaming, you understand. I knew there was a war on and that I would be in it before long, but I wanted just a few more months. It was the end of my being a kid, that summer of '42; it probably would have been the last of that, war or no war. I had met a girl named Gloria Spannenberg at a dance, and I was falling in love. She worked at the Bank of America and was tied up days. Mornings I played tennis at the L.A. Tennis Club, and afternoons I bet the ponies. Evenings, I took her out dancing. Gloria was always a great dancer. It was one great time as I prepared to become the champion.

Then in August, I got appendicitis. It isn't like now, where they put you on a conveyor belt and have you back on your feet in time for the eleven o'clock news and sports. By the time I was healed in 1942, Forest Hills was over, Schroeder was the champion, and I was ready to get shipped out in the Coast Guard. It would have been impossible to convince me at that time, but as I'll explain later on, that was all a lot of good luck for me.

5

Battles of the Sexes

The one good thing you can say in favor of the old under-the-table system was that it presented an honest appraisal of a player's box-office value. If the tournament promoter figured a kid was worth X-amount, the kid had two choices. He could either take the money and play or take the money, tank in the first or second round, and take the rest of the week off. It was a textbook marketplace, and promoters knew what the tennis fans wanted.

The vogue then was mixed tournaments, and the expenses were going 80 to 90 percent to the men. If Roy Emerson was drawing $1,500 for a tournament, then Margaret Smith was getting maybe a hundred and a half. This wasn't prejudice, it was just good business. The only prejudice practiced in tennis against women players is by the fans, who have shown repeatedly that they are prejudiced against having to watch women play tennis when they might be able to watch men play. For the Opens in France and Australia, the dames can't get inside to play the stadium courts until maybe the semifinals when they're running short of men's matches. When I helped run the Pacific Southwest, which always had a top female field, I watched carefully and saw the truth: namely, that people get up and go get a hot dog or go to the bathroom when the women come on.

Oh sure, there are exceptions. You put Chrissie up against Martina, the fans will stay. They will watch the champion: Moody, Marble, Connally, Court, whoever. To me, for the years ahead the single most valuable property in tennis is Tracy Austin—which is why I advised her family to sign with Donald Dell. Billie Jean was always an explosive type, always a draw. And the fans will watch the women at Wimbledon, I don't dispute that. But then the fans will watch the tennis at Wimbledon, no matter who's playing. In 1973 when the best male players boycotted, attendance went up because the fans were sticking up for their tournament. The British fans would pack Centre Court to watch two rabbits play tennis.

But outside of these few exceptions, forget it. In the early days of open tennis, the marketplace splits of the purses still went on the order of the shamateur breakdown: 75 to 90 percent for the men. And from all I've seen, that is fair enough. It is fair in terms of fan interest and also in simple division of labor. At Wimbledon or Flushing, the men play about 80 percent of the total stadium court time. The men put up twice as many players (from a pool of about ten times as many competitive players), and they play more sets and more games per set. In France the purse split is $300,000 to $50,000 for the men (the best female players have been playing team tennis), and in Australia the cut is $200,000 to $50,000, but of course the dames share equally with the men in the U.S. Open and nearly so at Wimbledon, and that is simply ridiculous. I don't think equal rights should jeopardize a fair marketplace.

The trouble is, when I say something like this I'm knocked for the wrong reason. I'm not a crusader against women's tennis. I'm just a businessman. Forget women's tennis for the moment. Do you think those golf women would be splitting prize money down the middle with Jack Nicklaus and the boys if they played tournaments over the same course?

If anybody is being cheated, it's the men. The women got equal prize money at Forest Hills a few years ago by having a commercial sponsor kick in the difference, upping their purse money to match ours. We on the ATP said fine, but if the girls can go outside to get some extra, can't we do the same? We had a sponsor already lined up, ready to kick in. Forest Hills said no, that would be unfair as they had already promised the ladies' sponsor exclusivity. So the men were denied more prize money because Forest Hills didn't want the woman's lobby on its back.

The Colgate Grand Prix goes all year long—more than ninety tournaments for men the world over, twelve months a year. Colgate has a similar program for the women, the Series Championships. It only includes twenty-four tournaments, and for most of the year it goes under a rock because the women have been playing World Team Tennis and the winter tour—originally Virginia Slims, then Avon sponsored. But Colgate is scared to death that somebody is going to tag it as discriminatory if it doesn't match the women's pool to the men's—so the dames get exactly as much as the men for about one-quarter the work and about one-tenth the exposure for Colgate. (Television isn't interested in the women players either.) Colgate holds the Series Championships in the fall at Palm Springs every year, and they can't put out enough paper to fill the place. In contrast, the Colgate Grand Prix Masters packs the Garden in New York every January.

Generally speaking, the women's tournaments that draw the best are those that play towns—Chicago, Detroit, for example—that don't have a good men's tournament.

It really doesn't matter how harshly or kindly I speak about women's tennis here, because I have been tagged as an ogre by the girls, and that is going to stick. I wish them all the luck in the world, and in fact, I have tried to help them from the beginning. In 1968, the first year of open tennis, Billie Jean and I were sitting together in the stands at Roland Garros during the French Open. We were discussing the sad state of women's tennis, and I suggested to her that the first thing she and the other girls should do was to form their own association and work up their own circuit. She agreed completely, and this is exactly what happened: they formed their own association and their own tour.

All the women tennis players should get down on their knees every day and thank Joe Cullman, the chairman of Philip Morris, because he bankrolled Virginia Slims, and that was the salvation of the sport. The girls eventually threw over the Slims Tour because Philip Morris wouldn't run things the way the Women's Tennis Association and Billie Jean wanted it, and that was a shame. Virginia Slims was the best run tour in the world, men's or women's.

But of course nobody ever pays any attention when I say something nice about women's tennis, because I'm stereotyped as a male tennis chauvinist pig. There are three reasons, I think, why I have earned this acclaim.

First, there is Gladys Heldman, the publisher of *World Tennis* magazine. Gladys was almost good enough to be a tour player herself—teaching herself to play after her children were born—and she is the wife of Julius Heldman, a ranking player of my vintage. Gladys started *World Tennis* in 1953 with two other players, Gardnar Mulloy and Gloria Butler, but eventually she took full control, and for two decades, right into the 1970s, Gladys was the most powerful tennis voice in America. She is also the smartest kid I ever ran into anywhere.

I had once considered buying a magazine named *American Lawn Tennis,* which was the forerunner to *World Tennis,* and it was a mistake that I didn't, because within the tennis establishment Gladys had what amounted to an editorial monopoly. And she loved it. Naturally she didn't rock the boat too much, because if tennis changed she might lose some of her authority. (And she was right too. When tennis finally went open, *World Tennis* continued to address itself mostly to the tight little inside circle, and a new broader publication, *Tennis,* came from nowhere to pass *World Tennis* in readers and advertising.)

Nevertheless, while Gladys didn't agitate in behalf of the

pros, she tolerated us and treated us fairly enough for the first six or seven years of the magazine's existence. Then around 1960, Gladys started to put the arm on me to buy advertising space. A tour required daily newspaper ads, citing specific times, dates, ticket prices, etc. Buying space in a national magazine was pointless for our purposes, and I told her so. "Gladys, I'm making the news," I told her. But thereafter I wasn't in the pages of *World Tennis*—or when my tour was covered there, it was negatively: the pros were bad for tennis.

Usually the tennis establishment said the pros didn't care for the game, that all we did was come into a town, take the money and run. And of course this wasn't altogether a false claim. But it was unfair. On a tour you have to play an average of four and a half times a week just to break even, so there was never a lot of time left to teach kids, and there was never a lot of money left to build tennis courts. But of course this is one of those phony arguments that the amateur tennis establishment dreamed up to use against the pros. Nobody knocks the Dodgers for not using their off days to help the kids in Los Angeles learn to play baseball. Our job, like the Dodgers, was to entertain fans by playing our sport well and making a living. In the bargain we created new tennis fans and stirred up interest in the game wherever we went.

In fact, I've devoted a great deal of my energy through the years to raising funds for junior tennis. The Pacific Southwest tournament annually produces $50,000 for Southern California amateur tennis activities, mostly for junior tennis. Nobody is ever going to shame me in this area.

Yet the USLTA and the establishment apologists like Gladys continued to label us as greedy carpetbaggers. It very cleverly diverted attention from the genuine argument: whether open tennis should be permitted. It held back natural progress. Remember, it was not the progressive United States, but traditional old England that first declared for open tennis. I think if Gladys had gone out on the limb for the pros and the open game, she could have turned the tide years earlier in American establishment thinking.

In any event whereas Gladys and I had never had women's tennis as the issue between us, we had our disputes, and when women's tennis needed a scapegoat, Gladys fingered me. It's always smarter to have an actual person to campaign against. The explosion came in 1970 at the Southwest, when the $50,000 total purse was allotted with only $7,500 going to the girls. Actually this was a decision of the full tournament committee. I personally argued that we ought to cut the women in for $10,000, but I was voted down. The majority wanted to attract more male stars, draw more fans, and make more profits that we could turn over to junior development.

Didn't I read in some magazine that that was supposed to be the noble purpose of the pros?

But when the Southwest only put up $7,500 for the dames, they pulled out, screaming at me, Gladys jumped in, screaming at me, and signed up eight of the women to $1 contracts. It worked out beautifully for everybody. With an all-male tournament for the fans to watch, our gross receipts went up, and, for her part, Gladys prevailed upon Joe Cullman of Philip Morris to start all-women's tournaments, which is what I had said they had to do. So if I really had been responsible for the girls getting a raw deal, you'd think that they would give me credit for starting them on their road to success. Instead, to this day, I'm a villain. The official Virginia Slims history still refers to the tournament as "Jack Kramer's Pacific Southwest." They won't let go.

There's a postscript to all of this too. A few years after the incident, when I resigned as Executive Director of the Association of Tennis Professionals, one of the first telephone calls I got was from Gladys Heldman. "Jack," she said, "we're going into business together—you and me."

"What are we going to do, Gladys?" I asked.

"Everything," she said. "The two of us can do everything in tennis."

And to tell you the truth, I thought about the offer seriously. Gladys and I would have made a helluva team. The only reason I declined was that I was cutting back on tennis business. I just didn't want all the aggravation. But just for the record, I would like all the ladies in tennis to know that the mother of women's tennis really wanted to go into business with that guaranteed pig, Kramer.

Oh well, next is Billie Jean—and specifically, the 1971 Pacific Southwest. After the withdrawal the year before, Philip Morris agreed to step in and donate $12,500 to the women's purse bringing it up to $20,000. Billie Jean got to the finals against her doubles partner (then) and her good friend Rosie Casals. They were playing for $4,000 first prize, $2,500 runner-up, a pretty substantial purse at that time. I was the tournament referee, but for the finals, I went up to the television booth to assist in the commentary for the local station.

The first set was close, and near the end of it Billie Jean got very upset with a call that the linesperson on one of the sidelines made. She kept fuming, she wouldn't forget it, even as the set went to a tiebreaker. On the second point, when the same linesperson—a female, by the way—made another close call against Billie Jean, she blew up. The woman had called a shot of Rosie's good. Billie Jean screamed that it was out. Then she screamed for the linesperson's removal, but the chair umpire backed up the official and refused to ban her. So then Billie Jean called for me, the referee, and when she was informed that I was in the TV booth, she got madder still. In my absence I had appointed a very knowledgeable tennis official to serve as referee, but that didn't satisfy Billie Jean. She yelled up to me in the booth and kept stalling so that the crowd began to get restless.

Part of the problem was that Billie Jean was the only person in the place who thought the ball was out. In fact, the videotape play-back showed that it was well within the line. So at last when Billie Jean saw she couldn't get any sympathy, she went to the line and prepared to serve again. But then just at that moment, something came over her—and just like that she decided to quit. Not only that, but as she stormed off the court she beckoned to Rosie, and damn if she didn't obediently follow Billie Jean. If she had stayed her ground, she would have won the $4,000 first prize, but she trotted after her leader, and we immediately held up the prize money for both of them.

I issued a statement about "their disservice to the public," saying that "professionals do not walk out on the public." Even Gladys Heldman called a press conference and harshly chastized both of them for their actions. Billie Jean King has done a lot of great things for tennis, and I'm the first to say that she has shown more responsibility to the game than a lot of our men's stars, but this particular time she acted completely irresponsibly.

The trouble is, though, that once again a scapegoat was needed, and Jack Kramer, up in the TV booth minding his own business, eventually came off in the annals of women's tennis as the bad guy.

Finally, what cemented my reputation as antiwomen's tennis came when Billie Jean had me thrown off national television. (For which I will be eternally grateful. Thank you, Billie Jean, thank you, thank you.) This, you will remember, was preparatory to the Battle of the Sexes between Billie Jean and Bobby Riggs. Chuck Howard, the ABC producer, had hired me to serve as Bobby's broadcast second. I was, after all, a natural choice. Rosie was going to act in that capacity for Billie Jean with Howard Cosell in the middle standing up for ABC, I guess.

Then out of the blue a few days before the match, Billie Jean informed Jerry Perenchio, the promoter, that she simply would not play if I were allowed in the TV booth. She claimed that her opposition to me had now changed. It was not that I was against women's tennis, but that I was against World Team Tennis, which was true enough, but it was a subject that wouldn't have come up in the course of Riggs vs. King. But, she was adamant. And so in the best traditions of free speech, ABC paid me not to work.

Not wanting to add to the controversy, I stayed in Los Angeles to help with the Pacific Southwest, which was on that week. Of course the night of King-Riggs, nobody gave a damn about our tournament, and as soon as the match came on television, most of the linesmen picked up and went into the clubhouse to watch it on TV. So not only was I kicked off the telecast, but I missed much of the early part because I had to call a line in a match between Cliff Richey and Ray Moore.

I got to the telecast in time to discover that the nicest thing Billie Jean ever did for me was to keep me home. Rosie was so bitter that she managed the impossible: she made Cosell appear to be America's sweetheart. Gene Scott, who had been rushed in to sub for me, seemed to be alternately astonished at her performance and then embarrassed for her.

Now as for Riggs, Billie Jean beat him fair and square. A lot of men—especially around our age—were so stunned when he lost that they figured he must have tanked. Budge is convinced of that. But what motive would Riggs have for that? Bobby Riggs, the biggest ham in the world, gets his greatest audience—and purposely looks bad? There's no way. If he had beaten Billie Jean, he could have kept the act going indefinitely. Next they would have had him play Chrissie on clay.

Of course the only possible argument to explain why a man of Bobby's ego would have tanked the match of his life, is that he bet huge sums against himself. But that's impossible. The whole world was focused on Bobby Riggs before that match, and it is inconceivable to think that he could have laid off big money against himself without it being discovered. Besides, while there was a lot of money bet on the event, it was almost all man-to-man stuff—or rather man-to-woman. The professionals wouldn't touch a gimmick competition like this one. In fact, in Vegas all they permitted was courtesy betting for good customers, what is known there as a "thin market." Even if Bobby could have concealed huge bets, he had no place to lay them.

So a betting coup makes no sense. Neither does another theory I heard, that Bobby had to promise to lose in order to get the match. I know that sounds crazy, but a lot of men still believe it.

No, Bobby got beat head-up because after he clobbered

Margaret Court he figured he could beat any of the dames without training. Here he completely miscalculated Billie Jean, who has always risen to the occasion. Also, Billie Jean has no one part of her game that makes her especially vulnerable to a man, whereas Margaret never had any spin on her second serve. She was too nervous to get the first serve in with any regularity, and Bobby could do anything he wanted with the second.

Actually I don't think Billie Jean played all that well. She hit a lot of short balls which Bobby could have taken advantage of had he been in shape. I would never take anything away from Billie Jean—because she was smart enough to prepare herself properly—but it might have been different if Riggs hadn't kept running around. It was more than one woman who took care of Bobby Riggs in Houston.

6

Mixed Troubles

The best female player I've ever seen was Helen Wills Moody. I never saw Suzanne Lenglen play at all, but Helen is clearly the best of the past fifty years. Second would be Pauline Betz Addie, who is terribly underrated, almost forgotten because the USLTA bounced her out of the game, and next would be Maureen Connally. That's the top three, far and away, with Alice Marble following them. Marble played the same kind of offensive game as Billie Jean, only she had a much better serve.

The top three—the top four counting Lenglen—all played a backcourt game, but I feel fairly confident that any one of them could beat Chris Evert on clay because all of them had more mobility than Chrissie does, and all of them could attack now and then. Tracy Austin, at fifteen, has a better forehand crosscourt than Chrissie, and it was always obvious that she could serve and move in naturally to volley—which is something Chrissie just can't do. Chrissie is so steady, of course, that even an aggressive player like Martina Navratilova must play well to beat her, even on a fast surface, but Chrissie doesn't have enough variety in her game to have been able to handle the really great players. Assuming Tracy keeps maturing, I would think that she would start handling Chrissie pretty soon, even on clay. Pam Shriver, the other young star who has such potential, is an entirely different sort: her strength is her offense. She reminds me of Alice Marble—and with so much mobility.

There is one thing you can already see in both Tracy and Pam that you can spot in all the top ladies—in Chrissie, in Billie. And that is whatever they may be like off the court, when they go out to play, they are killers. You watch Chrissie, say, when she's receiving serve. She's a cutthroat, her eyes are like slits. And all that stuff about adorable little Tracy, with her pigtails and her braces. Watch her face, she's ready to go for the jugular.

Moody was the toughest. I remember at the Pacific Southwest in 1941, when she was thirty-six years old and Ted Schroeder was teamed up with her in the mixed doubles against Sarah Palfrey and me. Some sort of scheduling problem arose, and as is usual in these cases, mixed-doubles has the lowest priority. So Perry Jones, who was running the tournament, came to us and told us that the mixed doubles match had to be put off till the next day. Sarah, Ted and I said okay and headed off. They caught up with us just in time. When Jones had gone to tell Helen the news, she had stared at him and said: "Perry, I came here to play." She meant it: play as scheduled or default. We played.

Helen and Ted beat us 7–5 in the fifth, with Helen lobbing Sarah to death down the stretch. That's the way to play mixed doubles: lob it to the lady in a spot where the man can't cheat and take it. Helen exploited the other woman as well as any man ever did.

I played tournaments with Helen after the war when she was in her forties. I remember in '46 winning a final over Tom Brown and Pauline Betz, when Pauline was at her peak. In contrast, the first time I played with Helen, I played singles against her. It was the Riggs-King thing in reverse. She was champion of the world at the time—she won seven Forest Hills and eight Wimbledons—and I was the national boys' champion, fifteen years old. I beat her, but Helen played a good game. She would have run today's women players into the ground. She played a backcourt game, like Chrissie, hitting topspin off both wings. She had a great forehand, and she could also hit a lob off her backhand that was so well controlled and so well disguised that it made her almost as tough on that side. I also played Helen Wills' great rival, Helen Jacobs, when I was a kid. She was good too; but she wasn't even in Helen Wills' league.

Pauline Betz, who later married Bob Addie, who was a sports columnist for the Washington *Post,* is the closest thing the ladies have to a Segura figure. Like Pancho, Pauline's best was always played at the wrong times and the wrong places. She won three straight Forest Hills, but they came during the war. She also won the first Wimbledon and another Forest Hills right after the war, so she was hardly unknown as an amateur. But just as she was reaching her peak in the late 1940s, the USLTA banned her. It was the closest thing to what the Olympic committee did to Jim Thorpe. It was a crime. Pauline had not signed a professional contract, but the USLTA came across a letter from Elwood Cooke, Sarah Palfrey Cooke's husband, suggesting that Pauline might play as a pro, and so she was ruled out as an amateur on the basis of intent.

The problem for Pauline was that she had no reigning pro champion to campaign against. All she could do was make a country club circuit, playing against Sarah Cooke.

So Pauline is pretty much forgotten, which is a damned shame, because not only was she a good player, but she was also the best company of all the tennis women. I can remember Pauline playing pick-up basketball against men at Rollins College when we were both there. At another extreme, she was a masters' bridge champion. She was a terrific golfer, great at ping-pong. On the court she was the best athlete I ever saw in women's tennis. They say Lenglen was a great runner, and I'm sure she was, but I can't believe any woman ever lived who could keep up with Pauline Betz. But more important, she was a terrific competitor.

In fact, Pauline was so good she almost broke the tour one time. After the war I beat Riggs on tour to become the pro champion, and then I clobbered Gonzales to keep the title. Riggs was a promoter by now, and we were looking around for somebody in the amateurs to challenge me, but nobody was ready. Sedgman was still a couple years away, and the best two Americans—Herbie Flam and Art Larsen—would have had no chance. Larsen was fascinating to watch. He had concentrated on tennis as mental therapy after serving long stretches in the front lines during the war. He was called Tappy because he went around touching everything for good luck, and sometimes he would chat with an imaginary bird that sat on his shoulder. This was good theater, but it never could have made a tour. Flam was a kid with no equipment, no serve whatsoever, but his heart took him a lot further than his racket could have. They met in the finals at Forest Hills in 1950, and I was so interested in the outcome that I went to the races.

But if there was no logical amateur challenger, Riggs and I started thinking that maybe we could do something with Segura. (This all gets back around to Pauline Betz; just keep bearing with me.) A lot of people had seen Segura playing the preliminaries on the Riggs and Gonzales tours, and he was fun to watch. Also, at least among good pro-tennis fans, he was establishing a reputation. On New Years Day of 1950, he beat me 6–3, 6–2 in the Palais de Sport in Paris, and then in June at the Skating Club in Cleveland, he beat me in the semifinals of the U.S. Pro.

The only reason I was in Cleveland was because Jack March, the promoter, gave me a Cadillac to appear. Riggs set up that deal and got $2,500 in delivery money. (So that was about $9,000 up front for me and Bobby, and I think the whole purse was $10,000.) But anyway, we played on a clay surface that had taken a lot of rain, and Segoo just ran me into the ground. The scores were 6–4, 8–10, 1–6, 6–4, 6–3, and not only was he the reigning pro champion, but I had been beaten for the first time in seven years in any kind of national championship. So Bobby and I figured we'd hype that and give Segura a tour against me.

Unfortunately there was one problem. There was no way he could handle my serve. Hell, once I beat him nineteen in a row. Also, as entertaining as Segura could be, that wouldn't do us any good coming into a town, because he didn't come in with a lot of amateur publicity—no Forest Hills or Wimbledon titles, no Davis Cup play. So we needed another attraction. And luckily Bobby and I had just what we needed: Gorgeous Gussy* Moran.

She had just gotten all that publicity at Wimbledon about her lace panties. People who didn't know Pancho Segura from Pancho Villa had heard of Gorgeous Gussy, so Bobby rushed in and signed her for a hefty guarantee of $35,000 against 25 percent—such a nice chunk that I had to agree to let Bobby cut me back to 25 percent too (with no guarantee). We gave Segoo $1,000 a week plus five percent, and now we were set . . . except for the detail of getting somebody to play Gussy.

Now here was where we went wrong. Pauline was available, she was a great player, and she was in no position to demand a big contract so we grabbed her at a straight salary. Bobby and I congratulated ourselves on pulling off a great coup.

Instead, it turned out that we had outsmarted ourselves—Pauline was too good for Gussy, but Gussy was still the name. But that won't work in sports. The headline star has also got to be the playing star. You can talk all you want about color, but winning is the real color. I haven't read a great deal about the colorful Ilie Nastese since he stopped winning consistently, have I?

The trouble with Gussy is that she had become an attraction with lace panties before she had become a champion. She had

*Everybody always spells Gertrude Moran's nickname with an *ie*—Gussie—except for Gussy Moran herself.

never been ranked higher than 4 in the U.S.—and was only
Number 7 when we signed her. A couple more years and she
could have been tough, but at this point in her career she just
wasn't any fair match for Pauline.

Then on top of everything else, Gorgeous Gussy just wasn't
as gorgeous as people were expecting. She was pretty (and, in
fact, I liked her looks better then, before she got a nose job),
and she has an absolutely beautiful figure. There was no doubt
that she was far more beautiful than the rest of the dames in
tennis. Unfortunately, after all the publicity, people would
settle for nothing less than Rita Hayworth in tennis shoes. And
Gussy wasn't looking to be a sexpot; she wanted to be a tennis
champion. If anything, she wanted to play down all the lace-
panty stuff. I knew we were really in for a lot of trouble when
Pauline not only clobbered Gussy opening night in the Garden
(6–0, 6–3 in all of thirty-three minutes) but also completely
outdressed her. For the singles Pauline came out in silver lamé
shorts and a shocking pink sweater, and for the doubles she
wore some kind of wild zebra outfit, while Gussy wore a very
traditional one-piece country club outfit.

We had gotten fantastic publicity too. In fact, in every city we
hit, Gussy would be all over the papers. Only nobody would
pay to see her play. In the Garden we only drew 6,526 (a
$16,960 gate)—much the smallest any tour opener ever did.
On the whole tour the only two places we did well were
Montreal and San Francisco. If ever I had any doubts, I
learned from this experience that tennis fans come out to see
tennis. Exploding scoreboards and giveaways are not going to
work in tennis. Tennis fans make up their minds well in
advance and 85 percent of the gate is advance sale. The lace-
panty publicity was worthless. All that mattered was that I was
clobbering Segoo and Pauline was routing Gussy. And it hadn't
taken Riggs long to figure out the situation. We took the train
down from New York to Washington, and the next day Bobby
came into my hotel room. "Kid," he said, "we have got a
problem."

Our solution was to try and get rid of Pauline. She was

married to Bob Addie by now, so Washington was her new home, but Bob had been called back into the service and Pauline was staying at the Statler. Bobby and I went to her room, and Bobby said: "Kid, isn't there something we can do to get you to sprain an ankle?" Pauline looked at us bewildered. So Riggs, the hustler himself, figured she must be negotiating. "All right, Kid, we'll give you a car if you'll sprain an ankle," he said. In response to this Pauline broke down and cried.

At this point Bobby caught on that his direct tack was not working exactly as he had hoped, and so he apologized for being so blunt and told Pauline to forget everything he had just said. But as we left, Bobby couldn't help but adding: "But look, Kid, at least try and make it close." Which Pauline was nice enough to try and do. But in doing so, all she really succeeded at was steadying her game. Before, Gussy might have had a good shot at Pauline on one of her bad nights, when she was going all out shooting for the lines. Now Pauline was concentrating and was damn near unbeatable. Poor Gussy, who was not that much of a drinker, started taking a slug of bourbon to relax herself before she went on the court. Plus Pauline was furious at Bobby and me. When Gussy finally did beat her in Milwaukee, Pauline left the court in tears screaming at Riggs: "Well, I guess you're satisfied now."

It was a disaster. Most of the time we cut the women to one set, and then after Segoo and I played, Gussy and Pauline came back and we played mixed doubles for the finale. I could have saved all those World Team Tennis owners a lot of money, because I learned a quarter of a century ago that you just can't make it when your main attraction is mixed doubles.

Twenty years later, when Billie Jean started accusing me of discriminating against women's tennis, especially when she had me booted off ABC, a lot of talk came up that I was still holding a grudge against women's tennis because of the Gussy tour. That's nonsense.

In fact, it was only a couple of years after the Gussy fiasco when I tried to sign another woman star, Maureen Connally. And here we could have had some great competition: Little

Mo, the amateur champion, just approaching her peak vs. Pauline Betz Addie, the pro champion, just at her peak (or maybe a bit past). I don't know who would have won. I rank Pauline over Maureen, but mostly because none of us knows how good Little Mo could have become. She won everything, and she never even got to be a woman.

I was negotiating with Maureen, and we had almost settled on a $100,000 two-year guarantee when she had the terrible horseback riding accident that ended her career. The horse she was on got smashed by a milk truck, which broke her leg. She wasn't yet twenty and already she had won Forest Hills and Wimbledon three times apiece. Her attorney, Melvin Belli, later had me testify for Maureen in her suit against the milk company, helping to establish how valuable a property had been permanently damaged in the accident.

You see, the zealots in women's tennis cannot understand that I am not against women's tennis. I am only against losing money in women's tennis. This whole notion that Billie Jean and her crowd have advertised—that "equality" between the sexes must extend to prize money—is simply ridiculous. Equal pay in the entertainment world, which is what sports is, is simply not applicable. It is like saying that if Barbra Streisand and Soupy Sales make a movie together, and both have the same number of lines, then he is entitled to as much money as she is. Or in a sports analogy, if they held the lightweight and heavyweight championships on the same boxing card, who is deserving of more money? Technically, Roberto Duran, the lightweight champion, may be a much better fighter than whoever happens to be the heavyweight champion, but that does not mean Duran should get more money. The draw gets the money. The payoff is on heavyweights in boxing and on men in tennis. The only difference is that nobody screams "equal rights for lightweights."

If you ask me, Billie Jean has cost herself a lot of money by being more concerned about technical sexual equality on the courts than with doing what will serve both sexes best. Now frankly, I didn't think World Team Tennis could ever succeed on the grand scale it sought because tennis is too much an individual sport. But whether I was right or wrong on that count, I knew it had to be doomed to failure the way it was set up because it placed too much emphasis on the dames. Technically of course, WTT played a fifty-fifty split: men's singles and doubles, women's singles and doubles, and one mixed doubles. It's even, all right. It's also foolish. It's going fifty-fifty with the lightweights in a world that would rather see heavyweights.

Worse, in actual fact the scoring worked to make the women even more important. Let's say Bjorn Borg would play World Team Tennis again. The chances are, in one set, on a fairly fast carpet indoors, that any reasonably good men's player is going to hold serve pretty regularly against Borg. He is going to win three or four games almost anytime out, maybe even get hot and play a deuce set or even win the set. They're playing no-ad, sudden death. I'm not saying that a handful of the best players would give Borg a respectable set. I'm saying that almost any fast court player in the top one hundred would be reasonably competitive under the WTT ground rules.

But this is not the case with the women. Once you get past the first five or ten, there is a tremendous drop-off. Chris Evert or Martina Navratilova will beat the women's Number 100 6–0—maybe 6–1—on an offnight. She is going to beat Number 50, Number 20 by the same lopsided score most times. So the top female player gives you more of an edge than the top male player, and therefore is more valuable. That's just plain cockeyed.

Okay, so now you know, as Billie Jean has said, that I am completely opposed to the idea of a team-tennis league. I'm so against it that: 1) as early as 1951 Riggs and I were trying to put together a team-tennis league, and 2) I was working on a truly international team-tennis league in 1973 when the WTT came into existence in the United States.

The first person who ever suggested the idea to me was Mickey Falkenberg, Bob's mother. Even then, around 1950, it was not an altogether original scheme. Tilden had proposed team tennis back in the 1920s. But I liked Mickey Falkenberg's suggestion, and Riggs and I began to flesh it out. It was our idea to go slow and build. We wanted to start off with four franchises in the east—probably New York, Boston, Phila-delphia and Washington—and play two out of three, two men's singles, one men's doubles. To stock the tennis teams we were going to have a draft. But the idea died because the arena owners had no interest. There were few good buildings in those days, and interest in the sport was relatively small, especially since we didn't have enough name pros to stock a league.

Then in 1973 George McCall, the former U.S. Davis Cup captain, came to the Association of Tennis Professionals with a new team concept. This time we were going to have a much greater number of franchises, sixteen, with two divisions of eight in Europe and eight in the States. But again we were going to take off slowly and try out the league in a limited time frame. Our thought was to try it for about three weeks in the fall, when (at that time) there were no competing tournaments. We were going to start off with a draft but then have a trading period so the various countries and U.S. cities could obtain local favorites. To further encourage national identity, we were going to offer the teams in Europe to the various national associations.

We even worked up a tentative playing format. There would be four-man teams, playing singles and doubles, but in order to keep a coach's manipulation to a minimum and to assure the best head-to-head matches, we were going to enforce a ranking system. A coach would have to play his Number 1 man against the other team's Number 1. From both a competitive and box-office point of view, we had the thing worked out pretty well.

Then at the Riggs-Margaret Court match, McCall told me that plans for a U.S. tennis league were proceeding well, and that he had a shot to be the commissioner. So we at the ATP dropped our own plans. We couldn't compete with tax dollars. The WTT sucked in rich guys on an ego trip looking for deductions, and they attracted players by offering guarantees.

98

We were going to make our kids play for purse money, just as in tournaments. So we had to give it up.

Whenever they want to feature the women and lose money in WTT, that's their business, but it upsets me because WTT competes against tournament tennis. WTT takes the stars of tennis, who attain that status by winning tournaments, removes them from tournaments, and then uses them to compete with tournaments.

On the other hand, I think things may be getting brighter for women's tournament tennis. It appears that there will be greater competition in the years ahead. Men's tennis must compete against baseball, basketball, football and soccer, as well as golf, while women's tennis stands virtually alone as the preeminent female game. And yet for many years it was men's tennis that kept producing top young stars—Connors, Borg, Gerulitis, Vilas, McEnroe. At the same time, for reasons I never could fathom, there were almost no new girls popping up. Now with kids like Tracy Austin, Pam Shriver and Anne Smith, the ladies will be getting more depth in their fields.

The ladies also have organized opportunities that the men don't have. Whereas the Association of Tennis Professionals has been restricted by antitrust laws, the Women's Tennis Association's power has never been challenged in court, and as a consequence it has more authority over the players. The suits that Jimmy Connors and his manager, Bill Riordan, brought have long since been settled, but the legacy remains. The lawyers haven't gotten in and screwed the WTA up, so it can run the game easier than we can. Women's tennis has also been very clever at attracting congenial sponsors like Virginia Slims and Avon that are promotional-minded and have pushed the tennis in order to help the product. Men's tennis sponsors have never tied in so well with the game.

Maybe most important of all, the switch of the U.S. Open from dirt to concrete has got to help the dames. It is bad enough watching the men play on that slow bubble-gum, but the women can put you to sleep out there. They know it, and really pushed to move the tournament onto cement.

Nevertheless, no matter how fast the surface, women's tennis can never become a superior spectator attraction. The problem is functional: in women's tennis the defense is always going to beat the offense. The top female players—Lenglen, Moody, Betz, Connally and Evert today—have all been backcourt players. Over the long haul they can beat the attackers. And this is always going to be the case, because the top offensive women can never be outstanding. They might get to the net, but they are neither strong enough or nimble enough to beat a good counterpuncher.

The men are exactly the opposite. Except on the very slippery surfaces, the best offensive players will win out over the best backcourt kids because the male athlete is quick enough and strong enough to cover the net. Chrissie beat Billie Jean even before she went over the hill. Billie Jean was really very lucky because the other top players of her time were also offensive: Maria Bueno and Margaret Court. It is a fluke that three offensive female stars would appear at roughly the same time.

It is a more normal situation now with Chrissie the one to beat. Martina will upset her occasionally, sure. But also keep in mind that Martina got beat indoors by little Tracy Austin the first time they played. Defensive women stars can be beaten by someone like Martina or Alice Marble or Margaret Court when their serve is on. Evonne Goolagong—so beautiful to watch, such a natural athlete—is also capable of beating any backcourter on her best days. Evonne is like Lew Hoad, capable of anything at her best.

But in the long run, the duller and surer that you play women's tennis the better your chances of winning.

7

Jake, We Have a Little Problem Here

The Grand Slam is a grand publicity gimmick for tennis. In 1938 Don Budge simply made it up to give himself something to shoot for. And he pulled it off.

Budge invented the tennis Grand Slam by selecting the championships of the countries that had won the Davis Cup. You need four to make a Grand Slam, and conveniently for Don there were just four Davis Cup champs—the U.S., England, Australia and France. Although France and Australia had been great Davis Cup champions, their tournaments did not come close to ranking with the fields at Forest Hills and Wimbledon.

Before and for years after Budge's lone appearance in the Australian, almost no top player from the northern hemisphere entered the tournament. Not only was it too far away but the expense money was low and the tournament was stretched over two weeks.

The French had a much more distinguished roster of champions than did the Australians, but most players were clay-

court specialists from the Continent. Until the last decade or
so, the grass-court players from the U.S. and Australia just
didn't consider the French as important as the other big titles.
Nowadays a champion really shows his stuff by winning on
various surfaces, so it looks like a knock at my own record—
and Gonzales' and Riggs' and Sedgman's and Vines', etc.—that
I never won the French. But I can defend that by saying at that
time no one really cared for anything but Davis Cup,
Wimbledon and Forest Hills. If I won the French nobody
noticed; if I lost it, it made headlines and my value diminished.

But let me give the devil his due. Right now the French
Open is the hardest championship in the world to win. It
attracts an extra good field now, there are more good dirt
players around, and it is best-of-five sets in every round after
the first two. You really have to grub it out. After playing
through the French (and the Italian too) in 1978, a match
against Connors at Wimbledon must have seemed easy for
Borg.

And that brings up the other side of the coin. What's the
easiest major championship to win? Wimbledon, by far.

I'm talking here about the favorite. If you're seeded Number
1, *the* tournament you should never lose is Wimbledon. In
horse racing they handicap against the favorite. At Wimbledon
the better the player the more advantages he is given.

First of all the grass is the best in the world. Nobody is going
to pull a freak upset because of bad bounces. The weather is
pleasant and cool. All the players—especially the favorites—are
primed and rested. The matches are all best-of-five, but points
on grass are relatively short so it is not as grueling as in Paris.
Also, at Wimbledon, the tiebreaker is not played until eight-all
(instead of six-all almost everywhere else), and the last set is
played out to its natural conclusion—no tiebreaker. Thus form
is more likely to hold up.

Wimbledon is scheduled over twelve days, with the favorites
given special considerations. As Wimbledon gets more and
more popular, it has become too crowded to play the big
names on an outside court, so players like Borg and Connors

play almost all their matches inside, and invariably, to satisfy the fans they are scheduled at the best times every day. Some kid who is not seeded will play the first match one day on court eighteen, the last match at dusk the next day on court fourteen, and then all of a sudden he is led onto Centre Court in mid-afternoon to face Borg, who has been playing there at that time all week.

The only time Wimbledon ever was a hardship for the players was right after the war when it was difficult to get all the right food in England. I took my own meat with me from America just to be sure.

Wimbledon also used to be easier for the favorites because its field was pale compared to Forest Hills. The fact is that Wimbledon's position of preeminence is really rather new. We all have a tendency to assume that anything from England is older than anything from America and therefore is steeped in tradition. And it is true that lawn tennis was invented in England and that Wimbledon is older than our championships—by all of four years. But our national association started before England's, and the Davis Cup is American. So Wimbledon has no significant seniority over the U.S. Nationals, and until very recently it was ranked as no more than an equal (if that) with our championships.

This all sounds practically sacrilegious now, but when I was an amateur I knew damn well that it was more important for me to win Forest Hills than to win Wimbledon. And Forest Hills was much harder to win. For one thing, the U.S. Open is always played at the end of the summer when players tend to be played out. It is sure to be muggy and hot. When the tournament was on grass at Forest Hills, the grass was plain lousy. This made for upsets and kept everybody on edge. The players tended to be out of sorts anyway because they did not get the blue-ribbon treatment they were used to in London and other places. As a matter of fact, when the ATP polled its members a couple years ago, it turned out that New York was the least favorable tournament site in the world.

In the days before jets, very few Americans and fewer still

Australians would make the trip to England. It was too expensive a gamble if you didn't have much of a chance, and even if you were a contender it meant the investment of a lot of time. Once Tilden won Wimbledon and established himself as the champion he couldn't be bothered to take up a large part of his summer on the ocean. As a consequence, a good grass player could breeze through the early rounds at Wimbledon, where your opposition was likely to be second-rate Britishers or clay-court specialists from the Continent. In contrast, at Forest Hills you had to meet all kinds of tough American kids who knew fast surfaces and were out to make a name and rankings for themselves.

By the 1960s, however, Wimbledon was firmly established as the world championship. This was really the reason why, in 1973 the Association of Tennis Professionals was forced to boycott it. The men who ran Wimbledon simply could not believe that anyone in the game—players especially—could possibly thumb their nose at Wimbledon. They always thought we were bluffing right till the very end, and then pride got in the way.

The whole boycott of '73 was all very sad too, because Wimbledon should never have been hurt by the players. Wimbledon put its prestige behind open tennis, and by doing so had brought open tennis into being and made players respectable and much wealthier. But ironically, the issue that brought about the boycott of '73 was an historical one, and somehow, I think, the players felt obliged to stand up for all their predecessors who had suffered from tennis officials and archaic national organizations in years gone by.

It is worth remembering. If nothing else, it's the only time in the history of any sport I'm aware of where the players have boycotted the world championship.

The matter turned on Nikki Pilic of Yugoslavia. He was his nation's best player, good enough to make the semi's of Wimbledon when it was still all-amateur. Another good Yugoslav player, Zelko Franulovic, had come along, so all of a sudden Yugoslavia had a competitive Davis Cup team for the first time since the war. Keep in mind too that national organizations can pay a lot of bills with Davis Cup matches. Pilic was playing Lamar Hunt's World Championship of Tennis circuit in the United States, and he and his partner, Allen Stone of Australia, were one of the better doubles teams. As the WCT season moved to Europe it appeared likely that Pilic and Stone would qualify for the doubles playoffs and would have to go back to North America for the championships in Montreal the first week of May. That same week Yugoslavia had a Davis Cup match scheduled.

When the Yugoslav federation—which was headed, incidentally, by the uncle of Pilic's wife—asked Nikki to play that Cup round, he gave a conditional yes, indicating that he would only play if he and Stone did not qualify for the WCT doubles championship. Keep in mind that Pilic had a contractual agreement with WCT and an obligation to his partner Stone. If Nikki pulled out, Stone could not pick up guaranteed prize money with a new partner. Pilic figured he and Stone would qualify, and as he explained to the Yugoslav federation, it probably wouldn't be a very good idea to use him for Davis Cup that week even if he were available because he had been playing on fast indoor surfaces for months, and the Davis Cup was scheduled on outdoor dirt. Pilic and Stone did qualify for the WCT doubles and Yugoslavia had to find itself another player.

Instead, the Federation ordered Pilic to play in the Davis Cup. You've got to remember this is the way it had always worked. If you lived in Transylvania, the Transylvania Tennis Federation could tell you precisely where to go, and if you didn't, the TTF would contact all other federations in the world and lock you out of tennis for as long as they wanted. In other words the national organizations were tyrants, and when Pilic refused to join the Yugoslav team, the Yugoslav federation notified the ILTF, who then advised all national associations to bar him.

The Association of Tennis Professionals had been formed the year before precisely to provide organizational backing for any player who would otherwise be defenseless against his national organization and the International Lawn Tennis Federation. I had been named the executive director of the ATP, which was the last job I wanted in the tennis world. I had had a lifetime of fighting and wanted to sit back and run my golf course in peace. But Ashe softened me up, and then Dell practically brought me to tears one night telling me that I was the only figure who could work well with all elements of the game. Okay, I have a soft spot for the kid, and I agreed to take the job if the board of directors voted for me unanimously and if I could take the job without pay. I felt that would help convince people that I wasn't taking the position just for power. I felt that if Kramer were a pro's volunteer, then an amateur's volunteer like Herman David, the working chairman of Wimbledon, would be more inclined to accept me and my organization. This worked too, until the Pilic business came up, because most federations (France being the notable exception) feared the ATP's growing power and invested it with grasping motives. Basil Reay, secretary of the Lawn Tennis Association of Great Britain and the ILTF alike was especially suspicious of the ATP.

The first I heard of the Pilic dispute was early in May when Philippe Chatrier, the head of the French Open and my best friend in international tennis, called me at home. "Jack," he said, "we have a little problem here," and then he sketched in the facts and the Yugoslav claims.

I said, "Philippe, if the ILTF bars Nikki, your tournament will be ruined because every ATP member will withdraw."

I suggested that Chatrier contact Alan Heyman, the ILTF president, and a very clever British lawyer and hold off on any suspension until a hearing could be held. Heyman agreed and this bought time for the French Open, but it only delayed a resolution of the dispute, because while Pilic stayed in the French draw, his would-be suspension was only passed along to the next tournaments: the Italian Open, Queens and Wimbledon.

I jumped on the next plane for Paris and found that an

ILTF Emergency Committee, chaired by Heyman, had agreed to hold a hearing. Dell, as the ATP counsel, and I were allowed to attend these hearings. The Yugoslav Davis Cup captain produced some letters from Pilic which when translated seemed to say exactly what he had claimed: that *if* he was free of his commitments he would play. The captain also testified that Pilic had assured him over the phone that he would definitely play; Nikki stoutly denied that.

Given the evidence, which was no better than unclear, Dell and I were sure that the ILTF would knock down the Yugoslav suspension. But a few days later, Herman David, the Wimbledon chairman, tipped Chatrier that the ILTF was going to rule for the Yugoslavs. The facts of the case were not important David said; but the authority of a national federation to control a player had to be upheld.

Pilic meanwhile was playing tennis like a demon and won his way to the finals, which were delayed to a Monday by rain. His suspension was not to be announced until after his last match so that his concentration would not be affected. I didn't wait. I flew to Rome and met with the board of the ATP and several other top players in the Holiday Inn that Sunday, the day before the Italian championships started—presumably, without Nikki Pilic.

The key people present were Cliff Drysdale, the South African who was the first president of the ATP; Arthur Ashe and Stan Smith, two founding board members; and John Newcombe, who was always a factor in any player meeting even if (at this time) he wasn't an officer. Drysdale asked for my opinion. "You can't let them get away with it," I replied. "Cave in here just because Wimbledon is involved, and it'll pop up again next year somewhere else."

The issue, you see, was quickly switching to Wimbledon. The Italians were supposed to bar Pilic first, but they accepted Pilic's entry—and only paid a small fine, quietly, months later. But the ILTF didn't really mind because it felt Wimbledon was the best ground for a war with the players.

Heyman and the others could not conceive that players

would boycott Wimbledon under any circumstances, but the events of the previous year made them all the more confident that the players would be there. In 1972 when Lamar Hunt and his WCT players decided not to play the French, all the major tournaments and national organizations bound together to lock the contract pros like Newcombe, Laver, Rosewall and Ashe, out of Wimbledon. The expulsion had cost Newcombe his chance at winning three Wimbledons in a row, which nobody had managed since Fred Perry in the 1930s (Borg finally did it in 1978). Without all these top players, Smith had beaten Nastase in the final. The ILTF reasoned that surely these guys wouldn't voluntarily give up another chance at the championship.

For the past thirteen years I had been the BBC's color commentator for the tournament so the ILTF and Wimbledon were just as convinced that I would not pass up a Wimbledon. I loved the job and realized that it kept me in the public eye and might sell my Wilson rackets. Whatever my feelings to Wimbledon, the ILTF blew them out of proportion because they incorrectly assumed that I could lead the players around by the nose.

When it comes to sports unions you've got big winners making hundreds of thousands of dollars a year alongside of hangers-on who are lucky to get through another year. And the players come from all over the world—all races, religions, languages, cultures. The ILTF was crazy to think that I could speak for the whole bunch of them.

Finally, there was Pilic, the *cause celebre* himself. All of the ILTF men know that no player was more unpopular with his fellows than was Nikki Pilic. He was stubborn and argumentative on the court, sure that everything he hit went in and that everything his opponent hit went out. Only the linesmen and umpires disliked him more than the players. Also, ironically, he was a political reactionary who was very much opposed to the concept of unions. The thought that Nikki Pilic would be saved by the other players banding together on his behalf was too much to expect. But of course that is just what happened.

At the meeting in Rome, I suggested that Drysdale approach Alan Heyman and get him to have a meeting with the player group and Herman David of Wimbledon. It was vital, I emphasized, that David realize that Heyman and the others were not just seeking a suspension of the one player, Pilic. They were using Wimbledon to force the ATP to back off from its demands that a federation could no longer control an independent professional tennis player.

But Heyman turned Cliff down. He wanted to maintain the pretense that this was just an isolated argument between one player and his national federation. And so, rebuffed, Drysdale got the support of the ATP Board of Directors to start circulating petitions in which those who signed agreed to pull out of any tournament that barred Pilic. Virtually all of the players at the Italian championships signed the petitions, and the press—most especially the British writers—supported the move.

Still, the ILTF and Wimbledon refused to back off, and almost as soon as I arrived back in Los Angeles, Drysdale was on the phone urging me to hurry to London. At Heathrow Airport, I was met by John Barrett, one of the ATP's advisory directors, and he told me that a meeting had been arranged with Heyman and David for the next morning. When I arrived thirty minutes early, however, I discovered that they were already in a premeeting meeting, and David, who had never been any friend of the ILTF and its hypocrisy, was getting the full powers of persuasion from Heyman.

When I suggested that the ILTF hand over the Pilic matter for independent arbitration, Heyman would not give an inch. He was adamant that Pilic had broken an ILTF rule, that a national association had suspended one of its players, and therefore, that the matter was out of his hands. In other words because of some stupid, archaic rule that had been written a half-century or more before to control some unruly un-sportsmanlike player, we were all trapped. That was the farce—and believe me, Alan Heyman loved it that way.

Poor Herman David and Wimbledon were caught in the

middle. David was a terrific fellow too, a former top British player, and Davis Cup captain, and obviously the tennis leader of his country. You could read the anguish on his face—and I'm sure all of this affected his health and contributed to his death a short time later. He had never liked the ILTF, but the All-England Club—Wimbledon—was under the authority of the Lawn Tennis Association of Great Britain which belonged to the ILTF, and therefore his hands were tied.

At this point I immediately informed my boss at the BBC and Mr. David that if the boycott did come off, I would never embarrass the network and the club by continuing as the color commentator. The BBC assured me that whatever happened, we would surely continue our long and happy association. (Since the boycott I've made one brief appearance at their microphones.)

By now I was meeting almost constantly with the ATP Board. Nothing broke the logjam, and so as a last resort we tried to obtain an injunction from the British courts. Heyman warned me that we were making a terrible mistake, and he was right. The judge declared firmly that he had no jurisdiction in the matter, and therefore the ban on Pilic had to stand. And as he departed his chambers, he advised the ATP that since we had brought the case before him, we should pay all the legal costs: $18,000.

The ruling did not surprise us, but unfortunately the British press and public took the no-decision ruling as a decision against us. Some of the very press who had been urging us to take this stand now turned on us. Since I was identified as the Number 1 villain, I took the most heat. It was a player's issue, and I thought it best that a player be speaking for us so more and more Drysdale stood up front. Besides, Cliff is especially articulate.

In all my years of tennis, I never met a player as smooth as Drysdale. He is as clever as he is handsome, the finest politician I ever saw in the game. I had been advised that Drysdale could be counted on to do the right thing so long as it is the right thing for Drysdale. In fact, I did lose some respect for him during a later dispute. It was the ATP's position that its players should only play for prize money, but as soon as World Team Tennis offered Drysdale a top contract guaranteeing him money win or lose, he changed positions overnight, and along with Newcombe, worked to get the by-laws changed. But never mind: Drysdale was the champion of the boycott. In the whole affair there were a lot of kids who reacted in fascinating ways— Newcombe, Ashe, Smith, Nastase, Rosewall—but none of them was more intriguing than Drysdale.

The night after we received the court's decision—Wednesday, June 20, five days before the start of the tournament— Drysdale convened the full board of the ATP and we thrashed things out till two in the morning. Then Cliff called for a vote, boycott or not. John Barrett abstained. John is an Englishman who works for Slazengers, the tennis manufacturing company which supplies the Wimbledon ball, and he simply figured that he was too involved in conflicts of interests. But the rest of the board voted to boycott. Included was Mark Cox who is British; plus Ashe, Smith and Jim McManus from the U.S.; Ismail El Shafei from Egypt; Pilic (yes, he was on the board) and Drysdale among the players; plus Pierre Darmon, the former French Number 1 who is now a tournament director; and myself. Afterwards Drysdale stood before the press and declared: "These are the hardest words I'll ever utter, but the ATP Board of Directors have voted to urge its members not to play in the 1973 Wimbledon championships."

The next day, Drysdale assembled the whole membership. It gathered in the face of the most biased press coverage. We were accused of everything except the one thing that counted, standing up for the rights of all players against an unjust rule. It was here too when Fred Perry (the great English champion—they took away his Wimbledon membership when he turned pro) deserted the players so completely, proudly declaring (in headlines) that "this player decision is not my cup of tea," whatever that is supposed to mean. "Imagine, I won Wimbledon in 1947, and King George V gave me my trophy personally, however, when I came back to visit the first time as a professional, I couldn't even get into the men's locker room. How do you like that for hypocrisy."

The turnout was a record; the vote was unanimous; the boycott was on.

Now came the crunch: holding individuals in line. Our task was made tougher too because the ILTF contacted those national organizations which had players at Wimbledon and got them to put the pressure on the kids to pull out of the boycott. The Continental Europeans got the most heat. The kids from the hard Communist countries had no choice. Alex Metreveli of Russia was not even permitted to be in the ATP, and of course he played and got to the final, where he was defeated by Jan Kodes of Czechoslovakia, who was likewise forbidden the right to belong to a union. The European federations generally retained more old-fashioned power. In many cases they were—and still are—connected with the government, so a player who went against the tennis federation was in effect breaking with his government. The top players especially affected by this were Orantes, Gimeno and Gisbert of Spain; Panatta and Bertolucci of Italy; Nastase and Tiriac of Romania; and, as well, the two top South Americans, Fillol and Cornejo of Chile. If a majority of these guys ditched the boycott it could start a stampede, and so we had to do a lot of baby-sitting with them.

In the end only Nastase bolted. And Ilie of course was the biggest name of the lot. He was seeded second, only after Smith, who had beaten him in a five-set final at Wimbledon the year before. He was the defender at Forest Hills, where he beat Ashe, and he was just coming off victories in the French (where he beat Pilic) and the Italian.

Almost as soon as Nastase voted to go along with the boycott, he started whining that he was getting pressure to play from the Kremlin on down. He claimed he would lose his passport if he didn't play. He knew what he had to beat to win Wimbledon—Kodes, Metreveli, a brash boy named Connors— and he wasn't going to let a little thing like loyalty to his friends stand in his way.

Everybody worked to keep Nastase in line. His countryman, Ion Tiriac, Dell and myself sat with him at dinner after the players' meeting, and one by one the players on the Davis Cup teams came over to him. Each promised him that if he stayed with the boycott and if this resulted in punishment from the Romanian federation, then they would refuse to play Davis Cup as a protest. You never saw such class—to a man.

In the end it did not touch Nastase. Just when we most needed to show a solid front, he announced that he was playing; that he was being "forced" to.

It is always difficult to figure out what effect outside circumstances have upon players, and certainly it is impossible to tell from one moment to the next how Nastase is going to respond. But he should have won this Wimbledon. He cheated his friends for the chance, and then when he didn't win, he was never the same.

Nastase is a fascinating kid. People are always amazed when they hear me point out that he is not a bad kid off the court. Dumb, yes, but even when he tries to be a bastard off the court, you can't hate him too much. I can remember in 1975 when he tanked a match disgracefully in the Canadian Open just before Forest Hills, so Don Fontana, the Canadian promoter, raised hell. We called a meeting at Forest Hills and the verdict was an $8,000 fine for Nastase. A couple of days later Orantes beat Nastase, who started walking back to the clubhouse. I just happened to be walking along minding my own business, but he spotted me and started screaming, "You dirty sonuvabitch, Kramer . . . I get you, you . . ." And worse, and on and on.

I didn't follow him to the locker room, and the next time I saw him a day or so later, he had completely forgotten about the episode. He didn't apologize, he didn't laugh about it—it was just forgotten.

I became a Dutch Uncle to Nastase, fining him and berating him regularly when I was the head of the ATP, so I got the reputation as the guy who "could handle Nastase." I was made tournament referee a few times largely on account of that, but Ilie and I could laugh and joke, and he never held any of my official actions against me. You see, he isn't a bad kid. Years ago I noticed a fascinating thing which always holds up. He never bitches at a call made at his end of the court. And that of course is the end where most players complain because that is where they can see the ball land. But Nastase argues with decisions made at the other end of the court. Of course he can't see them. But if he hits a serve and it feels good, and the linesman calls it long, Nastase has a fit because the ball *felt* good . . . therefore it must *be* good. Everything is emotion. He is the most primitive personality I've ever seen on a court.

Ion Tiriac is the one who screwed him up, I think. Tiriac is famous for being Vilas' mentor, but he is Nastase's countryman, and at the time Nastase appeared on the scene Tiriac was already a national hero in Romania. Tiriac had no speed, had learned tennis very late in life after being a hockey star, and there was no way in the world he could play world-class tennis. But he did, with his guts. If you gave Nastase Tiriac's heart, it would be the end of competitive tennis.

Tiriac wasn't jealous. He realized that Nastase was ten times better as a player. He would coach him and bring the Davis Cup to Romania. With Nastase, Tiriac could be a national hero far beyond what he could manage without Nastase. So Tiriac set out to give Nastase his football mentality; to play to win at any cost. And as it turned out, it worked against Nastase. It was like handing him a ticking bomb that kept exploding in his own hands.

I never hated a player in any sport more than I hated Tiriac at the '72 Davis Cup in Bucharest. He beat Gorman and he almost beat Smith, and he didn't deserve to be on the same court with either one. This was the moment he had been planning for years, and he used the home-town pressure to scale new heights. Only a player like Smith, who refuses to get rattled, could have survived the show that Tiriac and the crowd threw at him. At the net, at the end, Stan said: "I've lost all respect for you today and I'm never going to speak to you again." But what did Tiriac care? He had done everything he had to to win, and that was all that mattered.

Unlike Tiriac, Nastase gets hurt when people are offended by his actions. When he starts out to break up the opponent's concentration, he ends up losing his own. Nastase is a naturally enthusiastic kid. He could never be an attentive student like Vilas is for Tiriac today. Nastase has to be himself, and Tiriac tried to make him something else, and it ruined him.

Nastase might have been great. For native ability he is in a class with Vines, Hoad and Laver. But when you rank him you can only talk about might-have-been. I would say that Nastase and Kovacs are the best players with the least records to show for it. Nastase possessed the finest anticipation and movement that I ever saw in anybody: he has the truest natural feel for the game. His serve is a damn sight better than it ever has been given credit for. He could never put volleys away, but then he didn't have to, because he was too quick for anyone to pass him and so fast he could catch up with any lob over his head. He is the only player I ever saw who owned the ultimate attacking defense of being able to hit a topspin lob from both sides. Santana could pull that off on his best days, but Nastase could always do it.

At the time he bolted the boycott though, he was the most crucial figure at Wimbledon. If just one or two more Europeans had followed his example . . . but no one else jumped, and Tiriac even got into the fray against Nastase. After Nastase choked in Bucharest, Tiriac gave up on him. When Nastase went against his colleagues, Tiriac blew the whistle on him. Nastase had said the Romanian federation had forced him to play. Tiriac said that was a lie (and, in fact, the ATP subsequently fined Nastase $5,000 for it).

The only other major player to desert the ATP side was Roger Taylor. Now Taylor is British, and so I think we all sympathized with the pressures that were working on him (and on Mark Cox). It is one thing to boycott the championship of the world but it is another to boycott your national championship.

Actually Taylor had even more reason to side with the ATP than did Cox. While Mark was well born, well educated, Roger was the son of a steelmaker from Sheffield who was a working-class union man. Mr. Taylor told Roger to stay with the boys, and I'm sure that's where Roger's heart was. But his sporting goods company and his wife told him to stay with his country, and he did.

Taylor was very unhappy after that. The players fined him $5,000, but I don't think they held a grudge against him; I think they understood the pressures he faced and were grateful they weren't in his shoes. I don't think they ever *had* to say anything to Roger, because he punished himself enough for his decision. He had been a good player—the first rank off the top—but he never amounted to a thing after Wimbledon '73.

We still had one more cliff-hanger involving the whole ATP. Almost from the moment on Wednesday when we voted to pull out, there were ripples of reconsideration. There were two highly respected players who began to emerge as spokesmen for this new position. One was Rosewall, who even then, was almost a venerable figure among the pros. Kenny has never been much of a political animal, but he was caught in the middle because he endorsed Slazengers, the Wimbledon ball, and the company was on him. More important, despite that sweet little face, Rosewall is a tough realist, and he knew damn well that he wasn't just giving up one Wimbledon. He was giving up possibly his last good chance to win (though in fact he got to the finals at age thirty-nine in the next year). If anything could be done to stave off the boycott, Kenny was willing to help. So was Stan Smith. He was Number 1 seed, Number 1 in the world, the defender, ready to open on Centre Court Monday. Smith had the most reason of anyone to play. Now there is no player more honorable than Stan Smith, so Stan Smith began to search for an honorable way to put Wimbledon back together again.

Drysdale was perfectly willing to see if we couldn't come up with a miracle, and so he called another meeting of the executive council for the next evening, Thursday. Four players who were board members attended: Cliff himself, Ashe, Cox

116

and Smith. Jim McManus could not be present because he had gone to Eastbourne to a small tournament there, helping make sure that nobody broke ranks. John Barrett and I were the two other board members, both nonplayers, who were also present, as Pierre Darmon had gone back to Paris.

But when I got to the meeting, Rosewall, who is not a board member, was in attendance. Nobody was going to turn Kenny away, but just the same, he had no business at a closed meeting.

But never mind, here come Cliff Richey and Charlie Pasarell too, and they are not on the committee, but they are out-and-out revolutionaries: boycott at any cost. So Drysdale has traded off Rosewall for Pasarell and Richey. It is out of order, but everybody is happy.

Just before the meeting, I had gotten a phone call from Newcombe, another defending champion with an excellent chance of winning. John was also very involved in player matters. This was certainly one time in tennis when most of the best players were the leaders off the court as well. (Do we miss that now.) Newcombe's a cutie though. As great a guy as he is, he can be selfish. I got my guard up.

"Jack," he said on the phone. "I understand that Drysdale has called another meeting to reconsider the boycott."

"That's right," I said. "It's about to start now."

"All right, just checking. I'm going to go out and have a few beers." I knew with the Aussies this meant an all-night session.

"I wish I could join you."

"I just want you to know one thing, Jack," Newcombe went on. "If the vote is to call off the boycott and go ahead and play, I'll play. I'll do what everybody else is doing. But I guarantee you if the decision is changed, I'm out of the ATP and I'll never have anything to do with a player's association again."

I felt pretty much like John. I told him I would pass on his message, which I did. He went out and got drunk, and three years later he succeeded Drysdale and Ashe as the ATP president.

The meeting itself was more tense than the one two nights before. At that time we still had some breathing room, and we were fairly agreed. But now there was more of a split, and there were strangers to stir the pot. Kenny talked about obligations and Pasarell and Richey screamed about the principle of player independence. Sooner or later the Wimbledon '73 boycott turned everybody upside down. Even Ashe; the most solid guy of all. This came when Drysdale finally declared that we would take a vote on whether we should take the matter back to the ATP for a full vote. Then Ashe lost his cool screaming, "If we even vote on it, I resign!" It's so funny now, but here we all were at the time—both sides—patiently explaining to Arthur Ashe about free speech and the rights of man. Arthur Ashe! Reluctantly, he agreed to a vote and promised not to resign if it went the wrong way.

Well, I could count. McManus, who was in touch with us by phone in Eastbourne, would stay for boycott and so would Arthur and I. But the two Englishmen, Barrett and Cox, would surely go for a new vote, Smith was leaning in that direction, and if it came up 3–3, I was sure Drysdale would play it safe and call for another membership meeting.

McManus, on the phone, Ashe and Kramer voted for not calling for another vote. Smith joined Cox and Barrett in asking that we take the matter up again before the whole ATP. Three-to-three. We all looked down at President Drysdale.

He paused. At last he said: "I abstain."

Brilliant! I almost fell off the chair. The vote was a tie. There would be no changes, but Drysdale had escaped being charged with being the one man who ruined Wimbledon. Did I tell you he was the slickest? It really was a master move.

And finally too, a postscript about Pilic. At the very last he began to feel guilty about the trouble he had caused. In remorse he told me that he had agonized about everything and had finally decided that the only correct thing for him to do was to thank everybody, withdraw from Wimbledon, and take his suspension like a man.

I was thunderstruck.

I got that crazy sonuvabitch on the next plane back to Yugoslavia before he could confess to anybody else.

I hung around for a few more days. My son John was with me—the poor guy: his first and only Wimbledon—and he learned what it was like to be with Hitler in the bunker. All the media kept quoting the hypocritical amateur officials, who would say the same thing every day: "What would you expect from a bunch of bastards who are only interested in the money and don't care about the game?" Even my old friends at BBC never made any effort to show the ATP's side.

Looking back, my only satisfaction ·is that I think many people—the press particularly—who were so cruel to me and the players now realize that one man only was responsible for the boycott: Alan Heyman. He is as astute as he is egotistical, and he could see power flowing from his ILTF to the players' ATP, and the argument between Nikki Pilic and the Yugoslav federation came as a godsend. So he used Wimbledon as his weapon to screw up our growth. Not then, not now do I blame Wimbledon or Mr. David. They had no choice but to do Heyman's bidding.

In fact, once the boycott was fixed, I wanted as strong a field of non-ATP players as possible, because I wanted to help Wimbledon, and I wanted somebody to beat Nastase. Just before the tournament started I got an overseas call from Raul Ramirez' father. Raul was still in college, at Southern Cal. He was not yet a professional, but his father wanted to know if perhaps his son shouldn't withdraw in support of the ATP. That was a nice thing for Mr. Ramirez to suggest, but I told him that Raul should stay in—we weren't trying to ruin Wimbledon . . . and maybe he could knock off Nastase.

The one I was really counting on though was Connors. I didn't have any dispute with the kid at this time, and I knew he could steal the tournament. Unfortunately he was only twenty and he was head over heels in love with Chris Evert. It drove his mother, Gloria, crazy, because she also knew what a chance he had. Behind his back she kept calling him "Barry Court"— Barry being the nonplaying husband of Margaret Court. Metreveli beat Connors, but I should have known that Nastase would find a way to blow his chance. He let Sandy Mayer, who was the new NCAA champion from Stanford, upset him in the quarters. After that I didn't care who won, and I left London.

My son John and I took a trip to Spain and Italy, where I tried to explain to the tennis officials that their players had no beef against them but had no choice except to go along with their colleagues. I felt the tennis people would have been perfectly happy to ignore the whole matter, but they were obliged by the sports ministries to take some action. What they did though was very civilized. Since the two nations were scheduled to play Davis Cup against each other, they both agreed to ban their stars—Panatta and Bertolucci from Italy, Gimeno and Orantes from Spain.

I was disappointed that Manolo Santana let himself be used to take Gimeno's place for Spain. He was sort of semiretired at the time, but he had always been a good friend of the other two Spanish stars and had played with many of the ATP members. I would have thought he would have joined the protest in his way by staying out of the Davis Cup, but then Santana was always a good businessman; he knew what was best for himself. When I offered him $50,000 to turn pro a few years before, he turned me down by saying that he knew he couldn't beat many of the best pros, and besides, he could make more as an amateur.

On the other hand, Philippe Chatrier, my great friend, who was then the French Davis Cup captain and vice-president of that federation, was the one high official who supported the boycott all the way. He also was a tower of personal support for me, and when it was all over we began working together to form a committee of equal support among players, tournament directors, and federations officials, who could run the game more wisely and fairly. The result was the nine-man International Men's Professional Tennis Council, which really rules the Grand Prix today. So at least something good came out of the boycott.

Looking back now, there is one more story. That is Stan Smith's. He was reaching the peak of his career; he was still only twenty-six, Number 1 in the world; and I think it is possible to speculate that had he played that Wimbledon, had he won it—which was the best guess—he might not have declined quite so spectacularly in the years that followed.

The week after Wimbledon there were two tournaments on the continent, and the one at Gstaad in Switzerland had a much stronger field. So we asked Stan if he would switch to the other tournament, at Bastad, Sweden. As always, he promptly agreed to help. The tournament there was played on clay— hardly Smith's favorite surface—but he won, which gives a pretty good hint that he was primed for Wimbledon.

But then he came back home from Wimbledon as an ex-champion, somehow he had lost the ability to win. Smith didn't win another tournament for something like two years. It was not like he collapsed overnight though. A whole year later in the semifinals at Wimbledon '74, he was serving for the match against Rosewall, up two sets to love, when he completely fell apart. That was the last nail in the coffin. That and Connors. He couldn't stand Connors, and that made it all the worse that he couldn't beat him.

But let me say this foremost about Stan Smith: he's a helluva man. His performance at Bucharest in the fall of 1972 must be the finest any individual ever performed in the Davis Cup. In the interest of helping international good will and promoting Romanian tennis, the USLTA had agreed that the match could be played in Romania. Our boys were furious. And they were intimidated by the crowd and Tiriac. At one point, Harold Solomon literally hid under a blanket in his hotel room, and Eric van Dillen kept threatening to pull out of the doubles almost to the moment he walked onto the court with Smith. The players were not only frightened of the Romanians, but they felt that their own association, the USLTA, had rejected them because the association had given up our right to play the Cup in America.

In the middle of it all Stan Smith was a rock on the court, as Dennis Ralston the captain was on the sidelines. Looking back, I guess that Stan was never so confident as he appeared to be. He depended heavily upon his serve, and without it at its best he was vulnerable. In 1971 he had shoulder problems. Omar Fareed, my physician, Charley Pasarell's father-in-law, is an internist, but he is also a tennis player and he knows tennis players. He examined Smith in France, found a second bursar in his shoulder, shot him up, and Stan got confidence in his serve again, going on to the final at Wimbledon before he lost to Newcombe in five sets. And then he won Forest Hills and the next Wimbledon. But bad shoulders never clear up completely. I'm sure that the next time Stan's began to bother him, he must have compensated in the wrong ways, and he lost his overpowering serve.

The special Smith problem was that when he was not in command, he was in greater trouble because he could not play catch-up. He didn't have enough all-court tools. All of this was exaggerated by the general switch from grass to clay, which came in about this time. So Stan's biggest weapon was blunted.

When you reach a certain plateau in tennis, you do almost everything automatically. I would hit down the line at a certain moment without really knowing that I had made a choice and carried it out. When things start to go bad for a player, the first thing he loses is that spontaneity. He starts to think a little, which is bad enough, but then he starts to overthink. That's what happened to Smith. And then after a certain number of losses, he couldn't march about with that air of confidence. Listen, let me assure you that you play better as Number 1 because most players cannot forget that fact, and thus they play worse. Once Stan was an ex-champion, the others wanted him all the more—which made it that much more difficult for him.

So a lot of factors are involved in his decline, and we can never assess exactly how great a role the boycott played. On clay, Smith could never have been the force that he was to the summer of '73. If nothing else, the boycott probably cost him another Wimbledon title—and that's a pretty big price all by itself. Stan is lucky though compared to kids like Nastase and Taylor. He didn't win, but he didn't lose anything important either. He was one guy who came out of that whole thing intact.

8

Lucky Loser

The two Wimbledons that I played, '46 and '47, were certainly mild by comparison with '73. Indeed, they were completely without incident except for a blister that cost me the first postwar championship. I have to say though I was probably lucky to lose the '46 Wimbledon—just as I was lucky to get appendicitis in '42 and clam poisoning in '43 at Forest Hills. It's trite, but sometimes defeats are good for you in the long run. And it works the other way too: a win at the wrong time can throw everything out of whack. As I'll explain in more detail later, the worst break that Pancho Gonzales ever got in tennis was winning Forest Hills in 1949.

As for myself, if I had not had appendicitis in '42, I'm fairly certain that I would have won Forest Hills. If I had, the Coast Guard would have put me in special services, and I would have spent the war playing tennis entertaining the troops. As it was they let me off duty now and then for special tennis events, but I certainly didn't get any special handling. Budge and I played two exhibitions in New York in 1944, as even the USLTA acknowledged that a world war could take precedence over the sacred amateur rules. In January, at the Seventh Regiment Armory, Don beat me 7–5, 7–5, as we raised $8 million for war bonds. That worked so well that in March we moved to the Garden for a Red Cross benefit. For that I was given all of a forty-eight-hour furlough. Beforehand, for practice at New London, Connecticut, where I was stationed, we had to stretch a makeshift net across a basketball court. But it was all worth it, because I beat Don three and two—the first time in my life I had ever played on canvas—before ten thousand fans.

I was also furloughed in '43 for Forest Hills, and here again, had I won it I'm sure the Coast Guard would have turned me into a poster boy. The Coast Guard didn't have the glamour of the other services. I had tried myself to become a Navy aviator, but I had been turned down because I only had twenty-thirty vision in my left eye. So I just strolled two more blocks to the Coast Guard recruiting station and signed on there; anything to escape the infantry.

When the Forest Hills of 1944 came around I was stationed in Japan on an LST ship, and I was still in the Pacific the next September. If I had won in '43, I'm sure the Coast Guard would have also let me play in '44 and '45, and I feel confident that I would have won both times (as it was, Parker beat Talbert both years). Thus, when the war ended I would have been the three-time national champion, and I probably would have turned pro right away, or right after the Riggs-Budge tour. My guess is that either of them could have handled me at that time. If so, the way things worked in those days, I could have sunk without a trace.

That is why I was lucky to have eaten at the International Club a couple of nights before the Forest Hills final of 1943. I ate some bad clams, and I got really sick. I was lucky to get by Segura in the semi's since he had been hot that whole summer. Then I had to play the National doubles finals, which were contested at Forest Hills that year because of the wartime travel restrictions. Parker and I won—beating Talbert and Dave Freeman, the ex-badminton star—but by the end of the match,

I was absolutely exhausted. I spent the whole next day in bed, but it just wasn't enough time to get all the poison out of my system.

My opponent in the finals was Joe Hunt, whom I had known since I was a kid in California. He came from a tennis family and had beautiful equipment; he had been an excellent prospect from a very young age, and he succeeded Riggs as the outstanding junior in Southern California. In fact, Joe was something of a hero of mine. He had always been very kind about playing me good practice matches when I was still only fifteen or sixteen. I never really knew Joe well, but (as I'll explain later) we ended up as a pick-up doubles team in the 1939 Challenge Round. Then in the weeks just before Forest Hills, he was stationed in Southern California, and we often played each other at the L.A. Tennis Club.

I was confident going into the Hunt match because I had been beating him about three sets out of four in these practice sessions, and I really felt I had his number. I might have sneaked past him too. We split the first two sets and I was up 5–4 and serving for the third set, but he broke me with a fine defensive effort and then he went on to win that set 10–8. Even with a chance to rest over the intermission, I had nothing left. I lost at love in eleven minutes, winning only four points. When I weighed myself back in the locker room, I was down to a hundred and forty-nine. I had started the tournament at a hundred and sixty-eight.

The funny thing is that Joe got a bad cramp near the end of the match, and he was actually on the ground after the last point. There I was, the loser, standing up dead on my feet while he was the winner, fallen in a heap. And sadly it was the last appearance of his in a major match. Joe was a pilot, and he was killed in a training accident a few months later.

From Forest Hills I returned to Long Beach, California, where I was stationed in the commissary. I was an apprentice seaman, what was called a "spud coxswain," but soon I earned a shot at officer's training and was shipped to New London. I was commissioned in March of '44, and shipped into action on

125

an LST with the Seventh Fleet in the Pacific. I made seven landings, the first one at Leyte, and I was in some real shooting. I was in the war. Shortly after the surrender we got caught in a typhoon, which is every bit as frightening as battle.

I matured a lot out there. I had married Gloria on April 12, 1944, just before I shipped out. Our first son, David, wasn't born until December 3, 1946, but even before the family began to grow I knew I had to grow up. I was a very popular officer because I preferred the mid-watch, from midnight to four, the one no one else ever wanted. I had a lot of time to think then. It wasn't so much a fear of getting killed; instead it was just the reality of the everyday existence I had to endure out there— twenty-two months on a ship far away from tennis. I certainly didn't come from a wealthy background, but I had gotten used to enjoying good times, making a few bucks playing a game that came naturally, so that it took being cooped up on a boat in the middle of the ocean in the midst of a war to realize what a chance I had.

It wasn't that I had wasted a lot of time and talent. I knew I had thrown away a chance at education, however, and if I didn't make it with tennis I was going to end up pumping gas somewhere. I think it was this realization that made me play harder for the rest of my career.

Before, I had just drifted. There had been some occasions when I was the kid Cocky, when I would get blown up and play like a fathead. But that was not usual. In the same way, I enjoyed myself, but I never ran wild. Probably the most spectacular episode in my night life came one evening when I was twenty-one, and I won a $25 bet by downing eighty jiggers of beer—one every minute for eighty minutes. (If that sounds easy, try it.) I stayed in shape, I worked at it. I suppose that all that was really missing was drive. You have to care to carry yourself past a certain level.

I think about the European players today. Orantes is about as gutty as you can get, and Borg—who knows what kind of a miracle he is? But most of them simply cannot measure up to the Americans in intensity. The Europeans grow up using old

126

balls on soggy courts so they swing too hard and develop overspin, but I know that can't explain the general failures of the French or the British to develop champions.

The European players get more spoiled than the Americans. Each country has only a handful of good players—so good players start getting endorsement payoffs and attention before they deserve it. If you want to sell a new racket or a new line of tennis clothes in Spain, you better line up a top Spanish player to endorse them. And how many good Spanish players are there? The American Number-50 might be as good as a Davis Cup player in another country, but he has to fight much harder to work his way up.

The American gets very little official help. In France the tennis federation has more than a $3 million budget. It helps the financing of courts in small towns, sends the best players around on a national tour, subsidizes purses, develops instructional films—and they can't develop a single top player. Never mind a Borg. They can't make a Panatta, a Cox.

Poor Philippe Chatrier asked me once: "What more can we do, Jack?"

And I replied, "Since you're asking me, I'd say the trouble is you're doing too much."

Before the war I was one of a few young stars, doing well enough in the insulated amateur world. It is very easy to get lulled into just getting by when you are in this situation, but I came out of the Coast Guard in January of 1946 determined to get out of the rut and put myself on the line.

The first real test was Wimbledon, and it should have been a lock for me. In this first European postwar championship, the field was as depleted as it ever has been in modern times, except possibly for the boycott year of '73. As the time approached I came up with horrible blisters on my racket hand. To this point—and I was almost twenty-five—I had always been pretty free of injury (if you don't count clams).

Before the war, rackets had been made with an extra little piece of leather at the bottom of the handle—sort of like a knob on a baseball bat. It was called a butt piece. Well it really wasn't necessary, and to save a few pennies the racket companies stopped putting them on rackets. I was the only player it seems who missed the butt piece. I had depended upon it to get a firm grip, and without it the handle began to twist in my hand.

I took the *Queen Mary* to England, and then I defaulted in the semi's at Queens to give my hand even more time to heal. It didn't. But worse, when I stopped playing, I stopped working out as well. Dinny Pails of Australia was seeded ahead of me, but I was sure I could beat him, because he was one of these players who always looked much better than he was. And generally, the field was so undistinguished at Wimbledon that year, that even with the blisters I might have sneaked through and stolen it.

But in the round of sixteen, I came up against a chubby little unseeded guy from Czechoslovakia. That of course was Jaroslav Drobny, who had spent much of the preceding years doing forced labor for the Nazis. He beat me in five sets, and my hands were raw at the end. I think if I had come in with strong legs I might have been able to put Drobny away, but he saved himself time and again by putting away every lob I threw up. Drobny is a lefty, and the percentages are to lob a lefty down the deuce court line, but he kept hitting these overheads for winners.

Yvon Petra, a big Frenchman who had never won anything else of consequence (and who never did again), and who had spent eighteen months as a German POW, eventually won this first postwar Wimbledon. Drobny and I had to wait our turns.

I got a few days off after the singles loss, and eventually Tom Brown of San Francisco and I won the doubles. I was mad at myself for not staying in good shape, and I could have accepted the blisters as another patch of bad luck except that they would not clear up. If I played, they got worse; if I didn't play, my hand would soften up and I would develop new blisters as soon as I started swinging a racket again. It was a vicious circle, and after another month or so back in the States, I was getting genuinely worried about my future.

Then in August, on my way up to Longwood for the National Doubles, I drove through New London, and I remembered that Gardnar Mulloy's father-in-law, a Dr. Chaney, lived there. I figured I'd let him take a look at the blisters. Now the kicker was that Dr. Chaney was a dentist, but at this point I was desperate.

We chatted for awhile and then he looked at my hand. He said: "Jack, have you ever tried putting something on the handle instead of on your hand?"

As simple as the suggestion was, it was original. Then he suggested I try something named Kiro-Felt, a thirty-nine-cent product of the Dr. Scholl company. So I bought a packet and Dr. Chaney showed me how to use it. It was a felt-covered tape and we put it around the butt end of the handle. After that I never lost another meaningful singles match as an amateur. Dr. Chaney didn't send me a bill either.

I used Kiro-Felt every time I played for the next few years, and then switched to moleskin when it came out. Not till the '50s did I ever again play with a naked hand. The first major championship that I won with Kiro-Felt was the Forest Hills of '46, when I beat Tommy Brown in the finals. Tommy was known as "The Frisco Flailer" (we had nicknames like that in those days), and he was strong off the ground with an excellent running forehand, but he was always my pigeon. I played him seven times, all best of five, and I beat him twenty-one straight sets. He was dead game. At Forest Hills, before a packed stadium of 14,000—the postwar sports boom—Tommy saved four set points in the first set, which went to 9–7, but then I polished him off three and love.

Tommy was a fine player, and there were some good ones around—Schroeder, Parker, Pails and Bromwich—but once I got the dentist to take care of my blisters, there really wasn't anybody in the amateurs who could give me a match. Except for a couple of tough five-setters against Parker, I seldom lost a set until I turned pro against Riggs. I was an offensive player playing all my important matches on grass, and I drove people right off the court. Tilden had his Little Bill and then the

Frenchmen—Cochet, Lacoste, Borotra—for competition;
Vines had Crawford; Perry and Budge had von Cramm; Riggs
had Kovacs. I had no superior challenge (although I think
Schroeder could have filled this role if he had thrown himself
into tennis fulltime). So I had to play my standard in every
match. Maybe that was why I made such a good pro—I knew
how to get myself up, night after night.

It was in here that my style began to be celebrated as "the big
game." That was fine for me, it gave me a simple image that
could reach a wider public, but it always peeved me that some
people considered me all serve and volley. First of all I was a
percentage player, and second, I could hit groundstrokes.
Except for Segura I had the best forehand in the game at that
time, pro or amateur. So you could say I had *the* best one-
handed forehand in the game. I could hit a forehand down the
line as well as anyone I ever saw.

It's a funny thing, but except for Budge we were almost all
forehand specialists then. It makes sense to be a forehand
player too because you can hit topspin better with it. Also,
while it is very technical and would require great detail and
diagrams, the forehand player has greater control of the court.
Take my word. If you look back, Budge excepted, all the best
offensive players until the present attacked with a forehand:
Maurice McLoughlin, Tony Wilding, Gerald Patterson, Big
Bill, Vines, Perry, Riggs and Hoad.

And then out of the blue it all changed: Rosewall and Laver,
Ashe and Roche, Emerson. Newcombe was more traditional,
with a fine forehand. Of the top kids today, Vilas and Gerulitis
are much the best at the backhand, but McEnroe is strictly a
forehand player. Connors and Borg are both unusual. Connors' backhand is better than his forehand, but I'm more
inclined to say that he really doesn't have a backhand—he has
two forehands, one one-handed, one two-handed. Borg's
backhand also gets more attention because he scores more
spectacular passing shots off of it, but for the meat-and-
potatoes, his forehand is the better side. The underslice
forehand that he threw at Connors in the Wimbledon final of

'78 may not have kayoed Connors, but it confused him and set him up for the kill.

I've never been sure why the backhand came into fashion. I believe that it is a matter of grip in a reaction to the serve-and-volley attack. All of a sudden everybody said now we must learn groundstrokes, we must hit the return of serve. Since most serves go to the backhand, it was natural that kids start learning how to hit the backhand and that they hold the racket in a backhand grip. That's only a guess, but I think it's a pretty good one. I would also guess that the faster surfaces will start to favor serve-and-volley games more. Since the best way to counter a server as he comes in is with a good overspin forehand, I think we'll see a decline in the number of good backhand players.

After I won the Forest Hills of '46 and won my two matches in the Challenge Round when we took the Cup back from Australia, everything was pointed toward the next Wimbledon. It was important to win under any circumstances, even more to redeem my '46 defeat and show the British how good I had become. It went the way I wanted it to—my amateur career reached a classical climax in the final. I not only won, but I displayed a method for winning, whether or not it was called the big game or percentage tennis. My opponent again in the final was Tom Brown. He was a little nervous at the first because we had to wait an extra fifteen minutes for the king to arrive and be seated. Tommy did not play very well, but it didn't matter. It was just my Wimbledon, and I could do no wrong. I gave him only six games, and I took only forty-seven minutes. I was the first Wimbledon champion ever to wear short pants, and no one has ever come close to winning so quickly either.

And now Riggs wanted me. I still had to defend the Davis Cup against the Aussies and defend Forest Hills, but it was obvious that I had no serious threats, and in anticipation of my victories late in the summer, I started to consider pro deals. The first serious offer came, strangely enough, from Bing Crosby Enterprises. Gene Mako, Budge's old doubles partner, made the contact. Crosby had always been identified with golf (and some with baseball), but this one time he and his brother Larry thought they could do well with a tennis tour. They offered me a $50,000 guarantee, against 35 percent.

That was a fair enough offer too. In fact, what I accepted was 35 percent and no guarantee. I took that from a promoter named Jack Harris. I went with Harris because he had experience in promoting tours, having run the Vines-Budge circuit and the second Vines-Perry tour before that. I signed on September 3, 1947, just as Forest Hills was getting under way. While I got the percentage I wanted, I had to pay all local expenses, food and hotels while Harris agreed to pay for all transportation between sites.

It's a laugh to look at that "contract" today: one page of paper, single-spaced, typewritten, in the form of a letter written by Harris to me. It was witnessed by a mutual friend, L.B. Iceley, the president of Wilson. He just signed his name in the blank space at the bottom, there being no provision for witness. There wasn't a lawyer in sight. Guys like Donald Dell or Mark McCormack would slit their wrists if the word got out that kids could sign contracts like this and make $100,000 without lawyers. But it was all legal. It made me an illegal amateur, formally, instead of the informal illegal amateur I had been. I had already won my two Challenge Round matches, so now we only had to wait for me to run through Forest Hills and then head off to play Bobby Riggs as the undefeated champion of the amateur world.

I almost blew the whole thing. At Wimbledon I had had a cakewalk, losing only one set the whole fortnight, but at Forest Hills I had close calls in both the semi's and the finals. In the semi's I had to meet Drobny, who was making his first American appearance, playing me for the first time since he upset me in England the year before.

First of all we had to start play on the grandstand court because Bromwich and Parker were involved in an extra-long match in the stadium. By the end of Forest Hills the grandstand court was no better than the average cow pasture, but neither Drob nor I could use that as an alibi since both of us played a strong offensive game, hardly letting anything bounce even under the best of circumstances.

But if the court didn't bother me Drobny did, simply because he was a lefthander. I always hated to play lefties, and he was the best I ever met in my amateur years. And sure enough, he got a break from me and ran out the first set and followed that with another break in the second. About this point Parker finally finished off Bromwich, so we moved into the Stadium. We both held serve and entered the seventh game with Drob ahead 4–2.

He was serving, and for the first time, I managed to get a break point. When he missed his first serve I decided to go for broke. I ran around to hit my forehand off his second serve, but he made a good shot and the spin carried the ball into my body. All I could do was shove awkwardly with a forehand, and the ball seemed to go off the wood. But I got lucky; the ball faded cross-court and landed just inside the line. I was back on serve and back in the match.

One of the first things you learn in tennis is never to let a wood shot get to you. But Drobny had a strange competitive temperament, and there were occasions when for no good reason he would get down on himself and stop trying. It happened here. I won the next fourteen games and was in the finals against Parker. (The same sort of odd behavior from Drobny happened at Wimbledon in 1952. He was playing Sedgman in the finals and won the first set comfortably. Then something snapped in his head and all of a sudden he stopped coming to the net behind his serve. Sedgman started attacking a little more often, and he went on to win with ease in four sets.)

After Drobny I should have had an easy time against Frankie Parker. I hadn't lost to him in several years on the grass, but he started magnificently, and I got caught in a daze—what the Australians refer to as a walkabout. Frankie won the first two sets, four and two. I can remember very clearly looking up into the first row of the stadium seats and seeing the sun shining on the top of Jack Harris' bald head. I could see the top of his head because it was bowed down in despair. The crowd was sensing a big upset and was going crazy. Although I was always a popular champion, crowds invariably go for the underdog. It's more exciting that way. And this day they cheered for Parker in defeat much more than they did for me, in comeback and victory.

I finally did get straightened out. Harris could sit up straight. I took the last three sets with the loss of only four games. But there was one last scare. In the final set, when I was ahead only 4–3, I hit the chalk with a backhand volley to save an ad Frankie held against my serve. No, at that point I didn't think I would lose. But yes, you get into four-all in the fifth against a guy who has been there before, and you never can be sure what will happen.

But I broke him then and finished it off, and now Riggs and I were set. It was just icing on the cake when I went back out West and won the Pacific Southwest in L.A. and then the tournament in San Francisco the following week. My last amateur win there was, appropriately, over Tommy Brown. Then Harris started cranking up all the publicity: will Kramer turn pro? Can Kramer beat Riggs? Kramer turns pro! Kramer to tour against Riggs! Kramer and Riggs to open in the Garden! You really had to ballyhoo a tour in those days, but Bobby and I were perfect to play up because we were different types of players and personalities, and because the element of mystery was considerable. We hadn't played in six years, since he beat me in the quarters at the Pacific Southwest in 1941.

While I was getting ready to start touring I made my first endorsement deal, which remains the best business arrangement I ever made. This is, of course, my long association with the Wilson Sporting Goods Company.

At that time I used Wilson's top seller, the Don Budge Autograph. It sounds like I'm just plugging Wilson, but believe me it really was a great racket and I wanted to sign with Wilson, so on the way back from Forest Hills to the coast in

1947 I stopped by Wilson headquarters in Chicago. There I met with L.B. Iceley, the president of the company, and with Bill King, the executive vice president in charge of sales.

There wasn't much to talk about. I wanted to sign with them, and they wanted to give me the same sort of deal that Budge and Riggs had. The only substantial difference was that Wilson was proposing to give me only 2½ percent on each racket that they sold, and I knew that Don and Bobby (and Elly Vines too) had all signed for 3 percent royalties. So I complained to Mr. King.

He replied: "Son, if I were you I'd take my advice and take that two-and-a-half percent."

"Why?"

"Well, I'm usually involved in selling to the large sporting goods dealers, and when it comes time to place a big order, which racket do you think I'll be pushing: a racket that carries a royalty of three percent or one that's only going to cost me two-and-a-half percent?"

I said, "Mr. King, the more I think about it, the more I think two-and-a-half percent is very fair."

And it sure was. That half a point I gave up put me and my racket in the big leagues. I also applied a little tip I had learned from Elly Vines. He told me to be nice to the dealers and the salesmen. I'd make it a point on tour to drop by the sporting goods stores. Wilson rackets came and went right on through to Connors, who endorses the metal T-2000 model, and Stan Smith, whom they just dropped. But the Jack Kramer model has never left the shelf in more than thirty years and it's always been a top seller.

All those sophisticated polls that are always taken to measure the popularity of tennis—I could tell you the extent of the tennis boom from one year to the next just by reading my royalty statements. While I was pro champion, I never netted more than $13,000 in any year. My take crept up a little from there in the late '50s. Eisenhower was in office, and there was more talk about sports and health. By the time open tennis

135

came in I was up to $50,000 a year, and from there it just soared. By 1975, my 2½ percent amounted to close to $160,000.

I keep expecting Wilson to tell me that it was a good ride together, but I'm not a player anymore and that they want to bring out a new model of some hot-shot who's playing. I dread it, but I guess it'll happen someday. But it's been great. Tennis is about the only sport where a champion can go on forever being a piece of equipment. There's a lot of kids around who probably think I'm some kind of brand name, who don't have any idea that a kid named Jack Kramer carried a racket before he became one.

9

From the Backhand Court

Before I leave the amateurs and get into "The Duel of the Decade," which is how they billed Riggs and me, I'd like to spend some time with doubles. If I could tally it, I'd find that a pretty high percentage of my court time was spent playing doubles, amateurs and pros alike.

I loved doubles, and I had the perfect equipment for it: the big serve, and more important the great, deep second serve. I also had topspin forehand, a good overhead, and I was quick enough. I anticipated well, which is necessary because doubles is more intellectual than singles. For all my right instincts though, I never practiced doubles much as a kid, even though I did win a couple of important doubles titles.

You'll notice that the Australians always do well at doubles. They're good mates—they get along, they practice and drink together—but most important, they play doubles regularly from an early age. Down there, there aren't enough courts— didn't used to be anyway—so that singles was a luxury. They'd play family doubles, club doubles, neighborhood doubles. By the time an Aussie has grown up, the moves are all second nature.

I learned the nuances of the game when I was seventeen from Welby van Horn, a cagey veteran of eighteen. Welby was a fine player who was limited by his asthma, but who always had the makings of a good coach. After he moved to Puerto Rico he developed Charley Pasarell and some other kids down there. That summer of 1939 Welby needed a partner; he noticed my attributes for doubles, and he took me under his wing.

I was all slam-bang slug away, and needed to learn that if you're going to succeed at doubles, you have to throw away a large portion of the traditional big game. Accuracy is more important than power. You want to hit the ball with a dippy overspin on it, lob more, use the alleys and use more angles. Bob Hewitt, who grew up in Australia before he moved to South Africa, knows how to play classic doubles better than any of the current crop. He hits so the ball dips over the net so that the other team is hitting up, so that Hewitt's partner, Frew McMillan, swoops out of nowhere and smashes the ball away with his two-hand shots. That's the way van Horn taught me to play doubles. It's a team. You must accept roles, and often the guy who sets up the point doesn't actually win it and get the applause.

Welby had a super forehand crosscourt, and he could cream second serves, so he naturally played better in the first, or deuce court. That left the backhand court for me, and I played there for the rest of my life. Years later when I teamed with Budge, even he suggested that I play the backhand side—and he had played there all his life. He figured that if I played the backhand and he the forehand, we would have my forehand and his backhand to play down the middle, where most shots are going to come.

Anyway, van Horn and I were an immediate success together, and in the Nationals we got all the way to the quarter-finals, where we gave Adrian Quist and John Bromwich a very tough fight—and they were the class doubles team of the world. Budge had turned pro (breaking up Budge and Mako). Quist and Bromwich won the Australian championships eight times in a row and were the Aussie team in the Challenge Round that was to be played later in the month at Merion, Pennsylvania.

Quist played the backhand court. He had a dink backhand that was better for doubles than singles, and he had a classical forehand drive with a natural sink. And he was fine at the net, volley and overhead. Bromwich was like McMillan today because as a kid John hit from both sides two-handed, and while he eventually had given up the two-handed forehand, he still hit backhand two-handed and could get anything back from the baseline. He had strokes very much like Connors.

With Budge gone the U.S. didn't have a solid doubles team, so Walter Pate, the team captain, was looking to concoct one. The Davis Cup squad consisted of Riggs and Parker, who figured to play the two singles against Quist and Bromwich, plus Joe Hunt and Mako, who were pencilled in for the doubles. Mako of course was experienced enough, but without Budge's power out there, he was something of an unknown quantity. Pate picked Hunt to side with Mako because Joe could hit with more power than either Riggs or Parker and also because Pate was very high on Hunt.

So that was the doubles plan: Mako and Hunt. After Welby and I gave Bromwich and Quist such a good fight, we split four sets with Mako and Hunt in a practice match, and Pate invited us to come down to Merion and be sparring partners for his team. Welby and I were thrilled, although to tell you the truth, I don't know if I was more excited to be with the Davis Cup squad or to be getting the nice *per diem*. We were so pleased with ourselves and our situation, that we immediately went out and clobbered the proposed Challenge Round team, Hunt and Mako.

This did not sit well with Captain Pate. But Riggs had an

alternative plan. He suggested to Pate that he and Parker play the doubles as well as the singles. In fact, this idea has a lot of merit in the general if not in the specific. Davis Cup is not all that grueling. Any young man in shape should be able to manage two singles separated by a doubles in three consecutive days of play. As a matter of fact playing the middle day instead of resting is liable to keep a player sharp for the final day's play. More often than not, if you throw a new guy into the doubles to play with kids who have already seen action the day before, the newcomer chokes. So Riggs wasn't just talking through his hat.

But a Riggs-Parker team meant two little guys with no big serves, and there was no conceivable way they could even extend Quist and Bromwich, much less hope to beat them on grass. Pate didn't figure to win the doubles point, but he didn't want to concede it. Instead, he decided to go halfway with Bobby's suggestion and substitute Riggs for Hunt. So the next day van Horn and I were sent out to test this new scheme, and we promptly beat Riggs-Mako worse than we had Hunt-Mako. Now the idea of playing Riggs and Parker all three days was beginning to look sensible.

In all of this it never occurred to anybody to play the two kids who were winning. Welby was playing so well that he kept on winning after Merion and went all the way to the singles finals at Forest Hills before Riggs beat him (and Hunt, the sixth seed, needed five sets to beat me). But Welby was only nineteen and I had just turned eighteen, and nobody dared play such young unknowns in a Challenge Round. The possibility went out the window anyway the next day when Welby came down with one of his asthma attacks.

Pate had figured that it was time to try Parker and Riggs together, so he made a pick-up team of Hunt and Kramer and threw us against the stars. It was no contest. On bad grass with our big serves, Joe and I knocked Riggs and Parker right off the court. Pate was desperate now, and he tried pairing Riggs and Mako again. Hunt and I whipped them as badly as van Horn and I had a couple of days before.

At last I came into the picture. While it was inconceivable that two teen-agers play together, one could be tolerated. Hunt was an established, ranked player. So just before the deadline, I was officially named to the team, and when the time came, Pate nominated Hunt and me to play doubles. This wasn't fair to Welby; like most Davis Cup captains, Pate could make a wrong move at the last minute out of desperation.

Nobody seriously thought that Joe and I might beat the Aussies, but we could help Riggs and Parker in the singles by making Quist and Bromwich work hard. If we were to retain the Cup as we were favored, the assumption was that Riggs would win both his singles, while Parker would pick up a third point by beating Quist, the lesser Aussie.

Unquestionably the pivotal match was Parker-Quist, and it was drawn for the second match of the first day. The Davis Cup is conducted in an archaic way. It should not be spread out around the world, different venues, different times. It should be patterned after the World Cup of soccer, with the sixteen top nations assembling at one site. (I would say seed the top eight and make the second eight qualify.) It would be fantastic for tennis—a great annual or biannual festival of sport—and the TV coverage would carry to hundreds of millions of homes around the world. Great tennis stadiums would be constructed to hold the Cup; countries would bid to host it. This idea is not original with me; almost everybody in tennis—except for the officials in the small nations who like the Cup the way it is—support this idea or some variation of it. Someday we're going to get it.

It's also ridiculous that the order of matches is drawn out of a hat. When the Dodgers and Yankees meet in a World Series do the managers put the names of their starting pitchers on little pieces of paper and let the pitching rotation be determined by lot? Of course not. Either a neutral referee should decide the order of matches—making the choice in order to heighten the interest and drama—or even better, the order of matches should be determined by the captains (so long as no player would have to play two matches in the same day).

141

This would insert a new level of strategy into a Davis Cup, and even better, the speculation on what the captains would decide would begin days before a match and build up the interest. This idea would also help even things up for the visiting team, because the visiting captain would be given the prerogative of making the first selection.

But enough of pipe dreams. In 1939, as in 1979, matches were determined by lot, and the draw put the two Number 1 players (Riggs and Bromwich) head-to-head in the opening match, followed by the Quist-Parker showdown. We thought Frankie could win, but we certainly weren't supremely confident, and so to help matters along, Quist, who loved to play golf, got a wonderful invitation from some American "friends" to play a round at one of Philadelphia's finest courses the day before he met Parker. I'm not certain that Captain Pate arranged this little extra exercise, but it sure didn't help Quist's tennis the next day because after Riggs beat Bromwich in straight sets in the opener, Parker handled Quist in four sets.

So coming into my doubles, the U.S. had a fat 2–0 lead. This meant that while I still felt the pressure to play well in this world spotlight, I certainly did not feel I had to win at all costs. I was so excited but as much as possible, I was pretty loose. At the time, I was the youngest player in history ever to appear in a Challenge Round, and to this day only John Alexander, who played doubles for the Aussies in 1968, has been any younger. He was seventeen years and five months, while I was eighteen and one month. (And with Open tennis you can be sure no player that young is ever going to play in a Davis Cup final in the future. With Open tennis, Budge would have played instead of Kramer, and Emerson instead of Alexander.)

Ted Schroeder was playing the Eastern circuit that summer. He was my best pal in tennis and he was my best and favorite doubles partner. When he heard about my good luck, he found a way to come down from Newport, and he stayed in my room, sleeping on the floor. We stayed up until five o'clock talking. I was wide awake, unbelieving. I was eighteen years

142

old, and I was going to play in the Challenge Round for my country. But I was so young, so full of energy, that I woke up with a couple of hours sleep ready to go.

It was September 3, 1939. Outside the world was falling apart, and I was too young and naive to know. Hitler was marching into Poland. Of course I didn't hear anything, but all during my match the fans could hear newsboys out on the street calling "extra," and on odd-game breaks they would go outside and buy papers.

A couple of weeks later, after Forest Hills, Bromwich and I drove Gene Mako's car across the country. I was going home to L.A., and John was going there on his way back to Australia and the draft. (He was later wounded in New Guinea.) We really were kids. He had just discovered banana splits, and we ate them the whole way across. I drove like most American kids, like a bat out of hell. I got arrested one time in Grand Platte, Nebraska, and they held us in custody there for the night. Now John was much more conservative. He was scared of cars coming toward him; sometimes he'd drive right over on the shoulder to make sure he gave a wide berth. He had that kind of play-it-safe touch in him, and as I said earlier, that was what eventually cost him his Wimbledon on match point ten years later against Bobby Falkenberg.

Hunt and I lost the match, of course, but we didn't do badly. We won the first set 7–5, and after they won the second, we led 4–2, a break in the third, before they got down to business and took us in four sets. But we made them stay out on the court for two and a half hours, and they had to beat us, because Joe and I didn't beat ourselves. I was capable of better. My backhand was sometimes unreliable, and they hit to it. But I— to use the words they always fall back on in the newspapers in these instances— "acquitted" myself well.

You can tolerate defeat by the best doubles team in the world, especially if your country wins, and we certainly expected to win the next day. But we didn't. The Cup went down to Australia and stayed there until Schroeder and I got it back in '46. The reason was that Quist upset Riggs in the first match of the last day, and then Bromwich routed Parker for the winning point in straight sets.

Except possibly for Forest Hills the next year, when Riggs was fighting the flu and lost the final to Don McNeill, the loss to Quist was surely the toughest loss he ever took. You must remember that Riggs was always eligible to lose to a more powerful player when the other guy was on. Most great players can, in effect, only beat themselves, but Bobby didn't have that luxury.

In doubles Riggs was a much better player than he was remembered for. When he reached the top, he could seldom get any bets down on himself in singles, and so he would most often do his betting in doubles. Earlier in '39 he won a lot of money at Wimbledon, betting that he would win the triple— singles, doubles and mixed. Hell, the first time I really believed I was a top doubles player was not when I was ranked or did well in a major tournament: it was in 1940 when Bobby Riggs offered me $1,000 to play with him at Longwood. He figured that I was still pretty unknown and he could get a better price playing with the kid.

Nineteen-forty was the year Schroeder and I teamed up. We won seventy-six of the seventy-nine matches we played, and we became the youngest pair in history ever to win the Nationals. Altogether I won four U.S. doubles and two Wimbledons, and while Ted and I never played together in London, he was my partner on three of the four occasions when I won the National doubles. Unfortunately we failed to win the one trophy I most regret never winning—U.S. National Championship Doubles bowls. Two partners had to win it together three times in order to retire the great bowls. They had first been offered in 1923, after Tilden and Vinnie Richards had taken down the previous bowls. By the time Mulloy and Talbert finally retired these great bowls, with their third victory in '46, they had just about every great name in tennis on them. George Lott, a magnificent doubles player, had his name on

144

the bowls five times—only never three times with the same partner. And there were Tilden and Richards, Wilmer Allison, Johnny van Ryn, Les Stoefen, Frank Hunter, Vines and Gledhill, Budge and Mako, Bromwich and Quist, von Cramm and Henkel, Talbert and Mulloy, Kramer and Schroeder. My Wimbledon and Forest Hills trophies are beautiful and most meaningful in what they signify in terms of personal accomplishment, but no trophy, ever, could mean so much as the bowls for the national doubles that Schroeder and I could never pull down.

We won the national doubles together in '40 for the first time and repeated in '41. Then the war came, my appendicitis knocked me out in '42, and the next year Ted was out to sea when I won with Parker. In the meantime, in '42 and '45, Gardnar Mulloy and Billy Talbert won the title, so coming into 1946, both our teams had two legs apiece, and we were seeded to meet in the finals. It may be difficult in these days of $400,000 tournaments and $500,000 TV matches to comprehend it, but all four of us desperately wanted to win that trophy.

And then, damn if Schroeds and I don't get upset in the semifinals. We should have won. The team that beat us was Don McNeill and Frank Guernsey—who was a good college player and a doubles specialist, but day in and day out not in our league. But then to everyone's amazement, McNeill and Guernsey stay hot for the finals, Mulloy and Talbert start to feel the pressure, and all of a sudden McNeill-Guernsey have a match point.

Schroeds and I were watching: Gar shovels an angled forehand crosscourt, Guernsey lets it go, the ball lands out, and Guernsey and McNeill run to embrace each other. Talbert, who is right there at the net where he could see the ball, shrugs in obvious defeat. All of this is very clear on the film of the episode. There is no question but that the ball has landed past the sideline chalk. Only at this point does it begin to dawn on everybody that the linesman has called the ball in. Mulloy and

Talbert are back in the match in a deuce game, Mulloy holds his serve, and they go on to win the match and the trophy. The kicker is that Schroeder and I won our third time the next year, but it was too late.

Recalling these events makes me realize how important good timing is. Just imagine the team of Bill Talbert and Gardnar Mulloy possessing the finest doubles trophies the game has ever produced, and they might not even rank among the great all-time doubles teams. It's true, they won the nationals on four occasions, but only in 1946 did they play against a strong field. Twice they won the war-time tournaments which had very weak fields. The reason I can't place Bill and Gar in the top eight to ten teams I've seen or played against was their style of play. They really didn't have a shot killer on their side. Most great teams have had a guy who could be the point finisher. On top of that Bill and Gar always seemed to be trapped in the back court, fighting two guys at the net. In doubles, the real teams control things by controlling the net.

But let's talk about Talbert and Mulloy in a more important vein. Both of these guys have a fanatical love for tennis. They both still play at every opportunity, for anyone. And sometimes Billy can hardly swing the racket due to various arthritic conditions.

Talbert has made two tremendous contributions to tennis off the court. First, he has shown all diabetics in the world that you can be a success in sports, even carrying that awful disease. He has also, for many years, been the dynamic promotional force that operates the U.S. National Open. Billy has really professionalized the emotional side of this most important U.S. tournament.

Why is this so important? Very simple. The profits have gone up tremendously, and this allows the USTA to send out lots of money throughout our whole country. Of course this sets up better junior tennis programs, which brings far greater numbers of good kids into the game, and therefore more good players. This ability of Bill Talbert's has really been great for tennis development.

Gardnar Mulloy—Jughead we called him—had the same sort of late-blooming career, but for different reasons. He didn't start to play tennis until he was into his teens, and as late as college, football had priority. He went to the University of Miami on a football scholarship. Old Jughead has gone on to span the ages. He's in his mid-sixties now and in perfect shape. He's Budge's contemporary, but very few people realize that because Gardnar did not make the top ten until Don had left the amateurs, and it was 1952 (when Mulloy was thirty-seven) before he finally made Number 1 in the U.S. He was doubles champion with Budge Patty at Wimbledon when he was forty-two.

Jughead made the finals at Forest Hills that year he was ranked Number 1. His opponent, unfortunately for Mulloy, was Frank Sedgman, who was clearly the best amateur in the world. And Sedgman crushed him, losing only six games.

But old Jughead didn't lose them all. It so happened that on the tour in early 1951, Riggs, the promoter, some way or another goofed up, and all of us had about four days off in Florida. When Gardnar Mulloy realized we had a break, he contacted his old pal Pancho Segura. Gardnar asked him if he could give him a hand by playing a friendly exhibition at the Hollywood Beach Hotel in Hollywood, Florida. Segura gave him the ok, and the hotel got out some publicity which produced a pretty good sized affair.

Mulloy apparently was having some problems digging up the necessary money to make his trip to Wimbledon and thought that, if he could make a real good showing against Segura and perhaps beat the top pro, some of his more wealthy admirers might contribute toward his European expenses. Gardnar further reasoned—why not make sure of this support by arranging a win? He approached Segura, and Segoo, being a real loyal friend agreed to sort of jump in the tank. Anyway—what the hell—it was only an exhibition.

At that particular time Segura had become one hell of a tennis player. And for Mulloy to beat him, I think Pancho would have to hold back. But only those of us who were playing against Pancho knew just how good he was.

Well, wouldn't you know, Riggs on hearing about the exhibition decided that he would not only like to see it; but, he might catch a few dumb Florida crackers and get his hand into their pockets. Unfortunately, as Bobby appears on the scene that day he has no idea of the conversation between Jughead and Pancho, so he's not hep to the fact that it's going to be a very loose Segura on one side of the net.

It doesn't take Riggs too long and perhaps too many insults thrown at Mulloy to get some substantial action; and, in fact he has a fairly sizable bet with one Danny Orenstein. Danny, of course, was a well-known gentleman in many ways and at the time owned the Terminal Cab Company in New York, with a couple of thousand cabs to his credit.

The match gets going and Riggs notices that Segura is not belting his two-hander with his normal ferociousness. He also notices that Segura doesn't appear to be too unhappy when he misses a shot or two. In fact, Riggs begins to wonder whether or not it's the same Segura he's been watching night after night playing me awfully close on the championship tour.

In any event, Riggs approaches Segura, tells Pancho that he's got some heavy stuff riding on his back and dammit, start leveling. Segura grunts something sort of like "I didn't tell you to get down" and goes about his business of making this exhibition very enjoyable for the Mulloy backers.

Riggs, by this time, is really mad; but, being a good gambler, he decides that the smart thing to do is get off of as many bets as he can. He was successful with a few of his marks; but, unfortunately was stuck with most of the wagers.

The boys made it close; but, eventually Mulloy won.

It was after the match, after the payoffs that Riggs, of course, was all over Segura with innuendos and accusations. Segura denied everything and kept telling Bobby to remember that it was only supposed to be an exhibition, and why did Bobby want to treat it as a Wimbledon final.

It was remarkable, whenever Riggs and Segura were together later and didn't have too much to talk about, Riggs would always bring up the Mulloy match. He was trying to get Pancho to admit that on this particular day Segura, the greatest tryer we've ever had in tennis, was playing to lose. Bobby used to say, "It's too late to do anything about it, I've lost my money; but, jeez all I want to do is know if I'm smart enough to know a fix when I see one."

Poor Segura, he was only trying to do a pal a favor and didn't know there was going to be any betting. I am pretty sure Gardnar didn't know either. It's just another one of those stories—when Riggs is around he can turn a Sunday school class into a gambling casino.

Mulloy and Talbert never won Wimbledon, but Gar finally won a doubles title there in 1957, when he and Budge Patty beat the top seeds, Neale Fraser and Lew Hoad. In those days, before television, the men's doubles was given a much brighter spotlight. It was traditional to play the men's singles finals on Friday, and then on Saturday the women's singles final and the men's doubles final were played. This was a good arrangement, because the men's doubles shored up what was often a weak card, when the two women weren't very good or very competitive. The only problem was that a player who made both the singles and doubles finals would have to play his semifinal doubles match late Thursday, then go on to the singles final the next afternoon.

I'm very familiar with this situation, because it happened to me once, and it later happened to Rod Laver and cost him a Wimbledon title. In 1947, when I qualified for the finals in singles against Tommy Brown, I was playing as a doubles team with Bobby Falkenberg. We had a semifinal match late in the afternoon before my singles final. We were playing two good Aussies, Geoff Brown and Colin Long, and as we walked out onto the court I told Falkenberg, "Bobby, if you want to win this, you better understand right now that we're playing mixed doubles this match—and I'm the woman and you're the man." My goal was to win the Wimbledon singles. There was no way in the world that I was going to jeopardize that by wasting too much energy or risking an injury at doubles. Falkenberg understood my position too, and he played like a madman out there—running all around, poaching, smashing aces. He carried us to victory. Then on Saturday, after I had taken care of the singles business, I played as hard as I could and together we beat Tony Mottram and Billy Sidwell to win the title.

This is the reason why doubles championships should be separated from singles, the way it used to be in the U.S. when the doubles were played at Longwood a month before Forest Hills.

Laver turned out to be a better person than me, when he got caught in this same fix thirteen years later. This was 1960, and I was working for the BBC as a commentator. Laver was scheduled to play Neale Fraser for the championship on Friday, while on Thursday night Rodney and his partner, Bob Mark, had to play a semifinal doubles against Dennis Ralston and Rafael Osuna.

These two kids were playing unconscious. They hardly knew each other. They had been teamed up just because they were going to attend the University of Southern California together, and George Toley, the coach, thought Wimbledon might be a nice place for the two of them to get some practice together. Here they were, beating everybody in the semi's and on the way to the title.

Laver played with Mark because they were good friends. Mark was a very average player, and he had no chance to win any sort of title unless his buddy carried him, which is what Laver did. Rodney wanted to get his friend a Wimbledon title so he tore all over the court, saving Mark, taking charge, trying to carry the game to Osuna and Ralston. The match lasted five sets, three of them to deuce: 4–6, 10–8, 15–13, 4–6, 11–9, and by the time Laver and Mark had lost, so had Rodney lost the singles.

The next afternoon, Laver was obviously worn out and Fraser whipped him. I'm sure he would have won going away if he hadn't concentrated on his friendship and the doubles.

The problem with doubles today is that there are too much money and fame in the singles, so that it is not worthwhile for any top player to bother with doubles. Borg and Connors never play. Vilas plays only to help his coach, Ion Tiriac, win a few bucks and get an entry into the singles draw. Of the good singles players, Gottfried and Ramirez are usually the best at doubles (and coincidentally they played together for several years), but too often the doubles winners are specialists like Hewitt and McMillan.

There is just enough money in the doubles pool to make winning attractive for the singles loser, but not enough to keep it all on the up-and-up. Doubles is a scandal in tennis today. A couple of kids get eliminated in the singles, they decide to dump their doubles so they can get on to the next tournament and get acclimated (especially if there's a change in the surface) so they have a better chance for a better payday in singles. So they tank. Some do it artfully, some make a joke out of it. There have been times when both doubles teams in a match have been trying to lose.

That's great for the integrity of the sport, isn't it? Of course it's tough to prove that a team is trying to lose, but it should be that any team that fails to make a sufficient visible effort in doubles should also have to give up singles earnings at that tournament.

The really sad thing about doubles is that the fans seem to enjoy it as much or more as they do singles—especially since so many more fans play doubles. But the press concentrates on singles so the promoters put more money in singles, the better players skip doubles, and the vicious circle continues.

If Hewitt and McMillan are the class doubles team today in the world, I would put Smith and Lutz as the top U.S. team, but I guarantee one thing, that the single American player I know I would put on my U.S. Davis Cup doubles team would be Jimmy Connors. I'd put him in the forehand court and watch him return every serve. He makes a great doubles player

151

simply for that one attribute. Since he never plays doubles anymore, people have forgotten that he and Nastase made a great team a few years ago. They won both Wimbledon and Forest Hills which is a rare accomplishment. Connors cared about doubles too, when he still cared about the money he could win at it. One time when Nastase started clowning around on the court and it cost the team a victory, Jimmy took a swing at Nastase in the locker room afterwards.

(Of course if you ask me how I would get Connors to play Davis Cup—doubles or singles—I always answer by saying that if I were ever made captain of the U.S. team, I would immediately appoint two coaches—Donald Dell and Gloria Connors—and one manager, Mark McCormack. Thereafter, we would get every player needed for every match, and we would never lose to anybody. Next question.)

The trouble with Connors and most all modern players at doubles is that they hit the ball too hard. Only Hewitt and McMillan really can play the game of softball and angles. The modern slambang style is the recent legacy of the good Australian teams, especially Emerson, Stolle and Newcombe-Roche.

Emerson was the best doubles player of all the moderns, very possibly the best forehand court player of all time. He was so quick he could cover everything. He had the perfect doubles shot, a backhand that dipped over the net and came in at the server's feet as he moved to the net. Gene Mako and Johnny van Ryn could hit a shot like that sometimes, but never so often nor as proficiently as Emerson. Of the old-timers, Toto Brugnon, the fourth Musketeer, had the same kind of style in the forecourt: a chip backhand and some kind of bolo forehand. And the man could lob. But Brugnon was nowhere near the all-around player that Emerson was.

Finally, all the strokes and the agility aside, the most important thing that Emerson brought to any game was a capacity to lift his partner. He was so well liked, and so able besides, that anybody he played with automatically moved up in class. If you ask me what I did best as a doubles player, I would respond in the same way: I lifted my partners. The two most crucial points in any game, in singles or doubles, are 30–all and 30–40. Those were the points I won by myself in singles, and those were the points my partner came to believe we'd win. My attitude was: if this kid can play the forehand court, then we can win together. And I could keep winning at doubles long after I was through as world's singles champion.

One of the more spectacular of many such arguments I had with Gonzales concerned my playing doubles on tour after I was over the hill. His tour with Budge, Segura and Sedgman in '54 was not a smash hit, so I started playing doubles regularly so that the people who still remembered me and wanted to pay to see me would have that chance. But when I started winning more than my share, Gonzales took after me one night in Cuba, claiming that it was unfair that I came into the doubles rested. I agreed but said that we would all make out better in the long run—even if I took a little doubles prize money every night—because if I played doubles I could keep my name on the posters and draw a few more bodies. Unfortunately Gonzales didn't want to hear my arguments.

I played doubles as late as 1959, when I was thirty-eight and Mal Anderson hurt his back. I was having dinner at a restaurant in Washington when I was brought the news, and so I went right over to the arena, with a full meal and too many drinks in me, and Gonzales and I beat Hoad and Ashley Cooper. And I held my own until Anderson could come back a few weeks later.

Finally, while I scream at the kids today for not treating doubles with the proper reverence, I must admit that we sometimes played fast and loose with doubles on tour too. The trouble was that it was the last act on the bill every evening, and it was always late when the doubles came on. In 1953 when I toured against Sedgman the last time, Ken McGregor played Segura in the animal act, and then Segoo and I played the two Aussies in the closing match. It was the finest sustained doubles competition I ever was in. McGregor and Sedgman are still the only men's doubles team to have won the Grand Slam (in 1951; and they won three-fourths of it the next year), and Segoo and I had become a damn good team ourselves.

But the program was too long, and we had to strike a deal. The four of us agreed that we would play the first set of the doubles fair and square. However, whoever won this set would get a free ride in the second. Actually we'd play the second set hard except for a couple of points where the first-set losers would contrive to lose to hand over a service break. We wanted to bill best-of-three, but we sure as hell didn't want to play three sets.

But then one night in Corpus Christi, Sedgman and McGregor double-crossed us. Segoo and I won the first set, and we were coasting along in the second waiting for our service break, when all of a sudden they broke us, the dirty rascals. My first reaction was that they had forgotten who had won the first set. But no, they just wanted to win. And they did, around one o'clock in the morning.

So now Segoo and I were mad, and we told the Aussies that if that is the way they wanted to play it, all right, best-of-three all the way. Sometimes half the crowd would be gone, but the four of us would be out there knocking ourselves out five or six hours after the evening's performance began.

We had a kid working for us then named Billy Sullivan. Very nice kid—he drove the truck that carried the court and the net and other equipment. He had a long haul out of Pittsburgh all the way up through New York state into Quebec, to the town of Sherbrooke north of the Vermont border. It was a tough overnight trip, and Billy crashed and was killed, going too fast trying to make up time.

But you know, the show went on the next night in Sherbrooke. We got a relief truck and a new driver, and they picked up the court and the rest of the stuff out of the wreck and got it to Sherbrooke in time for us to play, right on schedule as advertised: Ken McGregor vs. Pancho Segura in the opener. But I've always thought if we hadn't started playing the doubles out, if we hadn't played so late that night in Pittsburgh, Billy Sullivan wouldn't have been going so fast to Sherbrooke and the kid might be alive today.

10

The Duel of the Decade

Nobody could have had a more bizarre professional debut than I did on December 26, 1947 in New York. I lost in four sets to Riggs at Madison Square Garden, and while neither one of us played the greatest tennis, that night honored Bobby and me more than any other in tennis history. December 26, 1947 was the day of the greatest snowstorm ever to hit New York. It started early in the day, it passed the depths of the great Blizzard of '88 by mid-afternoon, and by the time Bobby and I hit the court around nine-thirty that night, there were twenty-five and eight-tenths inches on the ground and drifts up to four feet.

There was no surface transportation so Bobby and I, and Dinny Pails and Segura, who played the opening match on the tour, had to hike over from the Hotel Lexington. Riggs always carried the most rackets of any player—seven or eight at a time, each slightly heavier in the head where he had added adhesive tape. He had so damn many rackets that he had to number them in ink so he could tell them apart. And here he is, lugging them crosstown in a blizzard. It was like an expedition to the South Pole.

We could not postpone the match so we beat our way through the rising snow to Eighth Avenue positive that we would be playing before a handful of ticket-holders. But when we walked into the Garden, we could hardly believe our eyes: there were thousands of people already there and more pouring in. A total of 16,052 tickets had been sold, and incredibly, 15,114 people showed up. The *Daily News* called it "the greatest tribute to an indoor athletic event in the history of sport." Nowadays they don't get 93 percent of the ticket holders to show up for an NFL game in bright sunshine in the middle of October. The gate came to $55,730.50, and while 20 percent of that was the wartime entertainment tax, the gross was about equal to the Vines-Perry debut a decade before which was the only other tennis match ever to break $50,000.

Riggs deserved as much credit as the fans. In practice he had been losing to Pails and Segura while I had been handling them with ease, but as soon as he got where it counted, he was a different player—steady in all departments. After Alice Marble introduced us, I promptly lost the first three games and a 6–2 set. In the second set, at 4–all, I had Bobby down 15–40, but he wriggled out of that and won the set 10–8. I did win the third set 6–4 and I was up a break in the fourth, but he came back for 6–4 and the match. I overhit, I missed lots of approach shots, and I couldn't pass Bobby at the net. I knew then that I was in for a rough go.

The next morning there was still no transportation so we walked to Penn Station, which was a long way and gave me a cold. No sooner were we settled on the train, going to Pittsburgh, than Riggs demanded a meeting with Jack Harris and myself. As soon as we sat down Bobby immediately announced that he wanted to renegotiate. Harris couldn't believe it: one victory and Riggs wanted a new contract. I had signed for 35 percent, and I made it very clear that I wasn't giving up a nickel. But Riggs wasn't holding us up, he wasn't being foolish. Nobody ever lived up to a contract better than he did, as a matter of fact. It was just a matter of Bobby picking his spots. He had an edge with his opening-night win in the big city, and he wanted to push it.

His point was, sure he had signed for only 17½ percent, while Kramer got 35, but that was the way the system worked. The new name got the big money. It was upside-down, it wasn't fair, but Riggs understood. But Bobby went on, if he kept beating me or if we played so close that we could start doubling the tour back through New York and the other major cities, then he should get a more equitable cut. Then Riggs said, rationally Kramer's name wouldn't mean as much anymore as Riggs' or as Riggs-Kramer together.

Now what he was saying was fair. He wasn't asking to reach into my pocket—or Jack Harris'—until much later down the road. But it was a heady move, a typically smooth Riggs ploy—taking the attack when he was on top—and both Jack and I agreed to give up 2½ points if we came around again. Bobby grinned with delight, every bit as proud of this victory as he had been of the one in four sets the night before.

I went back to my seat. In a few hours Riggs had beaten me out of the big match before the big-city press, and he had beaten me out of 2½ percent. And I sat there thinking that I had better win this tour. If I did not I was as useless in tennis as yesterday's newspaper. Wimbledon, Forest Hills, the Davis Cup—none of it would mean a damn. Budge lost one tour by a couple of matches and he is buried. It made me struggle. There is no greater incentive than the threat of extinction.

It didn't help me any that Riggs beat me in our next match, 8–6, 6–1, in Pittsburgh. (We only played best-of-three after New York.) But I got him the next night, 6–4, 6–4 in Cleveland, and all of a sudden things were bright again, especially since we drew record gates in both places. We were very competitive, which helped. Bobby went up 3–1 at our next stop, Dayton, where the lights were bad. He knew how to play the dark better than I did. But I caught on. A place like Uline Arena in Washington had low-hanging lights that hurt Bobby's lobbing, and I beat him in straight sets. I finally caught him after nine matches, 5–4, but then he got hot and won four in a row. Then I came back, and led 12–9 when we hit Florida at the end of January. We had three matches there, outside on clay, and Riggs won them all to even it up at twelve apiece. We split a couple more, and just before we came into L.A., I won a terrific match on the wood in Phoenix. Nobody could break serve. The scores were 14–12, 4–6, 18–16.

That put me up fifteen matches to fourteen, and our home town was ready for us. The box seats at the Pan Pacific Auditorium were going for $12.50—remember, 1948 dollars. The "mistake" Bobby and I made was that we came in almost even. We compounded that by splitting our two matches in L.A. That *convinced* all the wise guys that we were fixing. Tilden was one of the worst skeptics. He didn't like the way I had made the serve-and-volley such a glamorous style; he had told everybody Riggs would undress me, and when it didn't happen, he convinced himself that *he* couldn't be wrong, therefore Riggs must be tanking.

On this particular tour, Bobby's reputation as a hustler overshadowed his reputation as a player—and this was long before he started all the hustle gimmicks—playing tied to dogs, wearing boots. Bobby brought his image on himself, but it wasn't his fault that he didn't look like a champion. Tilden, Vines, Perry, Budge, myself: we were all big, tall, lean powerful boomers, while Riggs was a scrawny little scrapper with a whiney voice. Bobby wasn't popular with the other players on the court either, because he would haggle about calls all the time, but everybody liked him off the court. He was too cocky, tough, and he had one really bad habit of toying with lesser players (although I'm sure he didn't mean to hurt their feelings intentionally). It rubbed a lot of people in the game the wrong way, and so he never got his due from within.

But people too often forget that the main idea in tennis is to win. I'm not talking about cheating—which Bobby never did— or gamesmanship, which he was not above. I'm talking about coming out on top. It does no good to fit into some preconceived classic mold of a "winner" if you then don't win. Kovacs looked the part, and Kovacs couldn't win. Riggs looked like he came in out of the rain, but he won, and I guarantee you he is the most underrated champion in the history of tennis. After all the hustler stuff of the last few years, I want to emphasize it all the more: if you remember one thing from this whole book, remember that Bobby Riggs was a great champion. He beat Segura. He beat Budge when Don was just a little bit past his peak. On a long tour, as up and down as Vines was, I'm not so sure that Riggs wouldn't have played Elly very close. I'm sure he would have beaten Gonzales—Bobby was too quick, he had too much control for Pancho—and Laver and Rosewall and Hoad.

What I gave tennis was the big serve-and-volley percentage attack game, and it really dominated the game for the next quarter of a century until the backhands and the ground strokes with topspin came in with the dirt. But do you know why I started playing this game? Because it was the only way I could beat Bobby Riggs. He forced me into depending on serve-and-volley. And later how did I learn to play on clay? Playing Bobby Riggs.

Here is how the serve-and-volley game really came about. Keep in mind that before this, even the big hitters like Tilden and Vines, would only come to the net behind a particularly strong first serve or after a forcing groundstroke. I picked up a lot from Schroeder, who had such undependable groundstrokes that he came in on almost every first serve and a lot of seconds as well. But even when I started touring with Bobby, even playing the fast canvas, I would hang back on second serves. That was the way the game was played.

But Bobby was a terrific fast-surface player. Here is another misconception. He didn't play some rinky-dink Harold Solomon style, pitty-pattying the ball around on dirt. He didn't have the big serve, but he made up for it with some sneaky first serves and as fine a second serve as I had seen at that time. When you talk about depth and accuracy both, Riggs' second serve ranks with the other three best that I ever saw: von Cramm's, Gonzales' and Newcombe's. He was aggressive natu-

160

1928. Helen Wills defeating
Edith Cross in the semi-finals
at Forest Hills. WIDE WORLD

1930. Bill Tilden training at
Grunewald near Berlin.
WIDE WORLD

1933. Fred Perry in action against Johnny Van Ryn at the Pacific Southwest Tournament. WIDE WORLD

1933. Ellsworth Vines defeating G. R. B. Meredith at Wimbledon. WIDE WORLD

1934. Winners and runners up at the Pacific Southwest, including: Alice Marble, Elizabeth Ryan, Gene Mako, John Van Ryn, Don Budge, Gene Stratford, Dorothy Round Little, Fred Perry, Ellsworth Vines, and Les Stoefen. THELNER HOOVER

1936. Don Budge winning the Pacific Coast title. WIDE WORLD

1939. Seventeen-year-old Jack Kramer after a third-round victory at the Sea Bright Lawn Tennis and Cricket Club. WIDE WORLD

1939. Bobby Riggs winning the singles title at Wimbledon by beating Elwood Cooke. WIDE WORLD

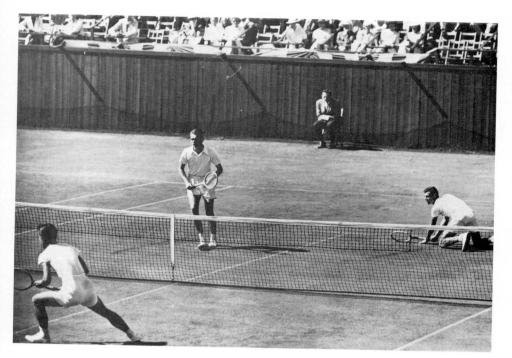

1941. Jack Kramer and Ted Schroeder retaining their doubles title at Longwood by defeating Gardnar Mulloy and Wayne Sabin. WIDE WORLD

1943. Jack Kramer hits the turf and loses his racket during his match with Sidney S. Wood, Jr., in the National Singles Championship at Forest Hills. WIDE WORLD

1947. Jack Kramer defeating Tom Brown in the finals at Wimbledon. WIDE WORLD

1947. As proud parents Jack and Gloria Kramer look on, young David Kramer settles right into the Davis Cup which his father has just helped win for the United States. THELNER HOOVER

1947. Jack Kramer and Ted Schroeder after winning the National Doubles title at the Longwood Cricket Club. WIDE WORLD

1949. Jack Kramer, Dinny Pails, Bobby Riggs, and Pancho Segura. These four former Wimbledon stars have turned pro—and will soon begin a series of exhibition matches. WIDE WORLD

SECTION A

1949. Some heavyweights meet at Forest Hills. From left, Paul Helms (Founder of the Tennis Hall of Fame), Maury McLoughlin (the original California Comet), Frank Parker, Jack Garland (U.S. Olympic Committee), Don Budge, Jack Kramer. H. LEE HASEN

1949. "Georgeous Gussy" Moran displays her lace-trimmed panties.
WIDE WORLD

1952. Jack Kramer practicing for his pro tour with Frank Sedgman.

1955. Promoter Jack Kramer does the serving and his pro tennis stars show fine racket form at Mamma Leone's restaurant in New York. The handy guys with the tools of their trade are, from left, Pancho Gonzales, Pancho Segura, Tony Trabert, and Rex Hartwig.

1958. Pancho Segura, Pauline Betz, Gussy Moran and Jack Kramer before a mixed doubles match at Madison Square Garden. WIDE WORLD

1973. Bobby Riggs taking his nutriments before his match with Billie Jean King. WIDE WORLD

1973. Bobby Riggs leans over to kiss Billie Jean King after she defeated him in the Astrodome.
WIDE WORLD

1970. Jack Kramer and his family. Back row, from left, Jack, David, John, Bob. Front row, Ron, Gloria, Michael, and their dog Sandy.

rally and he had superb anticipation. He could keep the ball in play, and he could find ways to control the bigger, more powerful opponent. He could pin you back by hitting long, down the lines, and then he'd run you ragged with chips and drop shots. He was outstanding with a volley from either side, and he could lob as well as any man. I had to learn to lob better myself just to stay on the court with him. He could also lob on the run. He could disguise it, and he could hit winning overheads. They weren't powerful, but they were always on target.

His strategy was to smother me. That sounds ridiculous, given my larger size and greater power, but Bobby had the confidence, the speed and the agility. When we first started touring he came at me on his first serve, on his second serve, and on my second serve. He could come to the net on his second serve by lofting a high-bouncer into the far corner of my backhand service box. I couldn't generate any real power, and with the high bounce, he also had time to get into the net.

On the other hand, my second serve didn't kick like Bobby's, so he could return that deep enough and follow into the net. Unless I was getting an unusually high percentage of good first serves in, I—the big server—was more vulnerable to service breaks. It was a crazy situation, and it forced me to learn to hit a high-kicking serve down the middle to his backhand in the deuce court. It forced me to think attack constantly. I would rush in and try to pound his weakest point—his backhand, which had control, but not much speed—pound it, pick on it, smash it till it broke down. For the first time it was kill or be killed. So the style I am famous for was not consciously planned; it was created out of the necessity of dealing with Bobby Riggs.

I was beginning to get comfortable with this new style around the time we hit Los Angeles. After we split there, we went up to San Francisco; I won there and a couple other places. Then we flew to Denver, and Bobby got something started with the stewardess, and that gave me Denver in the third set. Then we went to Salt Lake City, where we played on a tremendously fast wood surface where my first serve skidded off like a bullet, and all of a sudden, from dead even I was up six or seven matches. That was it. In the one week the whole tour had come apart.

Now that I had checkmated him, he had to try something new. He had to gamble off my serve. He started trying to slug his returns, and that meant he had no margin for error. He could only beat me at his very best.

The trouble with any extended tour, probably in any sport, is that it will not truly reflect the rivalry. If one player is 10 percent better than the other, I guarantee you he will not just win 10 percent more matches. Rather, he is more likely to win 50 percent. Once a player establishes himself over the other, the opponent has to change his game in some way or he is conceding. But anytime you change your game, you are giving up a sure strength to gamble on something new, and the chances are you were better off. In my case, when I changed it made me better, but that is rare.

As I lengthened my lead, Bobby grew quickly demoralized and gave up. He started tanking. At least nobody was accusing us of fixing to keep it close any more, but as my lead lengthened the interest in the matches diminished. By the time the five-month North American tour ended we had played eighty-nine matches before 332,977 fans and grossed $503,047 (after the local promoters got theirs, my 35 percent came to $89,000). It surely would have been even more had Riggs been more competitive the last couple months. After the 16–15 start through L.A., I went 53–5 the rest of the way to finish 69–20.

But hold on. Bobby Riggs did not just tank because he was a beaten man. As always, he had an angle. As soon as he realized that he couldn't beat me on tour, he decided to set me up for the U.S. Pro Championships at Forest Hills that summer. As I've mentioned in talking about my match against Budge in the semifinals of the '48 U.S. Pro, this was the only American pro tournament of any consequence—and it was in New York. What Bobby planned to do was get me overconfident on the tour, then beat me at Forest Hills and immediately start

162

claiming that he was still the *real* champion.

He almost pulled it off too. Not only did Budge give me that battle in the semi's, but even in the quarters I had to fight for my life against Welby van Horn. I was 4–all, trailing on my serve in the fifth set before I pulled it out. Riggs had a much easier draw, he beat Kovacs easily in the semi's, and he was ready for me. But I took him 14–12 in the opening set, then closed him out in four, and there no longer could be any question but that I was the champion.

This may sound peculiar but Bobby Riggs is one of the most honorable men I ever met in my life. He promoted my tour with Gonzales and my tour with Segura, and I never signed a piece of paper with him. You could absolutely trust his word.

By the same token, Bobby is always looking for an edge. If you played cards he would try to get by without anteing and he'd try to peek at your hand. To him, that's just part of the game. I remember one time in Sydney when Segoo, Pails and I were going out to dinner with Bobby. In the hotel corridor Riggs suddenly suggested (as if this had just occurred to him) that we lag coins to see who pays for the dinner. Segoo, Dinny and I carefully toss these huge Australian two-bob coins. Then Riggs stands up and moves over to the side of the corridor. The carpet was not quite wall-to-wall. It fell a few inches short on either side. So Bobby just rolls his coin down this little track. It runs up to the wall, hits against it and lays down flush to it. You see, nobody had said you *couldn't* roll your coin.

Bobby was like that in every activity. With the dames he was never content just to hand out a good line when he could "get engaged," so Bobby got engaged in a lot of towns. If the girl he was chasing looked like she might be interested in another player, Riggs would tell her (sadly and in the strictest confidence) that the poor fellow was gay. He was especially partial to rich women. For a long time he had a girl traveling with him named Judy who was a straight twenty-dollar tipper. Buy a Coke, she'd tip a twenty. Bobby was priming her to bankroll a South American tour, but one day Judy and all her twenties just disappeared.

Riggs' other passion was gambling. He'd bet on anything, all of which is well known. But he wasn't a compulsive gambler in the sense of people who have a betting disease. Bobby was a winner. He is still a sixty-year-old pixie who has spent his whole life playing games and having fun.

For all the women and all the betting though, Bobby wasn't ever much on booze—and he was always in much better shape than people imagined. He never liked the taste of whiskey, and the only time I ever saw him drinking was with dames. He thought drinking helped his sex. Since he didn't like to drink but did like sex, he solved the dilemma by lining up three glasses in a row: one Scotch, one Coke, one iced tea. Then after he sipped the Scotch, he'd screw up his face and chase it with a Coke and tea to kill the taste.

He'd never get mad. For anger, the best he could do would be to literally foam at the mouth. When he got worked up and started screeching in that little voice of his, small flecks of spit would form at the corners. There was one time in Philadelphia when we were on tour there in '48, when the sheriff or somebody came into the locker room and hit him with a warrant. Oh he was foaming like a mad dog! Then the guy came right after me in the shower. "Are you John A. Kramer, better known as Jack Kramer?" When I acknowledged that, he slapped the papers on me too.

I was more puzzled than upset, since I hadn't set foot in the City of Brotherly Love since 1939 at the Davis Cup, and the papers involved a commitment Riggs had made in 1942. But since we were playing with Bobby, they hit us all—Segura, Pails, me, even Jack Harris—with some kind of conspiracy charges. Walter Annenberg, the publisher, was suing, and his lawyer was Richardson Dilworth, who later became the mayor of Philadelphia.

Finally I found out what the dispute was all about. Riggs had been a leader in an early attempt at forming a player's association, and the association had made a deal for its players to compete in a tournament for Mr. Annenberg's newspaper, the *Philadelphia Inquirer*. Well this player's association, like all

164

the others before the ATP was formed, folded, and Riggs forgot about the commitment. Walter Annenberg did not.

I never did quite figure out how I could be hit for something in 1948 that had happened in 1942 when I wasn't concerned, but with Annenberg and Dilworth lined up against us, we were advised to cop a plea. Besides, they had one major player to testify against us—who else but our old pal, Fred Perry? The judge let Segura and Pails off the hook, so long as Bobby and I promised to play in three pro tournaments that the Annenberg papers were promoting. That was the settlement, and it was fair enough.

If Bobby had any drawback, it was his complete faith in his ability to win in the end. He was not a choker, but then a lot of other athletes who also aren't chokers do not delude themselves into thinking that they absolutely *will* win every time. (All of this is complicated even more by the fact that then, when he did lose, nobody ever lost more graciously than Riggs.) Anyway, the fact that Bobby had trouble even conceiving of defeat was what often landed him in trouble.

As an example: Bobby and I had a dispute with Schroeder in 1949, which I will recount in the next chapter. For now it is only important to know that Riggs felt Schroeder had let us down, and so in the bargain, to fuel his anger, Bobby also convinced himself that Schroeder was a choker. Now whatever Ted is, he is a great competitor. Most of his life he spent scratching out victories where he had no business even being in the match. But Bobby knew better: he decided Schroeder was a choker, and all he wanted in life was to go head-to-head with him in some game, preferably golf.

Finally in 1957 in New York, he cornered Schroeds and got him to play a round. I backed Schroeds and lost $200, but it was a good match. Fair enough. That night Gloria and I and Dinny Pails had dinner with Bobby and his wife, Priscilla. Bobby was feeling at his best for having whipped Schroeder, we all had a few drinks, and soon enough we started reminiscing. Riggs made a passing reference to the Budge match at the '48 pro championships, saying how amazing it was that I won

165

that fourth set despite having dropped my serve twice. Casually I disputed him, saying Don had only broken me once in that set. Bobby sat up in his chair. He smelled blood. "Twice," he snapped. "I'll betcha the money you owe me from today."

Now having known Bobby long enough, I should have had the sense to call a cab right there and get the hell away from him. But I was positive. I was so positive, in fact, that I not only put the $200 up, I gave him 10–1. Bobby gobbled that up, and not only that but Priscilla, who knew her husband well enough to sense when he had a pigeon on the line, piped up, "I want a thousand too."

At least I had the good sense to turn that down, even though I was dead sure I was right. How could Don Budge break anybody twice in a set on the grass and not win the set? So the next morning, hung over, I dragged down to *The New York Times* and began going through the microfilm. At last I found Allison Danzig's account of the match. It went something like, "Donald the Red, the valiant former champion, flashing his full repertoire of classic strokes before an appreciative assemblage"—Al was always a big Budge man— "finally wilted in the fourth set despite twice breaking Kramer's serve." There it was: read it and weep. I'm out another two thousand to Riggs, $2,200 all told.

I went back to see Bobby. Now he's got me. But listen, he tells me: he's going to give me a break. He only wants half the money up front. With the rest, all I have to do is back Schroeder in a series of golf matches out in California. But he was too cocky. He was positive that Ted Schroeder could never beat him at golf, so he gave away too much in his confidence. Bobby made it $100 four ways even; $100 four ways, a stroke a side; and another $100 four ways, with Schroeds getting two strokes a side. Too much.

The rest of the deal was that they were going to play for a whole week, a round a day. And when next we were all in California we met at Oakmont golf course and started off. My father and I joined the two players so I could watch the action and my bankroll.

166

It was no contest—especially since they were playing on Ted's home course. The first day, Schroeds won $200. He was a little tight, playing for my money. The second day $400. The third day, Schroeds took Riggs for $500 more. He knew the greens, the distances. At this rate, by the end of the week I was going to have my whole $2,200 back, plus interest.

So the fourth day: tee time and no Bobby. The minutes pass. At last he shows up, very apologetically, explaining that his doctor had disqualified him from any further competition. He was like a kid with a note from home excusing him from school. The doctor said Bobby had appendicitis. But, we all asked, if you have appendicitis, how come you're not in the hospital getting operated before your appendix bursts?

Bobby thought that one over for a few moments. "The doctor says I have latent appendicitis," he said.

11

Schroed

Riggs' dispute with Schroeder had been caused by the events of 1949. We needed a new challenger for the pro tour that year. Bobby knew he was finished as a valid contender, but he couldn't bear not to be in the action, and so he had taken over the management of the tour from Jack Harris. Then he caught my attention with an offer of 35 percent of the gate. Bobby consulted me about a lot of things. Since I was the champion, I was in many practical ways his partner, but he was the real promoter.

Gonzales had come out of nowhere to win Forest Hills in 1948, and he was an exciting player, controversial, a big hitter, but he was only twenty years old and far too undeveloped to go up against me night after night. We wanted him to mature so he could make a really good opponent in another couple years.

So, for the moment, Bobby and I figured that our best shot was Ted Schroeder. The three of us were all from the L.A. area and had known each other for years. Ted and I were the same age and were identified in the public mind together, for we had been such good doubles partners and had won the '46 and '47 Challenge Rounds.

Schroeder had taken up tennis as a kid because he was so brilliant in school that he was jumping grades too fast for his own good and his parents thought a sport might slow him down. He went at tennis like a demon. I can remember that he would collapse in tears if he lost his serve. Schroed has always been a man of extremes: emotional, outspoken, devoted. One time a few years ago, I overextended myself in some business deals and found myself needing $30,000 in a hurry. Ted and I always talk on the phone a couple times a week, and so I mentioned my problems to him. Very casually he volunteered that he'd loan me the money. Naturally I assumed that he had it lying in the bank.

Later, I found out that he didn't have that money on hand. He called his banker at home and told him he had to have a $30,000 mortgage written on his house that night. The banker said that was impossible. But he knew Schroed well enough to know that this was important to him and that, anyway, Schroed would not accept a turn-down. Don't ask me how he did it, all I know is that the very next morning a messenger arrived in L.A. with a $30,000 check made out to me.

That's the kind of friend Ted Schroeder is.

As a player Schroed had weaknesses with his groundstrokes. Long before the rest of us, he was rushing the net because he couldn't rely on his backhand or forehand. But he was a disciple of Cliff Roche and percentage tennis, and he had the ideal attacking grass game: a terrific overhead and volley (especially the backhand) and that most valuable of all tools, a strong second serve. Also, Schroed was tough physically, at a time of long best-of-five deuce sets, and he was a great fighter. The funny thing was that early in a tournament, Schroeder could not help himself from trying to play a classic game, imitating Budge. He would try gorgeous textbook strokes, staying back, trading groundstrokes, and then he'd fall behind and have to fight his way back, scratching and hustling, playing like Ted Schroeder. In the doubles final at Seabright in 1940,

Ted and I lost the first two sets to Riggs and van Horn and were down 5–0 in the third, with Welby serving. We pulled it out. That was a day's work for Schroed. And it killed Riggs; he'd bet $50 on himself and Welby.

As much as he loved tennis Schroed never gave his life to the game the way I did. He never saw it as a future, because he had an education. He graduated from Stanford. As I've mentioned, because he was so completely honorable himself, he found it difficult to tolerate the hypocrisy in the game. He hated the Eastern establishment officials so much that it was nothing for him to skip Forest Hills, his own national championship, and he certainly couldn't be bothered with giving up all the time necessary to play Wimbledon.

So to many people, he was a shadow figure. The Forest Hills he won, in '42 in five sets over Parker, gave him top U.S. ranking that year, but both the title and the Number 1 tended to be forgotten as the war moved along. Considering that and his antiestablishment opinions and the fact that he bothered to play only a few tournaments, Ted certainly would not have been selected for the 1946 Davis Cup squad if I had not interceded in his behalf. In so many words I told the Davis Cup committee that if Schroeder wasn't included then I wouldn't play either.

The whole thing was further complicated because Australia still held the Cup—from 1939 when Quist upset Riggs, and Bromwich whipped Parker—which meant that we would have to travel to Australia. In those days it was not just a matter of flying down a few days before the matches started, and then jetting back the next morning. At that time the plan was to go down weeks before the Davis Cup—which was played right after Christmas—and get acclimated by playing in Australian tournaments. That way too, the captain—Walter Pate again—could watch his men in action and pick the team to play on the basis of current ability, not past reputation.

The war had changed things a little. Instead of a turnover in players, the USLTA still had to deal with the same players—only we were older and more independent. We were married men for the most part and had spent the last few years fighting a war. In the past it had not been uncommon for captains to declare all wives *persona non grata*. Sometimes this policy was made against all wives because one was considered difficult, and sometimes it was just a matter of there being too many wives and prohibitive expenses for them.

In any event, Frankie Parker insisted that his wife, Audrey, go to Australia with full expenses, and when I found out about this I hit the roof. If there were money available to pay for her trip then there damn well ought to be an equivalent amount set aside for Gloria Kramer and Ann Schroeder. I argued that this should be the case whether or not our wives wanted to use that money to travel. In fact, neither Ann, who had a young son— John, who is now the PGA tour golfer—nor Gloria, who was expecting in December, could go. But Ted and I needed the money. The salary from Ted's job was going to stop while he was away from work, and Gloria and I were going to have to pay all living costs from the nominal $75 a week that I got from the Wilson Meat Packing Company.

Walter Pate tried to cool me down, saying there were no funds available for this type of request and that it was almost surely against the amateur expense rules. But I wouldn't give in and neither would Ted. Finally the USLTA solved the problem by rounding up a few wealthy tennis patrons who contributed money equal to Audrey Parker's expenses for the Schroeders and Kramers. (One of the major donors was Fred Small, the gentleman from Cumberland, Md., who had first paid me for playing a match. Thirty years later, Gloria and I still count the Smalls as among our greatest friends.)

Finally our team, with Audrey Parker, headed off for Australia in November. Parker, Tommy Brown, Gardnar Mulloy, Billy Talbert and Schroeder were all on the team; and Pate made it clear to us from the first that the only thing set in the lineup was that I would play one of the singles spots. Parker, Mulloy, Brown and Schroeder all had a shot at second singles; and Mulloy and Talbert, Schroeder, Parker and I were competing for the doubles berth. When we left, Pate was

171

leaning toward a doubles pairing of Parker and myself. In the Interzone final that he had played against Sweden at Forest Hills late in the summer, he had used Talbert and Mulloy in the doubles, and Parker and myself in the singles. That was a pretty strong lineup, and we won 5–0.

Certainly Parker was assuming that he was set as the Number 2 singles player. Maybe somebody had led him to believe that, but I know it couldn't have been Pate. "Cap"—as Budge had titled him—was Don's man, and he didn't feel quite so confident without Budge and Mako around. I very distinctly remember an early team meeting in Australia, when Pate (with his distinctive stutter), declared: "B-b-boys, I want you to know that we seven are going to pick our team together."

Things did not look bright for us down there because I came up with tennis elbow and had to lay off for awhile. In the Victorian championships, the prelude to the Davis Cup, I only played doubles, and Schroeder and I lost to Bromwich and Colin Long. Ted beat Pails in the semi's and lost to Bromwich in straight sets in the finals, but he wasn't the least bit worried. I hadn't played Bromwich since before the war, and Schroeder told me after his match: "Don't worry, you won't have any trouble with him at all."

My elbow was healing, and to tell you the truth, I wasn't worried. I thought I should beat Bromwich, and I was positive I could beat Pails, who was untried in this kind of competition. Besides, Danny was not suited to Davis Cup play; since he just couldn't psych himself up for a big match. I was sure Schroeder could beat Pails for the third point. I was very confident, but the Aussies were just as sure. They were favored, especially by the bookmakers.

Ten days before the Challenge Round, Pate named Kramer, Parker, Schroeder and Mulloy to the official four-man squad. By eliminating Talbert (as well as Tom Brown), that gave the doubles assignment to Schroeder and me—Parker and I had not worked out together—and it left only the second singles to decide. A day or two before Christmas, Cap called a meeting to thrash this out. There was tension from the very start because

Parker immediately announced that the whole meeting was unnecessary. "I was led to believe that I would play the singles," he said.

Pate said, "No, that's not true." Then, while Frankie sulked, Cap asked for our opinions.

As the Number 1 player, I spoke up first and most emphatically for Schroeder. I said he was playing best, and that to beat Bromwich or Pails you have to attack on your serve, something Frankie doesn't do. "But the main thing is that Frankie doesn't ever upset anybody. He doesn't get upset himself either, he just plays the same level every match. Here, that's not good enough. Schroed plays over his head in big matches." (The only time I ever remember Frankie upsetting anybody was the next year at Forest Hills when he beat Bromwich in the semi's.)

Talbert was next to speak, and he agreed that Schroeder was the choice. So did Brown. Then Pate turned to Mulloy. Everybody in the room knew that he and Schroeder couldn't stand each other. Gar started out by saying that he thought he should be the selection. But if the choice was between Schroeder and Parker, he didn't have any doubts. "Schroeder plays the singles," Mulloy said.

The news flabbergasted the Australians. They had counted on Parker as the choice, and if not him, then Mulloy. A typical response came from a tennis expert named R. E. Schlesinger, who wrote for *The Melbourne Sun*. His comment: "Before it was announced that Schroeder would be America's second singles representative, I felt confident that Australia would defeat America by three rubbers to two, but now there is a decided possibility that the final tally will be four rubbers to one in favor of Australia."

Furthermore, the reports going back to the States indicated that our squad was dispirited, which was not true. Parker wasn't happy, but he was a good team man, and he worked Ted and me hard in practice.

The whole business was settled with a first-round knockout. The analogy is apt too, because a Davis Cup match is more like a boxing match than it is anything in tennis. You've got to fire up and start swinging. A tournament means a slow build-up, easy matches in the beginning, getting tougher, preparing you for the last rounds. But for a Davis Cup, there are weeks of sparring, and then the real thing starts with the first ball.

The first match at Kooyong Stadium, Melbourne, in the Challenge Round of 1946 was Bromwich vs. Schroeder. I reminded Ted not to get trapped into coming in too quickly— which was, of course, his usual game—because Bromwich could clip those returns over the net so they'd sink like a rock at your feet as you rushed in.

If Schroeder had to play Bromwich the first day, I knew it was best for the team if they played at one-thirty. Ted was always an early riser, and as intense as he is, it was better for him to play early in the day. Nonetheless, Bromwich took him 6–3 in the first set and the Aussies accepted it as the beginning of a predictable victory. But then Schroed got his attack rolling. He took the net, and he ripped through the next two sets, 6–1, 6–2. Bromwich came back after the break, broke him right off, and when Ted couldn't get back into it, Bromwich won it at love. But the fifth set is always where Schroed thrived, and he won 6–3. Kooyong was stunned. It was Schroeder's greatest win; it gave us the Cup right there. It hardly attracted any notice when I beat Pails in straight sets later that day.

But the Aussies still had '39 to remember. They had been down love–2 and pulled it out on a foreign court. They figured to win the doubles to start back. But ironically, here they made the wrong choice. All of the criticism had been directed at Pate for selecting Schroeder, but in fact, it was now the Aussies who botched it. The captain this year was not Hopman, who had won the Cup for them, but Gerald Patterson, the beloved old champion, and Patterson picked Adrian Quist to team with Bromwich.

Quist and Bromwich were the perennial national champions, a great team from the past, but Adrian was getting old, and Bromwich had just won the Victorian while teamed up with Colin Long, who was a fine doubles specialist. Anytime you had

174

Bromwich in your forecourt, you should win. If Earth were playing in the all-time Universe Davis Cup, I'd play Budge and Vines in my singles, and Budge and Bromwich in the doubles. That's what I think of Johnny as a doubles player. It is also worth jumping ahead here to note that eight months later, when Schroeder and I defended the Cup at Forest Hills, the only point the Aussies won was the doubles, Bromwich and Long defeating Schroeder and Kramer in four sets.

But this day, in Kooyong, Quist was a terrible liability. Schroed and I pounded him unmercifully—Schroeder crunching overheads everytime they tried to lob their way out of something—and we polished them off in straight sets for the 3–0 lead. (Now that the issue was settled, Pate replaced Schroeder with Mulloy in the next day's singles, and Jughead beat Pails. Neither Bromwich nor I wanted to play the last meaningless point, especially when rain postponed it for another two days, but the pressure was on us, as our nations' Number 1, to go through with the match, and at last we did. I won in three sets, so officially we whitewashed them 5–0.)

The '47 Challenge Round, my last, went off without incident. I beat Bromwich and Pails in straight sets again, giving me twelve sets for twelve in the two Challenge Round singles I played, and Schroed won both his matches too. Once again he beat Bromwich on the opening day—this time the second match, in four sets—and then he took Pails in five sets on a slippery turf, going from sneakers to stockings to bare feet to spikes along the way. It was as good a Challenge Round match as there's ever been. In '48, after I turned pro, Parker took my place in the Cup, and he and Schroeder won both their singles, again over the Aussies. By now, except for Gonzales' one big win, (the upset at Forest Hills in September, 1948 when Schroeder didn't play), Schroed was clearly my successor as top amateur in the world. Whatever doubt there may have been in favor of Gonzales was removed in May of 1949 when Ted beat Pancho in straight sets in the finals of the Southern California, the big spring tournament.

Riggs and I were positive that if we could provide Schroed

with some real incentive to win Wimbledon and Forest Hills, he'd carry them both off and stand out as the undisputed challenger to my professional title. After he beat Mulloy to take the championship of Queens right before Wimbledon, Bobby, Schroed and myself met at the Atheneum Court Hotel in London to strike our deal. I urged Schroed to take a guarantee against a percentage, but he wanted a flat guarantee of $25,000, which I kept telling him was stupid until Riggs told me to shut up and let the kid have what he wanted. So we signed a letter of agreement to tour the next winter, Bobby went back to the States to start lining up arena dates, and I stayed on in London as company for Schroeder. (I would say that I stayed to be his coach except that he would not listen to me when I tried to be one. I just sat on the sidelines and sweated out his cliffhangers.)

He started out by almost tossing the whole thing away in the first round of Wimbledon against Mulloy two days after they had met in the Queens final. (And for all their dislike, they played as a doubles team all the way to the final.) Mulloy won the first two sets 6–3, 11–9, but Schroed came back, one, love and five, despite a hand cramp in the fifth. He kept up his usual Perils-of-Pauline routine all the way, saving a match point to beat Sedgman, going five against Eric Sturgess in the semi's, taking Drobny in five sets in the final, and Riggs and I are home free. We have got the Wimbledon champion signed.

A couple of weeks later, on July 18, I was in Scarborough, England when I got a call from Schroeder from his home in La Crescenta, California. He wants out of the tour deal. I argued with him—Schroeder still has the telephone bill showing that it cost him $288—but without any luck. He just kept telling me that he had decided that he wasn't up to the travel grind that a tour demanded. "Don't make me unhappy, Jack," he finally said. So what could I do?

Years later, Schroed told Gloria, my wife, that the thing that really ate at him was the thought of having to get up for a match every day. He didn't think he had the temperament for that, and so he feared that the tour would end up as a disaster for all of us. Schroed thought he was doing us a favor to pull out early.

The rest is a point of some dispute. I remember that Schroeder told me during this phone conversation—and then told Bobby when he called him—that he would take himself out of action altogether, including Davis Cup and the U.S. Nationals. That way there was a better chance for another hero—quite possibly Gonzales—to emerge that we could assign in Schroeder's place. Ted insists that he promised only to stay out of competition all summer until the Davis Cup.

I'll give Schroed his day in court here, but whatever he thought he said, I know damn well that both Riggs and I were under the impression that he had taken himself out of the Davis Cup and Forest Hills. I know that because a couple weeks later I get a call from Riggs. "That sonuvabitch has double-crossed us again," he whined. I could imagine the little foam forming on his lips.

"What sonuvabitch?"

"Schroeder. He's agreed to play Davis Cup."

And he did. He hadn't played competitively since Wimbledon, two months previous, but he steps right into the first match and comes back from being down two sets to one to beat Billy Sidwell in five. Then he beats Frank Sedgman in three. Riggs is furious. Not only was Schroeder winning, but he was stealing the spotlight from the other U.S. singles player, Gonzales. By now the only tour alternative to Schroeder was Pancho, or Gorgo, as we started to call him this summer.

That was because Gonzales, the U.S. champ, got wiped out at Wimbledon in the round of sixteen by a run-of-the-mill Aussie named Geoff Brown. As a consequence, Jim Burchard, the tennis writer for the old *New York World-Telegram*, wrote that Gonzales was a cheese champ. Well the players started kidding Gonzales about that, and somebody referred to him as a Gorgonzola cheese champ. I don't know why, but the tag stuck, and we started calling him Gorgo. And a lot of us still do. It's a little ridiculous that one of the best players in history has a nickname derived from his being a bum, but it was one of the few things that never bothered Gonzales.

Gonzales was still only twenty-one, and even with his two Challenge Round wins, I wanted him to grow up and play me a couple years later. When I got another call from Riggs, whining that Schroeder was going to play the Nationals, I told Bobby to take it easy, that maybe this thing was turning to our advantage.

I knew damn well that Schroeder wasn't trying to rewrite a better deal. On the other hand, if he won Forest Hills after he won the Challenge Round singles for the third year running after he won Wimbledon, he truly was so much more a valuable piece of property that we could offer him a better percentage arrangement, and he simply could not turn it down. Besides, having gotten himself in this predicament with all these victories, how could Schroed possibly turn Bobby and me down if he won Forest Hills?

I arrived back in the U.S. on the day of the semifinals at Forest Hills and went directly to the West Side Tennis Club. Schroeder was playing Billy Talbert. There was no way Billy, with his diabetes, could beat a conditioned player like Schroeder, especially in a grueling tournament like Forest Hills. But as I arrived, late in the third set, Talbert and Schroeder were a set apiece, and I watched Schroeder blow this one too.

I went into the locker room after Schroeder. "What the hell is the matter with you, kid?" I asked. He only looked up at me sheepishly. "You sick, Schroed? You're not doing anything to his forehand. Damn if you don't look to me like you're tanking."

Schroeder looked away from me, and then he went out on the court and dusted Talbert off in two sets.

In the other semi, Gonzales scraped by Parker. Frankie had the kid beat, tried too hard in a couple of unimportant games, got tired, and let him get away. As I said, Parker always found

178

a way to do just what he was supposed to. There were almost never any surprises.

Ted was at the height of his powers and Gonzales shouldn't have been a match for him. But it was not to be, although how Schroeder lost the match after the first set is beyond my comprehension. This was the longest set ever played in a final at Forest Hills. It lasted an hour and thirteen minutes. Five times Pancho had a set point. Once, leading 15–14, Gorgo had triple set point, love–40, on Schroeder's serve. And Schroed won 18–16. On that wave, he ripped through a second set 6–2. It was a lock.

In the third set, however, Gonzales got an early break. Up two sets, there is no way a mature player like Schroeder— especially one who had learned percentage tennis from Cliff Roche—would contest this third set on the grass. The book called for Schroeder to relax, let Gonzales have the set; then with the intermission, come back relaxed and win in four. Instead, Schroeder fought like a tiger for every point but lost 6–1. Ridiculous. But still I didn't worry. Considering all the funny business with Talbert the day before, I should have gone down and talked with Schroeder during the break. I didn't. I honestly didn't think it was necessary. And when they came back, Gonzales won the fourth set at two and put Schroed on the defensive.

Actually, Schroed didn't buckle. In the fifth set, they held serve to 4–all before Gonzales broke him, and the match point, after almost five hours, was a bad call. Schroeder hit a forehand down the line that was clearly in, but called out. Afterwards in the locker room, the poor linesman was in tears, so distraught at his error that he came into the shower to apologize to Schroeder.

I'm not saying Schroeder tanked it. He swears he didn't, that he could never throw any match. But given the circumstances, I think it is very possible that Schroed unconsciously tanked as the convenient way out. That's crazy, but I still think it's possible. I remember so very well that when Bobby and I went

179

down to commiserate with him in the locker room, the first thing he said was: "Now, I guess everyone will be happy." And that was terribly out of character—especially after the match he had just been through.

Sheepishly, Bobby and I moved around the lockers to where Gorgo was dressing and asked him if he might be interested in turning pro and playing me in all those arenas we had lined up for the winter.

Schroeder wasn't finished playing after Forest Hills. He had made his choice about his commitment to tennis, but for the next couple years he continued to play a few big tournaments and he continued to play Davis Cup. In 1950 he lost his two singles, as Frank Sedgman and Ken McGregor took the Cup back Down Under, and in 1951 he was again on the team.

Frank Shields was the captain this year, and since I was down in Australia at the time, he asked me to help coach the team. He was sure—and he was right—that I could get Schroed to play one more time. The team also included Vic Seixas, Tony Trabert, Dick Savitt and Ham Richardson.

The sensitive focal point was Savitt. He had won Wimbledon a few months before, but he really wasn't all that good a player. Sav had gotten lucky in the draw. Herbie Flam upset Sedgman, and then Savitt beat Flam in the semi's and Ken McGregor in the finals. McGregor was one of the weakest players but one of the nicest guys who ever played for me in the pros. As nearly as I could tell, all he ever wanted to do was save up some money, go back Down Under and play Australian-rules football, which in fact, he played better than he did tennis. And that's what he did.

So Savitt had won Wimbledon, and even though he had a bad leg at Forest Hills and lost to Seixas in the semi's, a lot of people thought his victory in July had guaranteed him a spot in the Davis Cup singles. Dick is Jewish, and so a lot of Jewish people were rooting for him. But Savitt was never really seriously considered for the singles.

For the Number 1 singles, both Shields and I wanted Schroeder. There just wasn't any question in our mind. We needed the experienced fighter. This tells it all: years later, at Alan King's Hall of Fame tournament in Las Vegas, Schroeder and Savitt were playing each other in a doubles match. On match point, Schroed serving, he missed his first serve and then aced Savitt with his second serve. Then he screamed: "And that's why I was a champion, and you never were!"

Sedgman had won at Forest Hills, giving Seixas six games, and he was way above any of our kids. The defeat at Wimbledon was a fluke. The only chance we had of upsetting Sedg was with a smart scrapper like Schroeder who knew how to stay alive, parry, and all of a sudden to raise his game if he got the chance. So the only choice was for the second singles. It came down between Trabert, who was set in the doubles (with Schroeder) and who had the most potential, or with Seixas who had more experience and also some good wins in Australia. No one even mentioned Savitt's religion; nobody even thought about it. That was only dragged up later, and poor Shields went to his grave a few years ago with people still calling him anti-Semitic.

We got a big break going into the match. The Aussies finally named Harry Hopman as the captain again the year before, and he had brought the Cup back. But in Australia he had a lot of second-guessers looking over his shoulder. The Australian tennis officials were usually just as foolish and misguided as the American ones. Sir Norman Brookes, the great old left-handed Aussie (their first Wimbledon champ), was at the head of the panel of Australian selectors, and they overruled Hopman. He wanted to play McGregor, but led by Brookes, the selectors picked Mervyn Rose, a lefty. Shields picked Seixas over Trabert, and Vic promptly whipped Rose in straight sets. Then Sedgman beat Schroeder, but it was four good, tough sets. Okay, it figured. But we still had a good chance. If Schroeder and Trabert could upset Sedgman and McGregor in the doubles and Schroeder could beat Rose, we would win 3–2.

This was definitely unlikely. Beating the Aussies at doubles would have been a major upset, but it was possible. Unfortunately. . . .

181

I'd have to say that I've only seen three pitiful performances in the Challenge Round. I mean so bad that you were embarrassed. Each was in doubles, and each was the same sort of thing: they played an old guy with a great past record, and he suddenly lost it. I saw it first with Adrian Quist in '46, when he played with Bromwich against Schroeder and me. The last time I saw it was in 1963, when the Aussies decided to play Neale Fraser with Roy Emerson. And I saw it this day late in 1951 when it was my friend Schroed. Trabert, the kid, played very well, but Schroed played so badly I wanted to cry for him. It's no fun being there when your friend suddenly goes over the hill, especially when you're his age and you've come along together. It is worst of all when he knows it. Schroed always knew what he had to do to win, and he knew very well when he couldn't do it.

So the U.S. was down two points to one, and there didn't appear to be any way in the world that Seixas could beat Sedgman in the fifth match. (And there wasn't; Seixas only won eight games.) But you never knew. Hell, Sedg might break a leg. Schroeder was scheduled to play Rose first, and he had to beat him to keep us alive. He had to beat him for himself too. Schroed knew it was the last important match he would ever play.

Schroed came to my room the night after the doubles, before his match with Rose. If you break down both our careers and our whole friendship, the friendship and memories go on, but what more is there really than this night at the end of a career, and that other night in 1939 twelve years before? That was the time when he came and stayed in my room just before I played my first Davis Cup match. Remember? He slept on the floor, and we talked until almost dawn. We were so excited, teen-agers, almost babies. And now here we were, so many years later, thousands of miles away in Sydney. There had been so much and we found ourselves talking about it all. We had both won our Wimbledon, both won Forest Hills. Together we had won a Davis Cup and defended it. And God, there'd been a whole war too, and wives

182

and children. And here it was at the other end, another hotel room, another very long night. Schroed knew the next day would be his last important one in tennis, and I knew that my days were numbered. The only reason I was still on top was because a new wonder drug named cortisone had been discovered at exactly the right moment.

At first Schroeder said he just wanted to play some gin, so I got out the cards. We played. I kept thinking he would get tired and go back to his room and sleep. Maybe he was too upset by how he had played in the doubles. I don't know. He didn't make any move to leave, so I just kept playing. At four o'clock—4:00 A.M.—he said, "let's take a walk." And so we strolled around Sydney till the sun came up and then came back to the hotel and had some breakfast. By then it was almost time to go to the courts. No sleep at all.

Schroeder must have been exhausted, and while I know, sure, it wasn't Budge he played, it wasn't even Ken McGregor—it was just Mervyn Rose—I've never been more moved by a match, by what a man could will for himself. He beat Rose in straight sets, but look at the numbers: 6–4, 13–11, 7–5. Everyone of them a battle. Schroed probably knew he had to win in three or he would collapse. I was sitting in the stands, and I got so excited that the referee, Cliff Sproule, thought I was coaching Schroed and reprimanded me. I was just cheering for him, for everything he had been.

It was a great way to go out, Schroed.

12

Little Pancho

Professional tennis tours began in the mid-'20s when Cash-and-Carry Pyle, the promoter, signed up Vinnie Richards and Suzanne Lenglen to play against lesser opponents, so the business was twenty years old when I got into it. But it had only gone in fits and starts. After Richards and Lenglen, there wasn't another good tour for five years, when Tilden turned pro and played against a Czech named Karel Kozelhuh. Then Cochet signed to tour against Big Bill, and thereafter virtually all the real champions went into the pros: Vines, Perry, Budge, Riggs (with Kovacs), and finally me.

From Richards right on through to kids like Ralston and Emerson in the '60s, it was a big deal when the amateur turned. It had a great effect on the world he was leaving, especially Davis Cup and the big tournaments. And curiosity was piqued: how would he do against the reigning pro king? The major exception to all this was Segura, who turned pro virtually unnoticed. Ecuador, where he was from, didn't even have a Davis Cup team, and anyway, he hadn't played that well in the amateurs. He is the only kid in the twentieth century to have won the Intercollegiates three times, but that was in the war years, 1943-44-45, when he was at the University of Miami and nobody paid a great deal of attention.

The major tournaments on grass were beyond his range then. He got to the semi's at Forest Hills in '43, when I beat him in four sets, but he lost without distinction (to Tom Brown and Drobny) the two times he played Wimbledon, and really, nobody took Segoo seriously. He didn't speak English well, he had a freak shot, and on the grass scooting around in his long white pants with his bowlegs, he looked like a little butterball. A dirty butterball: his pants were always grass-stained.

You talk about guys who weren't used to grass courts and could only play dirt; well Segoo was born on dirt. He grew up in a sugar cane house with the good earth for a floor. He was known as *pata de loro* (parrot foot) for the funny way he walked; and after he almost died at his premature birth, he had rickets, double hernia and malaria, plus he was discriminated against. He is what is known in his country as a *cholo*—Spanish and Inca blood mixed. The only reason he ever got near a tennis court was that his father was a caretaker at the club in Guayaquil. Everything about Segoo is a freak. He shouldn't be alive, and he certainly never should have been an athlete. It drives him absolutely crazy when I say this, but the truth is he's never been very good at anything in the world except hitting a tennis forehand. But otherwise, he's no good at golf. He's afraid to really swing the club. He can't dance. And after forty years, he still can't speak English. (I'm kidding, Segoo.) He could never figure out backgammon. He could play a little gin rummy, but whenever Riggs dealt cards, he always called a game known as Indicators (which is sort of like Hold 'Em, the game that's so popular today) because Bobby was convinced that Segura really didn't know how to play it, even after playing thousands of hands.

But I'll tell you this about Francisco Segura. There is no kinder gentleman around anywhere on this earth. And there is no one who has ever loved the game of tennis as much. We are

almost exactly the same age. Segoo, Schroeder, Pails, Tom
Brown, Drobny and I were all born in 1921. I don't think there
was a vintage time like that until the 1950s, when Connors,
Vilas, Gottfried, Dibbs, Stockton, Solomon, Tanner and Sandy
Mayer all were born within a period of about a year and a half.

The first time I ever played Segura was in 1940, in the
Eastern Clay Courts at South Orange, New Jersey, and
although I won, I was fascinated by his terrific two-handed
forehand. Possibly Budge's backhand was the better stroke, I'll
have to accept that judgment. But put a gun to my head, and
I'd have to say the Segura forehand because he could disguise
it so much better and hit so many more angles. As great a shot
as Connors' two-hand backhand is, it is nowhere near as tough
as Segura's forehand because Pancho could hit just as hard but
with more control.

Segura's trouble was that he never learned to exploit this
great weapon because he used it too often. He didn't know
how to pace himself and pick his spots. Perhaps he was too
quick for his own good; he was so fast he could run around
anything and get to his forehand. I probably played him two
hundred times so I know his game damn well, and I would say
that he probably hit his forehand four times as much as his
backhand. And remember to take into account that people
were trying to hit to his backhand. Certainly if you have a good
shot, you should try to hit it more often. I hit my forehand
two-to-one over my backhand. But Segoo went too far and
wasted himself in the process.

Nobody was ever in better shape, either. At forty he could
still play near the top of his game, and he worked out every
day. He had to; he couldn't stand not being on a tennis court.
Probably he played more matches against top players than
anyone in history. Besides my couple hundred, he must have
played Gonzales a hundred and fifty, and Budge, Sedgman,
Riggs, Hoad and Rosewall all around fifty apiece. I beat him
about 80 percent of the time, and Gonzales also held an edge
over him. He was close with Budge. Pails beat him 41–31 on
the Kramer-Riggs tour, but that was when Segoo was still

learning how to play fast surfaces. With everybody else, he had the edge: Sedgman, Rosewall, Hoad, Trabert, McGregor.

I would have to qualify all this praise, however, by adding that I just don't know how Segoo would do in a five-set final at Wimbledon or in a Challenge Round. He was never there. It's unfair that he never got the proper acclaim, but it's true that he never had to face the pressure situations that earns acclaim. The one year that he toured with me on the top of the bill, Segoo was noticeably less colorful and more grim. There is no doubt in my mind that Segura was a better player than Rosewall. Kenny never won a Wimbledon either, but he played all the big ones and won the most. If you could match Segura and Rosewall in their prime in the finals at Wimbledon, I'd have to back Kenny.

But not one of those great heroes I mentioned—not Tilden, Vines, Budge, Riggs; not Kramer—not one of those big shots ever contributed as much to professional tennis as Segoo. He never had an amateur career, and so he cared more for the pros. And he was the one pro who brought people back. The fans would come out to see the new challenger face the old champion, but they would leave talking about the bandy-legged little sonuvabitch who gave them such pleasure playing the first match and the doubles. The next time the tour came to town the fans would come back to see Segoo.

The one year he played the feature men's match against me was the time we also had Gorgeous Gussy, so even then Segoo didn't get top star billing or pay—just 5 percent plus $1,000 a week. Unfortunately, it was no contest either. I beat him fifty-eight matches to twenty-seven. Segura's problem was that no matter how well he played, he couldn't overcome my serve. Against most players, even the good servers, he could break them down by running around their second serves and pounding the forehands back. You had to get in a high percentage of good first serves to beat Segura, but in my case—and this was also true of Gonzales—we had such depth and control on our second serves that we could keep Segura from using his big weapon (and especially in the deuce court). So

Segura and I were a classic case of the tour imbalance that develops. Once I beat him nineteen straight.

Damn, but he would get mad. One time we were driving through the South, and he started screaming at me: "Jack, you big sonuvabitch, you could never beat me if you don't have that big serve." I screamed back at him that he couldn't even get to a court without buying a ticket if he didn't have that freak forehand. And we kept at it awhile, laughing and hollering. But at last he got to my pride, and I agreed to play him the next three matches at a handicap.

The deal was that I would not follow my serve to the net. I would have to let the ball come back on the return and bounce before I could come in to volley (and of course, he had to play by the same restrictions). The first night of the three matches was in either Baton Rouge or Birmingham—I can't remember which—and I beat him in a close match. It was the fairest test, too, because the next stop was Charlotte, and he beat me there in a terribly dark building that penalized ground strokes. Segoo— "Sneaky" we called him sometimes—he had eyes like an owl. And then the third night, I beat him in Norfolk, but he didn't get a fair shake there because there was very little runback space behind the baselines, so he couldn't scamper about and take his big windup.

The fans seemed to enjoy these three matches tremendously, and nobody I knew of caught on that I wasn't playing my normal game. Still, through the years whenever we polled fans about making changes in the game, they always voted heavily to keep tennis the way it was.

To be honest, I don't believe I could have played tennis the way Segoo and I did for the three nights because it wore me out so, running down all those groundstrokes. It was much more grueling than putting a lot into a serve and following it in. Rosewall was a backcourt player when he came into the pros, but he learned very quickly how to play the net. Eventually, for that matter, he became a master at it, as much out of physical preservation as for any other reason. I guarantee you that Kenny wouldn't have lasted into his forties as a world-class player if he had not learned to play serve and volley.

If I got the edge over Segura in those three one-bounce matches, he took a measure of revenge against me somewhat later in Hawaii. This was the one time in all my life when I didn't go all out in a singles match. I admitted that we sometimes fudged on doubles, advertising best-of-three, but only playing best-of-one for real, giving the second set to whomever won the first. Well this one time in Hawaii, Segoo and I did the same thing in singles. It was in Hilo, on the Big Island, it was pouring rain outside and in the arena it was hot and stuffy, with maybe two hundred people on hand. We were both exhausted from traveling, and we just didn't want to play three sets. So we agreed to play one for real, and Segoo won that set. Fine, now it was my job to tank the second. And you know what that sneaky little brown sonuvabitch starts doing? He purposely starts making errors, screwing up all over the place. Have you ever tried to lose to somebody who is not trying to win—and make it look good? It is much harder than trying to beat somebody who is playing beautifully. Finally, with great effort, I was able to out-lose him. I served a double fault on break point. I had to. I could tell he was ready to slam my second serve into the net.

This was one of the few times Segura ever had any leverage. The other kids had the titles, all he had was the ability to beat them. But he got his just reward one time. We were down in Australia, and I found out that I had mixed up the calendar and that his contract ran out while we still had two scheduled dates to play. We needed him, and as soon as he realized he finally had me over a barrel, he really held me up. I had to give him 25 percent, which meant that I went into the promotion contracted to pay out 105 percent of my share of the gate . . . and they always called me such a tough businessman.

It is hardly like Segoo had to work for slave wages. During the 1950s there were at least six or seven years when he made in excess of $50,000 a year playing for me—and remember, $50,000 was a lot more twenty years ago. There were very few baseball, football or basketball players making $50,000 then.

Of course he had to work most of the year, and no matter how you cut it, a tennis tour was a tough way to make a buck. It was also all upside down. Because the amateurs had all the prestige and publicity, the challenger got the lion's share of the money. Try to imagine Muhammed Ali taking half what some kid was offered. There was such little professional continuity that the amateur had to get a big pot right away to "lure" him into the pros. Everybody knew the chances were that a player would only get one big payday. If the champ beat him, his market value immediately dropped to zero.

As an offshoot of this necessary arrangement, the finances of the whole tour were cuckoo. In the U.S. and Canada, you had to play four and a half matches a week to break even. Ideally, at a little faster pace—five matches a week for ten weeks, fifty matches or so—it would be perfect for the promoter. But you couldn't stop at ten weeks because whereas the promoter, the challenger and the champion had all made nice percentages by then, you couldn't attract the salaried people and the extra players to give up regular employment and come aboard for such a short stretch. You had to keep going, eternally it seemed, to get all those people a little money. As we got larger, we needed a full, year-round staff, which meant more over-head. Worse, once you had played ten weeks, you had almost certainly hit all the major markets. You might try to double back into a large city twice if you had a really top attraction, but generally speaking the act only played once. So after the first ten weeks, you were not only promoting just to break even, but you were doing it in high-school gyms in small towns.

We played the opera house in Saratoga, New York once, where the back wall was eighteen inches from the baseline. Near Springfield, Massachusetts we played in a gym where basketball stanchions were set two feet behind the baseline so you had to run around them to get from one side of the court to the other. You could be sure that both players used a back-and-forth strategy—nobody was hitting any drop shots.

The normal split—almost everywhere but Madison Square

Garden which always demands more from everybody—was 55/45. Our cut was the 55 percent of the gross, while the arena got to keep 45. The local promoter also had to pay all the expenses. We made a few more bucks selling souvenir programs. Right after the war, when I first started touring, the government had a special 20 percent amusement tax, and so there was a strict accounting of all tickets sold. But once the tax went off, you were very vulnerable to the local promoters taking advantage of you. It was tedious work, but the only way to make sure that you were getting a fair shake was to get a manifest of all the tickets printed and then count the deadwood—the tickets not sold—when the matches were through.

Generally speaking, most of the arena people I dealt with were very honest. As often as not, we just had handshake deals. The only place I almost called off a performance in a dispute over terms was—where else—Madison Square Garden, the opening match of my last playing tour against Sedgman. Most promoters knew they had us at a disadvantage too, because we had commitments somewhere else the next day. If they wanted to stiff us, it would be very expensive and time-consuming for us to sue, and we would be trying to obtain justice in their back yard.

Sometimes a promoter would take a bath, and then you had to make a difficult decision. Should you let him pay you less than the guarantee? Jack Harris, my first promoter, taught me as a rule of thumb that if the guy had tried and if you thought you'd like to come back again and you could use this man, then let him off the hook. Better to take some of the heat and give the guy a break if you could be sure he would work extra hard for you next time around.

It sure wasn't perfect, especially when the contracts got more involved and guarantees and percentages changed depending on what country you were in. I needed a computer to keep it organized, but they didn't have them then. Most of the time, the "home office" of the Kramer tours consisted of my mother keeping the books back home. One time in Cincinnati when Riggs was promoting, we couldn't find a local promoter we liked so we decided to handle the local end ourselves. We didn't get the crowd. So I had to go to 9–7 in the third to beat Segura and paid $1,300 for the privilege. Another time Jack Kramer, the boy wonder promoter, managed to work it out so he was paying 102½ percent to his people.

I gave an agent in Europe 10 percent to line up a tour. Trabert was in for 35, Gonzales for 20, Rex Hartwig for 17½. I had to get a fourth to keep the commitments. I offered Sedgman 17½ too, but he wouldn't take it so I bumped it to 20, thinking surely that Trabert would go back 2½ points, trading off for a stronger tour and a bigger draw. But his brother was a lawyer and he wouldn't give in a nickel. So I had to eat 2½ percent every night, and the better we did, the more it cost me.

Another time, I ran a big round-robin tournament, scheduling all the key matches for the weekend. Segura was through all his matches on Friday, and by the time he finished he had clinched first place. So we played the good dates, Saturday and Sunday, to see who could finish second.

Bobby Riggs was my promoter for two tours, the one with Gonzales and the ones with Segoo and Gussy. Bobby's problem was that he didn't have any discretion. Tour dates were like women—he would take a shot at them all. If Riggs saw three guys standing around a gas station kicking tires, he'd try to sell them a date on the tennis tour. He did work hard.

On the Gonzales tour in 1949-50, I beat Pancho 97–26. Count it—that's one hundred and twenty-three matches. Pancho and I were both punchy for the last few months. The only thing worse than losing a tour 97–26 is having to win one. Finally, one night in Palm Springs I cracked. I started belting balls over the fence and then I started screaming, "I'm losing my mind! I'm losing my mind." Which was accurate enough, but I was terribly embarrassed. Here I was, supposed to be Mister Etiquette, and I was carrying on like a crazy man.

Riggs came into the locker room to see me afterwards. "All right, Kid, I'll end it," he said. "But I gotta fill a few dates through Dayton." He had some top guarantee at Dayton, and that was still weeks away. Pancho and I kept stumbling along.

The preliminary match, the ones Segura starred in for most

of his career—we called it "the animal act." There was a great disparity in payoff. Segura and Pails, for example, were playing on the Duel-of-the-Decade tour for $300 apiece a week, and paying their own expenses out of that. So I made $8,800 opening night in the Garden, Bobby had to settle for $4,400, and those two kids grossed less than I made that one night on their whole tour in the States. But if you wanted to play professionally, it was the only game in town.

In the East, where we almost always kicked off in the Garden, we traveled mostly by trains. Then as the distances grew greater and the train schedules less convenient, we switched to cars. The deal with Jack Harris was that he would pay all inter-city transportation, so he came around to Bobby and me and told us he could get us a good deal on a couple of DeSoto station wagons. We took that and he threw in $50 a week for gas and incidentals for both of us. This helped the kids in the animal act since they could ride with us. Having our own cars also made it possible to leave a town at our own convenience. Often the ideal time to travel would be in the dead of night right after the evening's matches ended. We were too keyed up to sleep then, but if we waited till morning we had to get up early to get to the next town and get in all our publicity engagements.

The best time to start a tour was in December, because that followed Forest Hills fairly closely and more important, it spread the tour over two calendar years so that you got a better break with the IRS. But that meant that we were starting off in the winter in the East and Midwest, so we often had to contend with bad weather. For a kid from Southern California I learned to drive in snow pretty well.

The court was carted from town to town in a one-ton panel truck. It was made of canvas, cut into two pieces about fifty-eight feet square, which made the court a little short. The halves were laced together at the bottom of the net. It was pulled tight on the sides by ropes that pulled through twenty-two eyes on each side. The driver was a regular member of the tour, and then the arenas would hire about a half-dozen workers (more in the big union towns) to put the court down under his supervision. The truck also carried the souvenir programs we sold and our ball supply. You would think that some tennis-ball company would have been delighted to supply our balls free for the publicity, but we weren't big enough. We could only get the balls at cost and then try to get some of that back by selling used balls at cut-rate prices to the fans.

The canvas court would last about three years, about three hundred matches, but after that it started looking shabby. At its newest, it was faster than the Supreme Court that is used on tour indoors today. The canvas had French seams too, so that if you hit one, the ball would shoot a little on you. If you felt very confident, you'd shoot for the seams. If the canvas was placed over wood, the bounces tended to be lower and faster, not unlike grass. Then, certain arena floors were of terrazo, and the ball would catch on that and sit up. Sometimes we played directly over ice, and strangely enough, that was a pretty good surface; the ball would sit up a little. The floor that went over the ice at the Montreal Forum was the one I remember the most because it was the worst of any big building. It fit together all wrong. The sockets were worn. We'd aim for the holes.

I have no idea, aerodynamically, why this is true, but the ball goes faster indoors. An expert might tell me I'm crazy, but from experience I know it's true. Furthermore, the bigger the building, the faster the ball goes. You could tell that in a place like New York, where we could never get the Garden to practice and worked out in a smaller building. As soon as you got into the Garden, everything you hit would soar long, like you were playing at a high altitude.

For all the advertising we did, tennis wasn't a sport you could hawk. The Gussy Moran tour proved to me that tennis people (at least at that time) wouldn't respond to anything but the tennis. Rarely would you ever get more than a 15 percent walk-up gate. The tennis fans bought their tickets well in advance, and this same small group tended to turn out for the tour year after year. Then there was a fringe crowd of sports fans who liked tennis but who would only support certain tennis attractions. Those were the ones that made the difference. Those were the ones who would pay to see me play Gonzales but wouldn't buy tickets to see me play Segura. As time wore on I found out that we could almost predict what the tour would draw anywhere around the country on the basis of how well it opened in New York.

Around 1955 we found that we could begin to fly regularly, and by then I'd saved up enough courts so we didn't have to ship them overnight long distances. Flying was a big boost because it meant that we could hit all the big cities right away when the publicity coming out of New York was the hottest. Oddly, we always drew the worst in Dixie, and we never got any publicity there. If we played Kansas City or Buffalo or Madison, Wisconsin, at least we'd get a paragraph on the wires; but it seemed as if the South didn't exist to the rest of the country, and if we played there, we just plain disappeared.

We played just about everywhere. For some reason I never played Wilmington, Delaware, or Idaho or South Dakota or Montana. I think those are the only states I missed. And also, I never played a match in Germany. On the other hand, I've made thirty-five trips to Australia, and at the time I was playing, going Down Under meant a forty-six-hour airplane trip.

It was a lonely and hectic existence. Considering that you had to be best friends with the people you were trying to beat for a living, we all got along remarkably well. Consider Dinny Pails and me. We played fifty-six times, and I beat him fifty-five times with one draw, but somehow we were able to forget that off the court. We always had to deal with the rap that we were fixed, but except for those isolated cases I've cited, it was on the square and we played damn hard every night.

After the matches we would relax with each other, have a few beers, play cards, because often as not we were somewhere alone and all we had for good company was each other. Of course you would know that I'm lying if I did not say that for many of the players, there were women. There were. A lot of the guys ended up divorced: Riggs, Segura, Budge, Gonzales,

Trabert. (Perhaps the toughest job I ever had as a promoter was trying to convince all the wives that the photographs of Trabert and Ava Gardner together in Australia were simply "publicity" to help the tour.) Maybe it was because they were separated so often from their wives, and maybe because of the separations there were other women. Probably it was both. Let's face it, in a business like a tennis tour, marriage is a high-risk proposition. Hell, my own was always hanging by a thread. I'll never be grateful enough to Gloria for bringing up our five boys while I was away so much.

Sometimes wives would travel with us. Frankie Parker married Audrey Beasley after she divorced his coach, Mercer Beasley. Audrey was very much Frankie's senior and had practically been his mother for many years. Frankie was always a loner anyway. Segura would always come to life when we crossed into a new country, because he would try to sneak up behind the Parkers as we came through customs so he could try and peek at Audrey's passport to find out exactly how much older than Frankie she was. He says he finally did get the answer. But theirs was a good tennis marriage that lasted many years, before Audrey died not so long ago.

In the pros we played cards as constantly as we had in the amateurs. As I said, Riggs favored a game named Indicators—five cards dealt to each player, then five cards dealt down in the middle. They would then be turned up to indicate the wild cards. It was a crazy game. I usually called jacks to back. Everybody had their favorite: Gonzales' was seven-card, high or low. Mervyn Rose, the Aussie, was one of the best card players. He had to be. The year he turned pro he won every amateur doubles tournament he entered, and he was at least a singles semifinalist at each tournament. He got with us, he won exactly one singles *match* in thirteen weeks, and he never took a doubles title the whole time even though he was paired with Sedgman. I remember one game in '58, we were taking an old DC-6 from Perth to Melbourne, and Trabert and Hoad, two kids who were unusual in that they seldom played cards, got bored and decided to pool £100 and come in. We had a pretty heavy group playing: Rose, Segura, Sedgman, Gonzales and myself. Trabert sat down, Hoad looking over his shoulder, they got in a pot, lost it, and were out the whole £100 in one hand.

It was a lot of fun—there are many great memories—but it was tough. People always ask me: could you guys beat the kids today? I say: could they have played with us? The kids today are sprinters; our breeding was for the tougher distances.

13

Big Pancho

As I mentioned earlier, the worst thing that ever happened to Gonzales was winning Forest Hills in 1949. There is no question that beating a top player like Schroeder from two sets down gave him a confidence he had never had before (he beat Ted again two weeks later in the finals of the Pacific Southwest) and moved him way up as a player. It also propelled him into the pros too quickly. At a time when Gorgo wasn't mature as a player he was pitted against Kramer, an established pro at his peak.

In the wake of Gonzalez' win at Forest Hills, we began the tour as quickly as possible and opened in the Garden on October 25, 1949, only a month after the Pacific Southwest. A fine crowd of 13,357 at an $8 top showed up, but neither the attendance nor the gross was up to the Riggs-Kramer debut.

I won that night 6–4, 3–6, 6–3, 6–2, and that was a fair enough sample of things to come. I beat Gorgo twenty-two of the first twenty-six matches, my last victory in that opening stretch being 6–1, 6–1 in less than a half an hour in a town named Waterloo, in Ontario. But actually Gonzales got better as the tour proceeded, and by the end he was a much tougher competitor, and possibly even the second-best player in the world . . . for whatever good that did him.

Although I was clearly the better player, we did have some good, long matches. And whatever you think of Gonzales, the man has the heart of a lion. At 5–all in the fifth, there is no man in the history of tennis that I would bet on against him; but against me on this tour, it was precisely the close ones that he couldn't win. In our first fifty matches, before Riggs exhausted us, I was 42–8, and of his eight wins, Pancho only took one in three sets. If he couldn't come out there smoking and blow me away, I'd beat him in the stretch. At this point, I think both Riggs and Segura could also have beaten Gonzales on a tour.

Pancho was just in way over his head. He had no idea how to live or take care of himself. He was a hamburger-and-hot-dog guy to start with and had no concept of diet in training. I had learned, for example, that if we got a couple days off in a row I had to almost stop eating or I couldn't burn it up. He'd eat at the same pace and I always beat him the next match. On the court Gorgo would swig Cokes through a match. My experience with soft drinks is that if you're playing hard and take one sip of a cold carbonated soda, you'll want another. (I had learned from Perry and Budge to bring sweetened tea to the court.)

Polite gentleman that I am, I helped Pancho with his Coke habit by making sure that there was a cold and unopened bottle waiting for him at the cross-over. I never said a word about the Coke until long after we finished touring—after I was through as a serious competitor as a matter of fact. Then in 1956, we were playing some tournament in Aruba, and at the odd-game break Pancho started swilling another Coke. I just stood there and said: "You know, Gorgo, you got to be crazy to drink that stuff during a match." He didn't say a word back—only stared right through me with those dark eyes. I think it had all finally dawned on him.

199

Also Gorgo was a pretty heavy cigarette smoker. He had terrible sleeping habits made even worse by the reality of a tour. He couldn't get to sleep after a match under the best conditions—and try getting to sleep every night when you're losing. So he'd take an afternoon nap, grab a hamburger and come out on the court dull and logy. If I won the toss, I always let him serve first because he was still half-asleep, and I could break him right off the bat. Then he'd start filling up on Cokes. He's lose again and have trouble sleeping again, and the whole cycle would repeat itself. Gorgo had no idea how to pace himself on the court either. One of the great ironies of that tour was that he was a kid in perfect health and I beat him on stamina.

Bobby had promised his wife Kay a mink coat if he made $50,000 on the Gonzales-Kramer tour. Kay got that coat because Pancho and I each took in $73,000 on the U.S.-Canada segment; we were both signed for 30 percent. That was good money, but not at the price Gonzales had to pay in return. The tour made him a has-been at the age of twenty-two.

That tour stuck with Gonzales too. He always has had an ego problem with me, even after I retired. I was still around, promoting and getting attention. I was like Marley's Ghost for Gonzales, there to remind everybody how badly I had beaten him. Also, I always got along well with the press because I understood what writers needed, and how we could work together for mutual benefit. Gonzales thought the press was out to get him. You could never explain to Gorgo that if they weren't writing about you then paying customers didn't know you existed.

It wasn't just the press. Gonzales could never talk to anyone except rarely and then he would be odds-on to be disagreeable. There was a time when Vic Braden was working for me out on the tour, and Vic's major job was to follow Gorgo around and apologize for what he had just said. Gonzales was suspicious of everyone. On one occasion the Gillette razor people offered him a quick $2,000 to do a razor commercial—sign a paper, fly to New York, spend a day filming it, and pocket two grand.

Gorgo was suspicious and just couldn't come to a decision. The ad agency man, exasperated and tired of trying to give money away, finally gave up and called me. I was on the next plane to New York.

As a professional competitor, Gonzales never comprehended that when you joined a tour you became, in effect, a major stockholder. The more publicity, the bigger everybody's cut. Even though he was usually the top name, he would almost never help promote. The players could have tolerated his personal disagreeableness, but this refusal to help the group irritated them the most. Frankly, the majority disliked Gonzales intensely. Sedgman almost came to blows with Gonzales once. Trabert and Gorgo hated each other passionately. The only player he ever tried to get along with was Lew Hoad. Everybody loved Hoad, even Pancho Gonzales. They should put that on Lew's tombstone as the ultimate praise for the man.

So Gonzales invariably stayed by himself—except on those rare occasions when he was on a losing streak. Then he needed some kind of company and would join the group for a sandwich and a beer.

One of the few people he enjoyed being with was his father, Manuel, who would join the tour now and then. He was a great old fellow. Gonzales never seemed to get along with his various wives, although this never stopped him from getting married. He married one of them—Madalyn Darrow, a former Miss Rheingold—twice. Segura once said, "You know, the nicest thing Gorgo ever says to his wives is 'Shut up.' "

One of the times he was married to Madalyn she decided to change his name. Madalyn discovered that in the Castillian upper-crust society, the fancy Gonzales families spelled their name with a z at the end to differentiate from the *hoi polloi* Gonzales. So it was Gonzalez for a time, and even now you will occasionally see that spelling pop up. I don't think Pancho gave a damn one way or the other.

By the way, Gorgo was not the poor Mexican-American that people assumed. He didn't come from a wealthy family, but from a stable middle-class background, probably a lot like mine. He had a great mother and there was always a warm feeling of family loyalty. If anything, he might have been spoiled as a kid. It's a shame that he suffered discrimination because of his Mexican heritage.

Anyway, even Pancho Gonzales has mellowed a little . . . although he can still be just as contentious as ever in competition. A couple years ago in the Grand Masters, Rex Hartwig, a wonderful fellow, beat Gonzales in a close singles match. The next day, when Gonzales and Whitney Reed played Hartwig and Sedgman in doubles, Hartwig made the mistake of saying "Nice try" when Gorgo failed on a tough shot. Immediately, Gonzales came to the net and accused him of trying to put him down by calling out "Nice try." Gonzales stopped only when Sedgman moved up to the net and told him to knock it off. Gorgo only picked on lesser opponents, so he would never mess with a top player like Sedgman. Gonzales never tried anything with me, but we always got along better on the court than off.

Now, at least with me, Gorgo can laugh at the way he was. One of the nicest surprises I get these days is when I go out to my golf course, the Los Serranos Country Club, and find Pancho there. It has become sort of his hang-out when he comes to Los Angeles, and I've told everybody who works at Los Serranos that Pancho is our Number 1 honorary member—no tabs. We get into some nice talks at the club and there is a special joy in that for me—that someone I battled so much is now a good friend. And also, he finally seems so much happier about life.

I get a laugh out of him too, because Gonzales more than any other older player is the one who complains about the way the kids today behave on the court. Of course, no one was ever worse to play against than he was. Even when he was trying to get an edge, there was an entirely different feeling playing against Riggs than against Gonzales.

It was all a game to Bobby. If he could influence the referee, con the linesman, bug the opponent, that was the same as rolling a coin down the track or sneaking a peek at the other guy's hand. He was never malicious; in fact, when I was playing Bobby, I would sort of get into the spirit of things. Because I was in better shape than he was, Bobby would always stall whenever he could, steal a few seconds extra at the cross-over. To call attention to his tardiness I made it a point to get back on the court as fast as possible.

With Pancho the tone was different. He could be mean, and he was even nastier when he fell behind. If he couldn't take it out on his opponent, he would be unmercifully cruel to the linesman.

In the '50s there was a lot of agitation to change the rules in some way to limit the big serve. Since Gonzales had a big serve, anything done to reduce the power of the serve was going to limit him. But Pancho took it as a personal vengeance. It never occurred to him that he was only being affected coincidentally in the greater effort to help the game.

For awhile, trying to make a better spectator game, we played what was called the three-bounce rule on tour. Essentially, it was what Segura and I had played for those three matches in 1951. Neither player could volley before the ball had bounced three times. This way a fast server like Pancho could not come in behind his serve, but would have to hit at least one ground stroke before making his advance.

The ironic thing was that by the time this rule was tried out Gonzales had become a much improved all-court player. He could operate successfully from the backcourt, and while the rule may have made him stay on court a little longer, he kept right on winning as always. You would have thought he would have been proud to show critics that he could win with another style. But he considered the whole thing a conspiracy and imagined that it was all a Kramer plot to get rid of him. (Actually, he was right—I did want to get rid of him—but this was not the way to do it.)

During this period when the pros were touring, there were only a few professional tournaments that survived. One at Wembley, in London, was played in September and always drew good fields and publicity. The U.S. Pro—the one I won in '48 when I beat van Horn, Budge and Riggs—was usually a class event, although as recently as 1963 when Rosewall won it the winner's check bounced. There was also a tournament held annually in Cleveland known as Jack March's International Championships.

For a time, after the U.S. Pro left Forest Hills, it sort of merged with Jack March's tournament. In any event in the '40s and '50s, Jack March ran a tournament in Cleveland. It bounced all around town, from the Cleveland Skating Club, to the Arena, to Lakewood Park, but at least it was always on somewhere. Guys like Budge and Kovacs, with no other showcase, would always prepare for Cleveland. Tilden borrowed money to travel from California and play there when he was sixty; in fact he died just after packing for Cleveland in 1954.

I only played in Cleveland once, in 1950, but there were other years when I kept the tour out of Cleveland so that the people there who liked pro tennis would not have any competition for Jack March's tournament.

March had been a player himself and had married into some Sperry Rand money, which gave him the opportunity to invest in pro tennis. He worked at it and he promoted well. Relative to other pro tournaments, the Jack March drew pretty good crowds. Twenty-five hundred was a mob for our sport then.

March was a crazy guy, and he would try anything. Sure enough one year he advertises that the Masked Marvel of the Tennis Court will meet the champion, Mr. Pancho Gonzales, in the first round. Can you imagine Bjorn Borg walking onto the court for the first round at a major championship to face a player wearing a mask and a cape? Well it happened to Gorgo.

The tournament was in the Arena and it was incredibly hot. I was sitting next to Segura, and as soon as the Masked Marvel appeared we both felt sorry for him. He had to be dying in that bag with the only slits being for eyes. How could he breathe? March had done a great job of keeping the Marvel's identity secret; the CIA should have such security. Unfortunately, as soon as the Masked Marvel hit one backhand practice shot, everybody who knew any tennis knew who it was. "Al-lllooooo," Segura and I screamed in chorus.

Eddie Alloo was a pretty fair player. He and I had been teammates together at Rollins College. Once in Tampa, he beat Bitsy Grant, me and Riggs in succession before Kovacs beat him. The reason we could recognize him with his mask was that Alloo had a backhand that looked exactly like Budge's. We called him "the little Budge." Anyway, the rest was anticlimactic. To keep from asphixiating, the Marvel kept disrobing as he went along, until everybody knew his identity. He put up a pretty good struggle—especially considering that his opponent could breathe and he couldn't. The stunt drew a few more fans and Jack March lived to put on another championship.

A guy who would use a Masked Marvel would try anything, and so when all the criticism of the big serve game began to heat up, Jack was ready. In 1955, he announced that all his matches would be played under ping-pong rules, with players only getting one serve. This was the first VASSS tournament—the Van Alen Simplified Scoring System, pushed by the Newport multimillionaire, Jimmy van Alen. Games were played to twenty-one, and you had to win by two.

Naturally Gonzales was furious. This was all the more proof that everybody in tennis was out to get him. But Jack March's tournament was the U.S. Pro title this year, and Gorgo had to take it or leave it. He came, and he beat everybody to get to the finals against Segoo. It didn't make any difference whether they were playing one serve or five, Gonzales was the best player in the world then and nobody should have been able to give him a serious battle. But Segoo won two close sets, and they came to the fifth tied two sets apiece: 21–16, 19–21, 21–8, 20–22.

Gorgo got full control at that point and went out to a 20–12 lead. Think about it: Gonzales has got eight straight match points coming. That is a world record, exceeding the old mark by five. Not surprisingly, with that cushion to play with, Gorgo got a little cocky. The players alternated serve in groups of five, and at 20–12, Gorgo had three more. He tried to finish Segoo off with an ace, missed that, then Segura hit a couple winners; and then it was 20–15, Segura serving. Gonzales still had five match points, but he went over, as he often did, and got a different return-of-serve racket. When it was hot and sweaty, Gorgo served with a loosely-strung racket so that he could get more twist and hop on the ball, and then he returned serve with a tighter one that made it possible for him to block serves back harder.

And now Segoo really went wild. Everything he hit was a winner. At 20–18, he played the most fantastic point I ever saw, lobbing the ball way up into the Arena overhead lights, somehow guiding it safely between them like it was a missile. Gonzales chased down the lob and bombed it back. Then Segura sent another sky job back through the lights, just missing all wires, bulbs and other apparatus. Again and again the ball got through the overhead minefield, and finally Segoo won his seventh straight point. Then it was 20–19, his last serve, and obviously Gonzales was shakey, as anyone would be if they had just become the first player in history to lose seven straight match points. The crowd was going wild. I have never seen Gonzales looking so scared.

And Segura, on the other hand, was a terror unleashed. With nothing to lose, he had played all the previous match points loosey-goosey. And now he was ready to tie it up. Gonzales tensed. Segura tossed the ball up, brought the racket forward, met the ball and sent it—plop, right into the net. There was dead silence in the Arena. Suddenly it was Gonzales who remembered the one serve rule. He leapt up in the air and dashed up to the net. He had won.

Segoo had served a single!

The worst thing that came of Gonzales turning pro before he was ready was that there was never any demand for me to tour with him again. At his best, if you break Gorgo's equipment down stroke-by-stroke, he was not that complete. He had a great first serve, one of the very best, and his second serve was so good he could attack off of it, but much of the rest of his success depended upon his competitive zeal. Still, I don't believe he ever could have beaten me on a tour, because he didn't develop his ground strokes sufficiently until I was out of serious play.

Had we toured again a few years later, it would have been close enough and exciting enough that we would have stolen all the thunder from the amateurs, and we might have forced tennis into an open game fifteen years before it finally came about. Pancho and I were both Americans. We both played a glamorous, hard-hitting game. I was looked upon as the clean-cut champion, all-American all the way. He was the scowling challenger, from an ethnic minority. I was the veteran hanging on, he was the kid coming up. There was something for everybody.

But after I beat him so completely in 1949-50, the promoters were convinced that we could never sell it again. Part of the problem was that Gorgo was personally so uncooperative with the promoters. When Tony Trabert won both Wimbledon and Forest Hills in 1955, I was still the pro champ. But after I signed Trabert, my first thought was to retire gracefully and bring in Gorgo to play Tony. I would promote. It made sense. Tony was the same sort of crew-cut nice guy type that I was, so I figured better he play a villain than another hero.

Just to make sure, though, I tested the waters and contacted my friends in the arena business, asking them whether they would prefer Trabert to play Gonzales or me. I was over-whelmed; the vote was almost unanimously for me to play. I was disappointed with their choice. I was thirty-four now, and my arthritis was beginning to trouble me. I was past my prime, out of shape, and I'd learned to drink a little whiskey. Besides, I knew my future was as a promoter not as a player.

Nevertheless, I started cranking myself up for the last hurrah against Trabert. I began my usual boxing routine, skipping ten three-minute rounds, working myself up to a hundred sit-ups. Even though I was thirty-four, I still believed I could beat anyone if I were fit. I always had a top match temperament. I always thought I could take anybody if I were in shape and if I concentrated, but likewise, I also believed I had to try hard to win.

I had to admit one thing about the last tour I had played—against Sedgman. I had lost my ability to regularly make the second good shot. You're going to make some spectacular outright winners now and then, but you take most points with one good shot to set things up and the next to finish it. Against Sedg, I suddenly discovered that too often I couldn't close him off with a second shot. That's the tip that a player in his thirties has started on the way down.

But I thought I had enough left for one more time around. I was sure I wasn't going to be the faded old champion they scraped off the canvas. I wasn't going to be Joe Louis picking up a final payday but getting clobbered by Rocky Marciano in the process. And then one day a couple of months before the tour was scheduled to start, I was working out at my office, when I got a call from Henrietta Gonzales, Pancho's wife at that time. She started telling me how wrong it was that I should be playing Trabert, that Pancho was younger, in his prime. He was probably the best player in the world but had no way to prove it if he couldn't play. Pretty soon, she broke down and started to cry, and it occurred to me that almost everything she said was true.

That was when I signed Gorgo to a seven-year contract, giving him 20 percent. He made $56,000 that first year, beating Trabert almost as badly as I had once beaten Gonzales.

I never missed playing, not at all. There were a few times in the next few years when I filled in for a kid who was hurt, but I did it without feeling any competitive emotion. I wasn't paying any training price anymore, and in my mind I wasn't really a professional athlete anymore. But before I gave it up, I had cared as much as ever, right to the end. Even the last year that I played as champion I can remember losing a tight match to Gonzales at Wembley. I was not in top shape; I had not expected to win. In the last set I had him 4–1 and 5–2, I let him get away, and it killed me. I was still the champion, and I came into that locker room and cried because losing hurt so much.

The instant I hung up with Henrietta Gonzales, I was through as a tennis player, and I've never felt those emotions again. I was very lucky that I had something else that I liked, promoting, to go right into. Old athletes never get over playing the kids' game.

14

Short Arms and Deep Pockets

My career very nearly ended five years early when I was twenty-nine. I had had a couple of cases of tennis elbow—such as the time in 1946 just before the Challenge Round—but they had always gone away with rest and treatment. Then late in the summer of 1950, I came down with a stiff neck. It would disappear at intervals, but unlike the tennis elbow, it would never go away completely. Eventually it moved into my playing shoulder as well, and sometimes I couldn't even raise the arm high enough to serve.

Before the tour with Segura, I began to worry about the ailment more seriously and finally went to see a doctor. He put heat on it and told me to rest for a week. I did. No help. I rested another week. No better. I took X rays. Nothing showed. Finally I went to see an orthopedic specialist, and he diagnosed my problem as osteoarthritis. It was a shattering revelation. He said that I had bony spurs, the calcification of a man of seventy. The good news was that the pain would not be constant. The bad news was that it would keep coming back. "To be very honest with you, Mr. Kramer," he said, "I can only conclude that you are in great danger of losing your career."

That did it, I couldn't stall any longer. I had to call Riggs and tell him to crank up Gonzales or somebody to take my place against Segura. For some reason though, I dropped by the L.A. Tennis Club on my way home from the doctor's office. (I was probably just trying to postpone the inevitable for another hour.) Quite by chance I met another member, Dr. Omar Fareed. We were pretty good friends, having met through Schroeder who had gone to high school with Omar. We started chatting, and in the course of the conversation I told him about the specialist's appraisal of my condition.

Omar listened attentively. He was (and is) an internist, but he specialized in arthritis, and he told me that he had samples of a new drug he was testing in his office. From what he had heard of this new drug, he thought it might help. Would I take a chance? Well, anything was better than calling Riggs with bad news, so I said I'd be the guinea pig. We went to Omar's office and he shot one hundred cc's of this white milky stuff into my hip. The next morning he gave me another shot in my left arm. He told me to go home and take a nap, and then meet him back at the club around four.

First he had me hit a few ground strokes. There was no pain. Then he had me hit a few easy serves. No pain whatsoever. Then he told me to let out, and I started hitting serves with full power. There was still no pain. It was incredible.

The milky white stuff was cortisone. I was probably the first athlete ever to be helped by it. If it had come along a year later, maybe just six months or three months later, it would have been too late for me.

For the next three weeks Omar tapered the doses off, and by the time Segoo and I played our first match I didn't have a trace of a stiff neck or sore shoulder. The only problem was that cortisone retains fluid in your system, and I had ballooned more than twenty pounds to one hundred and ninety pounds.

211

On the court it was bad enough that Pauline whipped Gussy; Segura ran me all over the place and beat me in straight sets.

Once the treatments ended, though, my body adjusted, and I quickly fell back to my normal one hundred and sixty-eight or seventy. I had to wear mufflers and scarves to protect myself from a chill, I carried a hydroculator with me and enough pills to stock a good-sized pharmacy. But thank God I was still a tennis player.

The fact that I had arthritis forced me to realize, however, that as a player I was on borrowed time, and I had to start looking ahead. I had not been pleased with the way Riggs had run the Gonzales tour, and the Gussy tour was a disaster. It proved that Bobby was just not thorough enough to make a good promoter, and I decided that the next time Jack Kramer toured for a promoter, the promoter would have to be Jack Kramer.

Riggs had originally gotten to become the pro promoter because I supported him. I had lost faith in Jack Harris, and Harris had not been shrewd enough to include an option in our contract. Our break came in South America after Riggs, Segoo, Pails and I had finished in the States. In the U.S., as I mentioned, we traveled mostly in the DeSoto station wagons, but it was stipulated clearly in our contracts that Harris had to pay transportation costs. In South America, where we didn't have cars and had to fly, this was going to be a big tab.

Harris said the players had to pay their own way. Not only that, but in those days if you bought four airplane tickets, you got a fifth on the cuff, and Harris was planning to bring his wife through South America on the Annie Oakley. We protested, and L.B. Iceley of Wilson was brought in to arbitrate. He ruled in the players' favor, but the whole affair left a sour taste in our mouths toward Harris.

We were all put out with him to start with because he was getting Pails and Segura for such low wages—$300 a week and their own expenses. True, nobody put a gun to their heads and made them sign, but we all felt Jack could have given them a nice bonus since the tour was such a success. Pails and Segoo hung on at the low wages because their deal was that once we left North America, they moved up to a percentage—10 percent apiece.

There was more trouble with Harris in South America. He kept assuring us that he was putting a fantastic tour package together for Australia, but by chance a telegram meant for Harris was delivered to Riggs, and it revealed that there was nothing at all set for Down Under. We really blew up.

"Everything okay for Australia, Jack?" Riggs asked him, setting the trap.

"Great boys. We're going to clean up down there."

"Take a look at this, Jack." And we sprung the telegram on him. Obviously we couldn't work together any longer, and he agreed to take his profits and go back home.

With Harris out of the picture, we decided to serve as our own promoters. We made up a new split. Transportation costs came off the top, then: 40 percent for me, 25 for Riggs, and 17½ for Pails and Segoo. Then we divided up responsibilities. We were in Venezuela when the break came, so Segoo went home to Ecuador for a rest. Pails flew to Australia to set up the tour there, Bobby went to New York to handle some business, and I flew to Hawaii to line up dates on the islands.

Mostly I just had to get away from the tour and go home. It was August by now, and except for a few days, I had been on the road since December and out of the country since June. It was especially tough getting up for matches in South America, since everybody down there assumed that everything is fixed, especially with pro tennis, since they still had vivid memories of Perry and Kovacs.

In many respects though, the tour was a better life outside the U.S. because we tended to play in country clubs rather than arenas. However, I can vividly remember two public places where we always played in South America: a dance hall in Montevideo and an arena in Luna Park in Buenos Aires. The two cities are in different countries, Uruguay and Argentina, but they're located just down and across the mouth of the Rio de la Plata, so we'd always play them back to back. We'd play the dance hall, then go across to B.A. in a boat, sharing a cabin, getting no sleep whatsoever. The arena at Luna Park had a roof, but for some reason there was a gap at the top where the sides met the roof, and the wind would come whistling in past the support columns. At night it could get freezing in that "indoor" arena.

On top of all this, the court was too fast and the lights too dim. I can recall one memorable night sitting around a blazing fire that was lit in a trash can at courtside. This was when Trabert was on the tour for 35 percent, I was promoting plus filling in as a player for 25 percent, and the rest of the package—20 percent apiece—belonged to Gonzales and Sedgman. We had a two-night stand in Buenos Aires, and they had beaten me and Trabert the first night so now they were playing in the "finals." Damn, but they were mad—Gonzales particularly. There was 60 percent sitting around the fire, laughing and warming our hands. Trabert would whistle at the good shots too, and he could whistle like a train coming through a tunnel. The 40 percent had to stay out on the court and play like madmen in the cold and the dark. Pancho finally beat Sedg something like 12–10 in the fifth.

The Number 1 problem with traveling abroad was trying to get paid fairly. There was always a premium on American dollars, so even if you struck a deal at the advertised exchange rate, it was almost impossible to get what you were supposed to. Anywhere, you were going to get screwed 25 to 40 percent when you tried to make the transition into dollars. In the early days of my touring you could save some by laying it off with Pan American. You'd bring in the local currency you were stuck with and buy airline space for future use, but eventually that loophole was closed and there were no options but to deal the best you could, usually on the black market.

Then too, if you got a lot of dollars, it was a trick to get them back into the States. When we were all splitting up in Venezuela, I was the cash carrier, and had $22,000 worth of greenbacks fitted here and there all over my body. The whole time in the airport too, Segura and Riggs carried on an argument that went for hours and involved, if I remember, the matter of $3. Riggs had some extra gut that Segoo wanted since he wouldn't be able to obtain it in Ecuador. I'm weighted down with bills, they're arguing whether to pay $11 or $8, something like that. Riggs loved it. By the end Segoo was practically in tears from frustration, so Bobby knocked down his price by two bits or a half dollar and, happily, went to catch his plane home.

The money exchange problem was always a nuisance. One time later that year, we played six matches in Cairo and Alexandria for a three-thousand-pound guarantee at a time when the pound was worth $4.04. It was an especially profitable visit to Egypt for Riggs, because our contact was a kid named Habib Sursock (who was related to King Farouk), and he was made to order for Bobby. He had made a pile of money (in canned fruit and Coke) and loved to play cards and golf, both of which he did badly. Riggs never let him out of his sight. But at last it was time to leave for England, and only then do we discover that we are not getting British pounds, we are getting Egyptian pounds. Okay, they're worth the same, so we take these huge notes and stuff them in a place unlikely to be checked out—Dinny Pails' jockstrap (that is, with him wearing it).

Sure enough, we get the loot into England and take it to the first bank we can find to exchange for English pounds. There, we are informed that it is against the law for a bank to change anything over a ten-pound Egyptian note. So, as usual, it's off to the black market where we make the exchange minus the usual service charge of about 35 percent. To top it off, just before we go back to the States, the pound is devalued from $4.04 to $2.80, so I end up with $1700 of the $3600 guaranteed me.

Pails was the first of the Aussies I toured with, and he was much like all the others. I'm not talking about his being quick, with nice groundstrokes; I mean he had a healthy respect for

215

money. The general attitude of the Aussies toward spending cash was best summed up once by Segoo when an Australian radio reporter asked him to name his single biggest thrill in tennis. "The night Frank Sedgman bought dinner," Segoo replied.

The Aussies' own expression was "short arms and deep pockets," and including Sedgman, the Aussie with the shortest arms of them all is Ken Rosewall. One time on tour we came to the Pakistani border, and they were in the middle of some border dispute. At customs there is a guy on the ground, bound and gagged. Apparently he had been caught smuggling. The local tennis man with us says, don't worry, this doesn't concern you, just make sure you declare everything. Now remember, we all carried lots of cash with us, always looking for the chance to trade up into dollars, so we were loaded.

But let me tell you, when I saw that poor guy bound and gagged on the floor, I declared every last nickel. I was declaring Life Savers and gum. We'd picked up some diamonds in South Africa weeks, months before, and I laid out every one of them. Little Rosewall came through customs right behind me, carrying a Qantas flight bag like it was his school lunch. He declared some souvenirs, a few dollars, some change. And do you know that little Kenny had $35,000 cash in that flight bag? Nobody was going to mess with his money.

The Australian government was close with its money too. Once I worked a deal with an Aussie horse owner, George Ryder, whereby he would take over part of the promotions Down Under, and in return he would ship racehorses to me in the States. Unlike Australian tennis players who are bred for distance, Australian horses seemed to be all early speed—at least the Ryder-breds were. But I had some that could really fly for five or six furlongs.

Fred Turner, who owned one Kentucky Derby winner, Tomy Lee, bought a colt from me named Drop Volley for $40,000, and he won some money for Turner. Then I had a filly named Service Line I liked just as much, so when Turner offered me $25,000 for her, I turned him down figuring I could get $40,000 for her too. Service Line immediately started foot-faulting down the stretch, and I was lucky to get rid of her for a claiming tag of $7,500.

There were some others we brought up, all with tennis names—Smash, Tennis Slipper, Tennis Queen—but the one we all thought would be the best was a huge black colt that we named—what else—Big Pancho. Unfortunately, Big Pancho found a way to damage himself, and sadly, we had to put him down before he ever even got to the races.

It was the natural parlay of the real Big Pancho's bad disposition and Riggs' love life that finally made me my own promoter. As has so often been the case in my life, what appeared to be a bad break ended up working in my favor. It came about this way. In the summer of 1951, before Wimbledon, Riggs asked me if I would be interested in having him promote a tour between Sedgman and myself. I replied that I didn't think Bobby was a capable enough promoter, and so I didn't want to sign with him. Then Herbie Flam upset Sedgman at Wimbledon, which reduced Frank's appeal, so I forgot about the kid for the time being. Riggs was itchy to promote, though, so at Forest Hills (which Sedgman did win), he met with Frank and Ken McGregor and convinced them to turn pro and tour with Gonzales, Segura and himself. Bobby squeezed me out simply by telling the kids: "Kramer's retired."

Of course I wasn't retired, but to this day Bobby says that was his understanding. He had called me up about a tour, and I remember telling him that I wasn't interested in a Riggs-promoted tour. He remembers only that I said I didn't want to tour. In any event he went ahead. Riggs gave Sedgman and McGregor 55 percent of the net—no guarantee—to split any way they chose; and then he, Segoo and Gorgo were going to share the remaining 45 percent of the net three ways even.

This was Gonzales' chance to get back in the limelight. He'd been nowhere since I whipped him two years before. He should have paid Riggs for the privilege of playing. So a few weeks later just as the tour dates were being firmed up, Gorgo comes to Riggs and tells him that he has to change the deal. Gonzales wants to take 2½ percent of Segura's cut and assign it to himself. "There's no goddamn way that Segura is worth as much as me," he tells Riggs.

Well at this point, Bobby was divorced from Kay, his first wife, and he had just met Priscilla Whelan, who was very attractive and also very wealthy. So Riggs figured he doesn't need the aggravation of Pancho Gonzales fouling up his happy life. Riggs wires Sedgman in Australia that the whole thing is off, and then Bobby goes off to get married and hustle golf games for the next few years.

By chance, at the time Sedgman got the word that he was cancelled, I was in Sydney helping Frank Shields with the U.S. Davis Cup team. I had already been in touch with Sedg regularly, trying to convince him that since Bobby had misrepresented my position—I had damn well not retired—Sedgman had been signed under false pretenses. But Sedgman was as straight a guy as ever came along. And to him, a deal was a deal. He wouldn't leave Riggs.

As soon as Sedgman got the telegram from Riggs, he called me. I told him that it was much too late to try to get tour dates for this winter, but we agreed to meet at Wimbledon and strike a deal there. So for a lousy 2½ percent, I got into promoting. The bad part of all this is that twenty-five years later, Gorgo still reminds me that he was the one who made me a promoter . . . God bless him.

Sedgman was the easiest deal I ever made, too. I had seen how he had stuck with Riggs even when he found out the man had conned him. He was a very solid guy—tried his best in every match he ever played. We met at the Atheneum Court Hotel in London, and our extended negotiations went exactly like this:

Kramer: "How much do you want?"

Sedgman: "Seventy-five thousand dollars."

Kramer: "You got it."

When we finally drew up the contracts for Sedg and McGregor it was a little more complicated. Sedg got 30 percent of the first $150,000, then 35 percent thereafter. McGregor got $30,000 against 10 percent. I planned a Davis Cup format, so I brought Segura in at $500 a week as my Davis Cup teammate. Sedgman beat Drobny to win Wimbledon, he beat Mulloy to win Forest Hills, and he won both his matches and the doubles with McGregor to defend the Davis Cup, 4–1. I was so scared I was going to botch a sure thing as a rookie promoter that I had trouble sleeping before the tour, but I hired a terrific secretary, Esther Koff, away from Wilson and brought in Bobby Riggs' ex, Kay, as business manager. We sailed from there.

"The Big Tour," as we named it, drew almost half a million fans around the world and grossed $860,000, more than a quarter of a million more than Riggs-Kramer. Sedgman probably doubled the $75,000 he asked for, and McGregor probably took home $60,000. Ken took that money, and opened a sporting goods store which is still going strong. Sedgman made more money out of squash courts, a confection named Sedgie Straws, and various other enterprises. Since he always stayed in shape, he came back as a big winner on the Grand Masters tour when he reached forty-five.

Since Sedg and McGregor were Australian and since they turned pro officially right after the Challenge Round, I planned "The Big Tour" a little differently. They had to hit the U.S. West Coast coming into America, so I decided we'd open in L.A.—my home town. Maybe the Garden was mad that for the first time a pro tennis tour didn't debut there. When we got to New York, right before we were to go on I discovered we didn't have the deal I thought we had. As I said, in almost all arenas the split was 55/45 for us. Now the Garden always had to squeeze a little extra. For Sedg and me, they demanded $3,500 off the top for advertising, which I had agreed to. But just before Segoo and McGregor were going to go on the court, I learned that the Garden was taking 55 percent. I had assumed too much and hadn't had the time to see the contract.

We had two consecutive dates involved, too. I was furious. Bad enough all the money I've had to leave behind in Pakistan and places like that. I wasn't getting taken on Eighth Avenue. I told Segoo and McGregor to stay in the locker room. There were nine thousand fans in their seats, but I wasn't going to cave in. I knew damn well that if the word got out that the kid promoter could be jerked around, I'd be fair game in every building in the country. We sat tight. They offered me 47½, and I wouldn't take it. Fifty-fifty. I agreed we'd go on and work out the contract in the morning.

Segura and McGregor hit the court thirty-five minutes late, and I fumed some more during their match. By the time Sedg and I went onto the canvas, I was a tiger and beat Frank one and two. He had no idea why I was so steamed up. The next morning when I resumed arguing with the Garden, I got 52½ out of them. I wanted to hold out for the 55, but I finally decided to settle.

It had originally been our plan in New York and the other big cities to play two nights and to switch around on the second day, like the Davis Cup format, with me playing McGregor and Segoo facing Sedgman. But after all the turmoil, I took advantage of the extra publicity and announced afterwards that Sedgman wanted to get another shot at me in New York. So damn if we didn't draw an even larger crowd the next day (11,000, grossing $62,000 for both days), but by then my juices had stopped flowing and Sedg beat me in three good sets.

This tour, which was to be my last one, was the only close one of the four I played—I only beat him fifty-four matches to forty-one. I went up 11–6 in the beginning, but he came back to go on top 18–17. But in the next month, everything went my way. We played some matches down south on clay, and I'd learned to play the dirt by then. Plus Sedg had trouble with a sore shoulder and a case of the flu, and I won seventeen of the next nineteen to go up 34–20. And I split with him from there.

But Sedg was a great competitor. Even when he got the flu

and the sore shoulder, he never quit. He was the quickest I've ever seen. He could attack off his second serve, or he could come in behind his little slice backhand—and once Sedg got to the net, forget it, because he was so quick you had to thread a needle to get anything past him. Anything he could get he would put away. Frank Sedgman hardly ever hit a second volley. If he got his racket on a volley, it was almost always a placement, deep and hard.

He was more aggressive the latter part of the tour, and he should have played it that way all along. This sounds rude, I know, but if Sedg had been a great player—in the very top rank—he would have beaten me. I couldn't hit the second good shot by then and had just gone over the hill. My arthritis acted up periodically all along, and I had to devote a lot of my attention to promoting. Still he couldn't beat me. He couldn't handle my second serve, and at the end, that was what saved me.

15

The Almost Champion

After Sedgman left the amateurs, the two Americans, Trabert and Vic Seixas, became the world class. But almost immediately the attention fell on the whiz kids from Australia, Hoad and Rosewall. They were born only three weeks apart in November of 1934, so when they burst on the scene early in 1953 they were barely eighteen and a half years old. Rosewall won the French, they won the doubles together there on dirt and at Wimbledon on grass, and a few months later they beat Trabert and Seixas in the Davis Cup, winning both victories under pressure the last day when they were down 2–1.

They were amazing, and they were also popular at the gate—especially Hoad, who was blond, handsome and strong, with an exciting power game. Obviously they were too young for the pros, and in fact, 1954 proved to be something of a sophomore jinx for them. Neither won a major title (Drobny beat Rosewall in the Wimbledon finals), and then Trabert and Seixas turned the tables and pasted them in the Davis Cup. In a thirteen-year period, this was the only time the U.S. won, except for 1958 when we had the Peruvian, Alex Olmedo, as the U.S. star.

All this left me in the middle. Hoad and Rosewall were too young, Trabert was still building a reputation, and Seixas was simply not good enough. He was like Mulloy; he had risen to the top on hard work and conditioning. Vic used to play a lot of practice sets with Segura, and Vic told me that once they played something like twenty straight sets with Seixas never able to take more than three games in any one of them. So for 1954 I had to go with the pros I had. I thought it was important to keep pro tennis in the spotlight.

I tried something different. Instead of an animal act and a feature attraction which was traditional, I thought maybe the fans would go for a mini-tournament format. I took the year off myself just to promote, and used four players—Gonzales, Sedgman, Segura and Budge, who was thirty-eight but still a name and still in shape. An equivalent four today would be Connors, Borg, Gerulitis and Rosewall. Pretty good show? We couldn't give it away. Our two dates in the Garden both drew less than 5,000. We would play a two-night series. The first night it was usually Gonzales vs. Budge and Sedgman vs. Segura. Then the next night, the winners and losers would play.

We played for purse money too. In the Garden the winner got $4,000, runner-up $2,500, third $1,500, fourth $1,000—plus there was a $1,000 doubles pot. (The percentages were about the same, with lesser amounts in smaller cities.) But it was apparent from the first that tennis fans were only interested in traditional tournaments which the amateurs had. Sedgman and Segura and Gonzales were all playing against each other for the first time on tour, and here they were, all three in the top four in the world, but people wouldn't come out. And I should have been in shorts, defending my title instead of just promoting.

Gorgo won the tour. He beat both Sedg and Segoo by the same count, thirty matches to twenty, while Segoo beat Sedgman 23–22 (Budge had only a few wins). But in the final analysis, all it did was cost me a lot of money to prove that Gonzales was the top challenger to me.

I needed the whiz kids. And they were perfect for my pro Davis Cup idea. This was especially true because the Americans had won the Cup in '54 so that the Challenge Round would be played in the States at Forest Hills in '55. There would be more interest in the Davis Cup, and it figured to be close. If I signed Trabert, Hoad and Rosewall right afterwards, and then took Seixas' place as the other American, we had a worldwide hit. My company grossed in excess of $300,000 with the Sedgman tour. I thought we could play an Aussie-American tour for a longer period, probably fifteen months, and if so, I saw no reason why the tour couldn't be the first to break $1 million, with my gross in excess of $500,000.

That was my scheme. All I needed was that the three kids have a good year in '55. Good?—it went like I had scripted it. Rosewall won the Australian championship, Seixas and Trabe the doubles. Trabert won the French singles; he and Seixas the doubles. Trabert won Wimbledon too, and the kids got into the doubles final against each other with different partners. At Forest Hills, Trabert got a triple, beating Rosewall in the final. But in the Davis Cup, both Hoad and Rosewall beat Trabert, and they whitewashed us 5–0. It was a dream. We were set to open in December with the Davis Cup champions on one side vs. the pro champion and the Wimbledon/Forest Hills/French holder on the other.

Trabe signed, and then while the kids were in L.A. at the Pacific Southwest, they signed. Harry Hopman handled everything for them. Hopman always knew exactly what was going on with all his amateurs. He had no children, no hobbies, and tennis was everything to him. Hopman always said he hated the pros, and he battled open tennis to the bitter end, but as early as the time when Sedgman and McGregor signed, Hopman was trying to get himself included in the deal so he could get a job with pro tennis in America.

He has never been my favorite guy. The minute one of his stars would turn pro, Hopman would turn on him. No matter how close he'd been to a player, as soon as he was out of Hopman's control, the guy was an outcast. "It was as if we'd never existed," Rosewall said once. If a pro tried to help Hopman and his old Australian team, Hopman would use him. There was a time in here when Sedgman, as a pro, volunteered to help train the Aussie team. Hopman accepted the offer, and then he took Sedg aside and told him that what Hoad and Rosewall needed was confidence. So he told Sedg to go easy on them, which he gladly did. After a few days, Hopman wrote an exclusive in his newspaper column revealing how his kids could whip Sedgman and how this proved once again that amateurs were better than the pros.

But Hoad and Rosewall needed an adviser as their captain. Hopman was obviously the man. I opened my books for him. He checked everything to make sure that what I was offering was fair. He approved and advised the kids to take it if they wanted to turn pro. They did. We called up their parents in Australia and they approved. We signed papers. I started lining up arenas for the greatest pro tennis tour in history.

A couple of weeks later, I got a call from Australia. The kids had changed their minds and had decided to remain amateur. I got the next flight out to Sydney. As soon as I arrived the situation became very clear—although Hoad and Rosewall had different reasons for reneging.

Lew had gotten married that year, and his wife, Jennie, was pregnant. She wanted her husband to be with her when the baby was born. She liked the idea of having a grand tour of the world with her husband as star. Paris, London, Monaco, New York, San Francisco—a couple of leisurely weeks at each stop, all expenses paid, good times, and a hard match or two every week or so. That appeared a great deal nicer to Jennie than her sitting home with a baby or maybe joining Lew for a few weeks of one-night stands—Toledo to Dayton to Columbus to Indianapolis—with Kramer or Trabert across the net every night.

Rosewall's pressure came not from family but from business. The Aussies had much more liberal amateur rules. (For example, when it first became apparent that Sedgman might turn pro in 1952 the Sydney *Daily Telegraph* got up a "wedding fund" of more than $12,000 for him. That sort of thing is illegal in the U.S.). Rosewall had worked for Slazengers since he had first gotten into tennis, and the firm was like a family to him. The officials there pleaded with him to stay amateur and to keep representing Australia. They raised his "salary," and got him another "job" with Carnation Milk.

From Hopman I learned that Rosewall had made up his mind to remain amateur. Unlike Hoad, and Laver too, Kenny could get distracted from his tennis by business. He wanted things settled, and he had committed to Slazengers. On the other hand, Hopman let me know that Jennie Hoad might be persuaded to drop her demands if I upped the ante for her husband. It was a squeeze play Hopman had worked up: now that you don't have to pay Kenny, you can take some of what you "saved" and pay Lew extra. But I wasn't going to play that game. I had signed him at a figure. My tolerance for Hopman—already low—hit rock bottom and has remained there ever since he tried to pull that on me.

So I went home empty-handed. It's worth remembering, too, that they were playing with fire. They had double-crossed me, and I had the signed contracts to prove it. I couldn't make them play, but all I had to do was wave those contracts in public and they were through as amateurs. I didn't, of course, because except for vengeance, it wouldn't do me any good. It would ruin me in Australia forever and would make it impossible for me to ever sign those men again.

I also had to do something with Trabert—which, as I've already said, turned out to be touring against Gonzales. Gorgo beat him so decisively that it reduced Trabe's appeal. My career was over, but if I could get Hoad and Rosewall for the next year, for '57, we could still crank out the Davis Cup format—the kids against Trabert and Gonzales. Hoad, meanwhile, had a super year. He won the first three legs of the Grand Slam (plus the Italian) before Rosewall beat him in the final at Forest Hills. In the Challenge Round, the two of them shut out the U.S. again.

But I still couldn't beat Jennie Hoad. Now that she had her baby, she wanted another world tour. Hoad was making top expenses, and they figured my money was good anytime, which was true. Hoad was potentially the greatest tennis attraction of all time. Meanwhile, Rosewall was ready to sign, and as much as I would have liked the two kids to turn pro together, I couldn't ask Kenny to let his life be decided by Jennie Hoad's whims. I guaranteed him $65,000 to tour against Gonzales—and he made $110,000. For the first time, we stayed Down Under and opened Rosewall-Gonzales in Australia right after the Challenge Round was finished.

And I did the only thing in my whole life in tennis that I ever regretted. It's still on my conscience, and while my wife says I should keep my mouth shut about it, I want it out in the open:

I tried to put the fix on to help Rosewall.

The reason why I want to own up is because if I tell the truth about everything—about how we sometimes only played one set in the doubles for real, about how we tried to get Pauline to go easy on Gussy—then perhaps everyone will believe me when I say that we were square 99.44 percent of the time. Pro tennis was my life for many years. A lot of great players played a lot of matches for all they were worth. It was real. It happened. The amateurs may have gotten more attention at the time, but we were the best, and I want us remembered.

I panicked with Rosewall. Keep in mind that at that time he was in Hoad's shadow; he was not yet the marvel of the ages that he has become. He was a cute little fellow with a dink serve, who operated mostly from the baseline. That great volley of his hadn't been developed yet. I was afraid that Gorgo would eat him alive and put us out of business the rest of the way. But like a lot of people I completely underestimated Rosewall.

Just before we opened in Melbourne, I went to Gonzales and offered him a deal. Gorgo was in the second year of a seven-

227

year contract with me at 20 percent. I said, "Look, Gorgo, if you find some way to carry the kid, it's worth another 5 percent of the gross to you." Gorgo agreed, although I'm not sure he really understood what I meant. By "carry," I just meant to keep it close in the beginning so we wouldn't scare the crowds away down the line.

Anyway, the dirty deed was done. But then, after the first four matches which went three to one for Gonzales, he came to me and called it off. "You gotta let me out of this, Jack," he said. "I can't play when I'm thinking about trying to carry the kid. I can't concentrate. It just bothers me too much." It was obvious that it did. It was also obvious that Rosewall was not the pushover I feared. (In fact, Gonzales only beat him 50–26, and it was always competitive.) So I told Gonzales to forget the whole thing and play it straight, still at 25 percent.

The kicker to all this is that, besides bothering my conscience all these years, the deal also almost cost me Gonzales. Later that year when he was trying to get out of his contract with me, his lawyer argued that Gorgo's contract wasn't valid anymore because I was paying him 25 percent instead of the 20 percent that had been stipulated. The judge, Leon T. David of the California superior court, considered that argument and then he declared for me. He said he was sorry, but he'd never heard of anybody claiming an injustice because somebody wanted to pay them more.

If Gonzales wanted to get rid of me, I was just as anxious to get rid of him. Hoad was obviously my knight to slay the dragon. Lew was more exciting on the court, and he was a dream off the court. Nothing fazed him. Of course that was a double-edged sword. Nothing ever excited him either, except possibly the biggest finals and Challenge Rounds when he was an amateur.

Hoad had turned me down twice, but suddenly, early in 1957, shortly after the Rosewall-Gonzales tour started, he had a friend call and tell me that Lew wanted to sign with me. At the time I figured that he saw all the publicity going to Kenny, so he got excited and wanted to get on board the train before it pulled out of the station. Since nothing ever excited Hoad about his own tennis, though, there was no logical reason to assume that Rosewall's tennis would interest him.

In retrospect I think Lew had encountered his first touch of back trouble, and Jennie had advised him to get the big payday in a hurry. Whatever the reason for his change of mind, I couldn't use Hoad then; I wasn't going to waste him without a big buildup. I told his friend who called me to have Lew look me up when he came to the States, and we'd work out something then. Right away Lew jumped on a plane to L.A.

I planned everything differently with Hoad from everybody else I ever signed. Here was a man who had pulled out on a signed contract once, who had turned me down a year later when he had top market value just because it wasn't terribly convenient with his wife—and now he had changed his mind again. When Hoad saw me in L.A. I was determined not to get past-posted once more. To seal the deal, I gave him a check for $5,000 and to be sure that he cashed it (to absolutely certify our contract) I sent Ted Schroeder, who worked for me at the time, to the bank with Hoad.

I paid Hoad well. I gave him a $100,000 guarantee against 20 percent. He agreed to join the pros after Wimbledon, and if he won there, the guarantee went to $125,000.

I also put in a performance bonus clause (the only one I ever wrote). Hoad's cut would go up 5 percent—20 to 25—every time he won a match. You see, I didn't think it ever hurt Hoad to lose, he just didn't seem to care enough. He always argued that it really pained him to lose, that he just had trouble maintaining his concentration, but it sure never seemed that way to me. He just did not possess the intensity that champions normally show.

Of all the top players, Hoad shared the most in common with Elly Vines. Both were very strong guys. Both succeeded at a very young age. Vines won Forest Hills when he was nineteen, and Hoad won both his singles in a 3–2 Challenge Round victory when he was only nineteen. Also, both were very lazy guys. Vines lost interest in tennis (for golf) before he was thirty, and Hoad never appeared to be very interested. Despite their great natural ability, neither put up the outstanding records that they were capable of. Unfortunately, the latter was largely true because both had physical problems. Lew was heavy in the thighs and he suffered groin pulls regularly, and then his back did him in completely.

When you sum Hoad up, you have to say that he was overrated. He might have been the best, but day-to-day, week-to-week, he was the most inconsistent of all the top players. Overall, he lost to Rosewall, to Gonzales, to Segura, to Trabert. He did win back-to-back Wimbledons, a French, an Australian, and he was 6–1 in Challenge Round singles, so he had a fine record. But generally, he is held in greater esteem than he deserves, I think, because he was so damn popular with everyone that people in tennis wanted to believe he was better. Even when Hoad was clobbering Gonzales, Gorgo wanted his respect and friendship.

But I didn't throw Hoad to Gonzales right away. As I said, I worked everything differently with this kid. When he turned pro after he won Wimbledon that year, I brought him over to the States for a quick kill at the gate with a couple of round-robins in New York and L.A. It was sickening, he had no defense at all. He won a couple, then lost nine straight matches.

Then I took him out of circulation. I made myself into a sparring partner, and with Rosewall and Segura we took off from the U.S., going to Europe, then to Africa and Asia. I was going to give Hoad an opening out of town. I was going to build him up, patch up the weak spots, get him so that he could knock off Gonzales. Gorgo knew exactly what I was doing, and he was furious. It didn't make Gonzales any happier that that fall of '57 I beat him at Wembley, 1–6, 6–4, 6–4. September 28, 1957—that was my last win over Gonzales and probably the last really big victory I had. For a guy who had been retired three years, it was a nice little afterglow.

What impressed me most about Hoad was how strong he was. Like a lot of strong kids, personally he was as gentle as a lamb. Once he went a whole day in Nairobi, then to Karachi, then to Lahore—more than forty-eight hours, two long plane trips, four tennis matches. And he never got anything to eat— just some beer and tea that he got on the planes and the Cokes they brought him on the court.

I always felt that Riggs and I played tennis with the fewest mental errors of all the top players. Hoad had the loosest game of any good kid I ever saw. There was absolutely no pattern to his game. I'd marvel at the shots he could *think of*. He was the only player I ever saw who could stand six or seven feet behind the baseline and snap the ball back hard, crosscourt. He'd try for winners off everything, off great serves, off tricky short balls, off low volleys. He hit hard overspin drives, and there was no way you could ever get him to temporize on important points. Segura went crazy just trying to get him to lob a little more.

But when Hoad felt like getting up, boy was he something. On that warm-up tour, Rosewall beat me something like twenty-two matches to four. I was thirty-seven years old and had been away from championship play for several years, while Rosewall and Hoad were approaching the height of their powers; 22–4 was about right. But instead, when Hoad and I played, I actually beat him thirteen matches to twelve. That was because he just didn't give a damn when he played me. There was no challenge in the old man. It was the same thing with Segura, and Lew lost a majority of his matches to Segoo. But it was different against Rosewall. He wanted to beat Kenny, and he did. Remember now, Hoad lost 13–12 to me while Rosewall beat me 22–4, but Hoad turned it around and won two-thirds of his matches against Rosewall.

Never was it more maddening than Wembley, which he played at the start of our death march late in September 1957. Traditionally, Wembley had been the world's Number 1 professional tournament, as important to the pros as Wimbledon was to the amateurs. This was largely on account of Sir Arthur Elvin, the head man at Wembley. That year I made a package deal with his organization to bring in Hoad,

231

Rosewall, Segura and myself for the tournament. Wembley also dealt personally with Gonzales, and then they filled out the rest of the twelve-man field with some European players. Hoad had won the previous two Wimbledons, the last one only a few weeks before, so he was the big attraction. For supplying him, Rosewall, Segoo and myself, I was guaranteed 50 percent of the gross. I contracted Segura for $1,500, win, lose or draw; and the two kids were going to get their normal percentage from me no matter how they fared in the tournament (Lew, of course, always rated 5 percent more for winning). Whatever happened, I was left with a very healthy cut.

What the British wanted was a showdown in the finals between Gonzales, the pro champ, and Hoad, the Wimbledon champ, so they seeded them one-two. Segura and Rosewall followed. I was unseeded, and who do I draw in the first round but Hoad. Lew was so popular, they put our match on BBC.

Try to figure out how I felt. By instinct, I hated to lose and as an athlete, I really got myself high for the match. But as a promoter owning half the gate, I was sure to do better with Hoad winning and getting to the finals.

Hoad solved my dilemma in the first set by playing so terribly I couldn't help but win. I took him 6–1. In the second set, the businessman in me took over, and I actually tried to get Lew back in the match by staying back on my serve. I'll never really know whether I would have gone all the way and jumped into the tank, because in the game after I broke him in the second set for a 2–1 lead, he stretched real wide trying to run down a volley, pulled a groin muscle and became almost immobile. There was no way I could lose from then on, and I took him 6–3.

As it turned out, even without Hoad the tournament was one of the best Wembleys ever, and the paychecks were fantastic. Rosewall beat Gonzales in the semi's and Segura in a tough five-setter in the finals to win.

But if Rosewall won Wembley, at least Hoad began to catch on. He started to work up to Gonzales. At least he was thinking about percentages. That was a revolution with Hoad. Perhaps most important, we had gotten Lew into the routine of being a pro, and getting used to the grind was the hardest thing for any rookie to deal with. Finally, we worked our way down to Australia and started final preparations.

We opened in Brisbane early in 1958. It was a smash hit. The ground shook everywhere we played. We had thirteen dates in Australia and New Zealand and set attendance records with ten of them. Hoad-Gonzales was such a duel that, looking back, I know it is what sealed my doom with the amateurs. It blew amateur tennis off the map. Would you pay to see Ashley Cooper vs. Mal Anderson for the championship of Australian amateurs or Hoad vs. Gonzales for the championship of the world?

They really fought each other. In Adelaide, Gonzales played with bleeding fingers, in Sydney with an aching forearm muscle. Neither would quit. For once in his life, Lew Hoad cared. The thing was so exciting that even he got swept along. We started off playing five sets, and invariably it went five sets. We had to kill the doubles finale, the programs went so long. Then I cut the feature back to best-of-three because I was afraid that I was going to kill them both if they had to go five every day.

And what made it so exciting was that Hoad was staying with him. Gonzales was up 5–4, but then Lew really got rolling and won the last four matches Down Under, and when we flew to the States he was up 8–5.

The first night, in San Francisco, Hoad won 6–4, 20–18 to go up 9–5. I thought he would blow Gorgo out right there, and the next match, in Los Angeles, Hoad won the first set 6–3, and then they fell into another marathon. This one went even longer than the Frisco set, 24–22, but this one Gorgo won, and then the match, 6–1 in the third. He was only down 9–6 instead of 10–5. We flew to New York the next day and drew 15,237, up till then the largest tennis crowd in U.S. history. They played best-of-five here, but after Hoad won a 9–7 set, Gonzales played like a demon and swept three in a row at love, four and four.

So that made it 9–7, and it looked like Gonzales was coming back. But no. After those back-to-back wins in L.A. and New York, Hoad took full command. He won nine of the next eleven matches. The tide had turned for him—no question. You see, most of the matches remained close, three sets. And Gonzales was playing well. Some nights he was playing as well as he had ever played in his life. They raised each other's games. But that was Gorgo's problem. He was playing beautifully, and he was getting beat. Near the end of February, they flew out to the Coast again for some matches, and I went out to the L.A. airport to touch base with them. When Gorgo got off the plane, I could see in his eyes he was a beaten man. I'd seen it before when I beat him on tour.

As I said before, when you go one-on-one night after night, one player takes charge. Hoad could serve with Gonzales, and he was every bit as quick. But he was much stronger. He could flick deep topspin shots with his wrist that Gonzales couldn't believe a human being could hit. Hoad also had a tougher overhead, and he had better groundstrokes. They both knew all this by now. The longer they played, the more certain it was that Hoad would win. I had a new champion—and he was blond and handsome and popular, and very cooperative too. If Lew Hoad could whip Pancho Gonzales, so too could he bring amateur tennis to its senses and force open tennis.

A few days after they came back to California, they moved out to Palm Springs to play at The Tennis Club. It was the height of the tourist season, and the word was out that there was a new champion in the making. By now, Hoad was up eighteen matches to nine. The demand for tickets was so high, I remember that we had to stick Sinatra way up in the back— and he was damned glad to get in the gate. Lana Turner was there with Fernando Lamas. Elizabeth Taylor was there with Mike Todd; it was just a couple months before his plane went down. It was the night of March 1, 1958, a cool desert evening.

Hoad never loosened up. They had been playing mostly indoors. It was a little chillier in Palm Springs, outdoors with the sun down. Gonzales beat Hoad. Then the next morning,

Lew woke up with a stiff back. The long drive to Phoenix didn't help, and he lost there. And the same thing the next night in Albuquerque, then El Paso. He just couldn't get loose with his back. We tried everything, but the only thing that helped at all was three or four days of rest—and we were playing every night. As Hoad went down physically, Gorgo's confidence rose and the assurance came back to his eyes. In about three weeks, he had caught him. The matches were still close, and every now and then Hoad was his old self. But too often he was tight. We could never be sure of the back. After awhile, I had to start letting the promoters work off a percentage of the gross to a percentage of the net because on some nights Hoad couldn't even play. Gonzales began to pull away. From 9–18, he went 42–18, and won the tour 51–36.

Of course I didn't know it at the time, but the era that Cash-and-Carry Pyle had started three decades before came to an end March 1, 1958, in Palm Springs. The amateurs were starting to go after me, and I had nothing to fight back with. Open tennis was still ten years away. We were heading into the Dark Decade of the sport.

16

The Way It Wasn't

To my mind the real "fix" in tennis was in the champion-ships, so-called because the real champions, the professionals, couldn't get in. Wimbledon, Forest Hills, all the big amateur championships were frauds. It was like running the high-jump championship of the world, barring all the kids who could jump seven feet, and then calling the guy who did six-eleven the champion.

From 1931, when Tilden turned pro at the age of thirty-seven, until 1968, when the game finally went open, virtually every player who won both Wimbledon and Forest Hills turned pro. The only amateurs who won the two major titles and didn't sign were Schroeder, Vic Seixas, Neale Fraser and Manolo Santana. Schroeder, as we know, passed up the opportunity. Seixas, Fraser and Santana were smart enough to realize that the only reason they won in the amateurs was because the best players had turned pro. As the 1950s wore on, it was possible for very average players to become great amateur champions. Ashley Cooper was another who won Wimbledon and Forest Hills, but when he joined the tour he had a great deal of difficulty holding his own. The same applied to kids like Mal Anderson, who won Forest Hills, or to Alex Olmedo, who won Wimbledon.

Anyone with any intelligence knew this situation existed. Olmedo was not only a Wimbledon champion but had also received an inordinate amount of publicity as the Peruvian who won the Davis Cup for the United States; but when he signed with me, I couldn't even get Madison Square Garden to give us a date to debut him. They knew it would be no contest if he played Gonzales; they knew that the "champion," Olmedo, was really only the tenth or eleventh best player, and they knew that the fans knew this too.

I've often wondered how the history books of this era would look if the real champions had been allowed to play in the championships. They say you can't rewrite history, but just this one time for the sake of justice, that's exactly what I'm going to do. In the two left-hand columns, I'm listing the players who did win Wimbledon and Forest Hills. In the two right-hand columns, I'm listing those players I think are most likely to have won if the competition had been opened to all players. This is dream stuff, and it is impossible for me to imagine when the upsets would have occurred. Somewhere along the line, players like Schroeder, Segura, Trabert, Emerson, possibly even Santana would have sprung a surprise and taken a Wimbledon or Forest Hills or two. But let me make up my history strictly on the basis of form.

Basically what I've done here is list the probable winners of Wimbledon and Forest Hills if they'd been open to pros and amateurs, next to the amateurs who actually won. When I've felt that a player was absolutely dominant—as I was, say, in 1949—then I've given that player both titles. If there was some question as to who was the best, I've given one title to one player and the second to the other (arbitrarily assigning Wimbledon to one, Forest Hills to the other—they could be

237

reversed). So here it is: on your left, history as it was, unfairly. On your right, history rewritten the way it probably would have happened.

	AMATEUR CHAMPIONS		KRAMER'S "OPEN" CHAMPIONS	
	Wimbledon	Forest Hills	Wimbledon	Forest Hills
1931	Wood	Vines	Tilden	Vines
1932	Vines	Vines	Vines	Vines
1933	Crawford	Perry	Crawford	Perry
1934	Perry	Perry	Vines	Vines
1935	Perry	Allison	Vines	Vines
1936	Perry	Perry	Perry	Vines
1937	Budge	Budge	Vines	Budge
1938	Budge	Budge	Budge	Vines
1939	Riggs	Riggs	Vines	Budge
1940	NOT HELD	McNeill	NOT HELD	Budge
1941	NOT HELD	Riggs	NOT HELD	Budge
1942	NOT HELD	Schroeder	NOT HELD	Budge
1943	NOT HELD	Hunt	NOT HELD	Budge
1944	NOT HELD	Parker	NOT HELD	Budge
1945	NOT HELD	Parker	NOT HELD	Riggs
1946	Petra	Kramer	Budge	Riggs
1947	Kramer	Kramer	Riggs	Kramer
1948	Falkenberg	Gonzales	Kramer	Kramer
1949	Schroeder	Gonzales	Kramer	Kramer
1950	Patty	Larsen	Kramer	Kramer
1951	Savitt	Sedgman	Kramer	Gonzales
1952	Sedgman	Sedgman	Gonzales	Kramer
1953	Seixas	Trabert	Kramer	Gonzales
1954	Drobny	Seixas	Sedgman	Gonzales
1955	Trabert	Trabert	Sedgman	Gonzales
1956	Hoad	Rosewall	Gonzales	Sedgman
1957	Hoad	Anderson	Hoad	Gonzales
1958	Cooper	Cooper	Gonzales	Hoad
1959	Olmedo	Fraser	Gonzales	Gonzales

	AMATEUR CHAMPIONS		CHAMPIONS	
1960	Fraser	Fraser	Rosewall	Gonzales
1961	Laver	Emerson	Gonzales	Rosewall
1962	Laver	Laver	Rosewall	Gonzales
1963	McKinley	Osuna	Gonzales	Laver
1964	Emerson	Emerson	Laver	Rosewall
1965	Emerson	Santana	Rosewall	Laver
1966	Santana	Stolle	Rosewall	Laver
1967	Newcombe	Newcombe	Laver	Rosewall

In some cases, I have had to be very arbitrary in selecting the winners, because there were years when three players were so close. In 1938 and 1939, for example, Perry could have been better than both Vines and Budge. In 1957 Sedgman could have been as good as Hoad and Gonzales, and in 1963 Gonzales, Laver, and Rosewall were all very close.

As you can see, a lot of things happened quite differently. Fred Perry would have won only one Wimbledon, and so I, not Fred, would have been the first modern player to win three Wimbledons in a row (in fact I would have won four straight, '48–'51 before Gonzales beat me 6–4, 6–7, 13–11, 6–8, 7–5 in the famous long final in '52). Budge would have won six straight Forest Hills and would have made it seven but for Riggs' comeback victory in '45, when Don was serving for the match at 5–3 in the fourth and then lost 7–5, 6–4. Gonzales also would have won seven Forest Hills and six Wimbledons too, giving him the modern record of thirteen. And little Rosewall—not only did he get a Wimbledon title, he would have gotten four to go with his five Forest Hills.

Oh it would have been very different. . . .

17

The Dark Decade, 1957-1968

The craziest thing about tennis during these years is that the fans continued to be attracted to the traditional amateur "fixtures," even though they knew that the pros had the best talent. In other forms of entertainment the fans have gone to where the talent is. Only in tennis . . . I never could figure that out.

Nobody disputed our claims either. Nobody every seriously suggested that Neale Fraser could beat Gonzales or that Art Larsen could beat me.

It was ludicrous. In 1957 Mal Anderson beat Cooper at Forest Hills. It was the equivalent of a good Triple A baseball game—the Syracuse Chiefs against the Rochester Red Wings. But the Triple-A tennis was front-page sports news. It drew large crowds and international attention. A few weeks earlier at the same site, Forest Hills, I brought in the major-league all-stars. I promoted a round-robin that featured Gonzales, Sedgman, Segura, Trabert and Rosewall, and starred Hoad in his pro debut. He won Wimbledon on Friday, played the men's doubles final on Saturday, flew to New York and gave a press conference on Sunday. On Monday, *Life* Magazine came out with an exclusive detailed story on Hoad's signing that I had given my old friend Marshall Smith, the sports editor there. Since *Life* went to print Friday and didn't come out till Monday, we took a chance on a leak. But they gambled too; when I flew into New York from Venezuela on that Friday, I had to go right to the Time-Life Building to assure George Hunt, the managing editor, that Hoad really was signed; I showed him the contract.

So we had a *Life* exclusive when the magazine was at its peak. We had a fantastically popular two-time Wimbledon champion just days after he had won the title; plus we had the controversial pro champ, Gonzales, ready to face him for the first time . . . and at Forest Hills. But we still couldn't make it go. There was slight press coverage outside of New York and nothing overwhelming within Manhattan. We ended up selling the Hoad-Gonzales match to CBS on an expenses-off-the-top basis, which is a fancy way of saying that we gave it away. We drew small crowds and lost a bunch of money.

I think I knew in my heart then that the situation could not be retrieved. Nothing seemed logical, so I felt that there must be a weakness within me. I could only think to myself: Jack, what have you done wrong?

I had done some things wrong. I had let the fat-cat amateur officials make me the issue. I had become a red herring. Whenever the subject of what is wrong with tennis would come up, somehow the subject would be diverted to a discussion of my merits (or mostly: my supposed demerits). The summary question would be: do you want to sell the whole sport of tennis to Jack Kramer?

I grew more and more frustrated as I watched the finest carryover sport in the world being strangled of its natural popularity by a bunch of hypocritical idiots who ran the amateurs. The last thing I wanted was to run all of tennis. I just wanted to make a living out of it. I couldn't have run tennis even if I wanted to. If the last decade has taught us nothing else, it is that no one man can run even a nickel's worth of tennis. That's the problem: no one can gain sufficient control to bring fair order to the game.

On the other hand it was indisputable that I did run pro tennis. (Donald Dell and some of the other kids still call me "The Czar" in honor of those days.) I don't suppose any one man ever so controlled a professional sport as I did. But if I ran it, I didn't run it into the ground. Despite our general lack of recognition, those players good enough to play pro did very well. In the late 1950s I had as many as seven players a year making $50,000 or more—and how many football or baseball heroes were making $50,000 then? And I'm afraid that as soon as I pulled out of the pros in 1962, the operation hit rock bottom. My trouble was that I should have hid under a rock and pretended I had no control. I should have been a real fifth-column type and tried to undermine the amateurs. My mistake was that I thought truth had the best shot. I was dumb enough to think that because we were the best, logic would prevail and so would we. Unlike most people who are wronged, I cannot pretend to claim that I wasn't heard. I got along with the press, and I had a platform everywhere.

Unfortunately I seemed to advertise the amateurs wherever I went. When the press wrote about me, they wrote about my victories in the amateurs. The same thing happened with the other pros. If Hoad came to town, no one wrote about his great match with Gonzales two weeks ago in St. Louis; no, all the ink was about his '57 Wimbledon or his great Challenge Rounds. We were locked in the past.

We trapped ourselves from buying any future. The longer we had to play one-night stands with the star-of-the-year policy, the longer we were kept from establishing real tournaments. Jack March was the only person in the United States who wanted to promote a professional tennis tournament. The rookies got the big money, based on what they had done in the big amateur events. How could we expect people to take us seriously if we did not pay our best the most?

Because no good player would turn pro without guarantees, it was virtually impossible for us to build tournaments because the part of the budget that should have gone to purses was gone off the top in the form of guarantees. Fix? The really ironic thing is that so much of the time—like the cold night in Buenos Aires when Gonzales beat Sedgman—our guys were knocking themselves out strictly for pride. The money was long since divvied up.

I always wanted us to get into tournaments. In 1953, over Easter in New York, I gave it a shot. I put on a four-man tournament at the old Seventh Regiment Armory for McGregor, Sedgman, Segoo and myself. I advertised it as a prize-money event because I was certain that nobody would believe that we'd play hard if there wasn't a purse distribution. In fact, all four of us were on set deals. And so, just before the tournament started I lost my nerve and called in the writers I knew, and I leveled with them. These guys knew tennis, they knew we really did play to win, and I think they all went along with the prize-money claim. What the hell, nobody cared anyway. We drew 1,500 for the final.

At that Wembley in 1957—when I beat Hoad and Gonzales both—just about everybody in the whole field was on a guarantee to me; so winning and losing didn't mean a damn in the pocketbook. But in the doubles finals, Segoo and I played the Whiz Kids and won the first two sets. I was ready to get out of there, and then Hoad gets interested, and he and Rosewall won the next three. We finished up at one in the morning, and the next afternoon Rosewall and Segura had to play the singles finals—it went five sets for Kenny—and I, age thirty-six, had to play Gonzales for third place. Our pay was already determined, but still all of us played our hearts out.

The trouble was we never played for tournaments, and so none were ever built. That's why I'm so against guarantees of any sort today. It is not that a guarantee will make a player lazy, although that may happen. No, for the good of tennis the money must go to the tournaments. If the tournaments are not strong, tennis will not be strong, and there will not be any guarantees to anybody in the future.

I was blameless in another problem I caused myself. Serve-and-volley was my style. It became the one way to play the game. Remember, I could hit a groundstroke, I could return serve. I didn't really advance to my ultimate big game until I was twenty-six, and in fact, in the latter part of my career I learned a whole other game—I became a fine baseline dirt player.

But too many of the kids who followed me only saw the flash and boom. They could only hit the big serve and rush pell-mell to the net. They had no defense. This fed on itself since they played kids who were playing the same game. The level of play declined, and it was boring to watch. (People who argue that tennis players get better all the time are never able to explain to me how Rosewall did as well against presumably a better breed in his late thirties as he had against an earlier crop when he was in his physical prime.) From Trabert to the Connors group, American tennis was its weakest ever. Fans never complained about the serve-and-volley style when people like Gonzales and Sedgman and Hoad were playing it. They only began to complain and lose interest in tennis when the level of quality fell off.

At least we tried to improve the pro game: we instituted the three-bounce rule. Jack March tried VASSS—Jimmy Van Alen's system—and one serve only. For a time I put in a special service line one meter behind the baseline. I didn't necessarily want to tinker with the game, but I knew it was boring. Looking back though, I can see that what we really needed was the best players playing in the best places. So long as tennis remained the only amateur game in a sea of professional sport, it was only natural that natural athletes sought sports other than tennis. I picked tennis. I didn't come from a tennis family. Neither did Riggs, Vines, Budge, Gonzales or most of the earlier stars. But from the 1950s on, tennis was simply not getting good athletes. The best tennis players the U.S. produced were virtually all the sons of pros (Buchholz, Richey) or the sons of devoted tennis-playing fathers (Ralston, Graebner, Froehling). Even Ashe, our only black star, fits into this pattern since he grew up next to a tennis court in a park where his father was a policeman. We have had better players recently, but this Connors' generation is also almost all from tennis families.

Only now, as we enter the 1980s after more than a decade of open tennis and sustained tennis popularity, will we finally start attracting our best athletes from outside the sport.

As the 1950s wore on, with no new American stars, the whole sport failed, amateur and pro together. For the Davis Cup, in 1954 at White City Stadium in Sydney, great temporary stands had to be constructed and there was a turnaway crowd of 28,000. A decade later the Aussies couldn't come close to selling the 12,000 permanent seats. In the early rounds of the French and Australian championships the crowds sometimes numbered in the hundreds. For the finals at Forest Hills, the stadium would be half-filled, and some of the press would leave the marquee, go up into the stands and sunbathe as they watched the championship. In the early 1950s, the top five U.S. tournaments—the national singles, doubles, indoors, clay courts and hard courts—all made money, producing at least half and sometimes as much as two-thirds of the USLTA's budget of $135,000. By the end of the decade only the doubles tournament at Longwood was in the black. The networks could not find a sponsor for the matches at Forest Hills—not even the finals.

Naturally, in the face of this disastrous turn, the amateur officials never considered that they might be doing something wrong. They just blamed Kramer and the pros for all their problems. I could have accepted this if I had been succeeding, but after Hoad hurt his back, I started to lose my shirt. In the next two years the tour dropped more than $75,000. Even then, in 1960 I donated 2½ percent of the gross to the USLTA to help them develop players. Tennis was in trouble and we all had to work together. But instead, the amateurs and the establishment press—led by Gladys Heldman—turned on me.

The disaffection of the Australians came early, and it hurt me bitterly. Australia had always been pretty good about accepting professional tennis. Down Under, I was popular—known by the term "Lerican," which means a big friendly Yank. Hopman was always tearing down the pros, but this anti-professionalism was not so institutional a bias as it was in the States. The Aussies accepted the departure of Sedgman and McGregor easily because they had Rosewall and Sedgman coming up. There wasn't even much heat when I signed Kenny after the '56 Challenge Round.

I scheduled a tournament at White City after Rosewall turned, and I worked up the draw so that he would meet Sedgman in the quarters. That was the match the Aussies wanted to see because the two stars had never met before in actual competition. The reason I wanted Rosewall and Sedgman to play in the quarters was first that I wanted to be certain that they would meet. Remember that at this point I wasn't all that confident about Rosewall's ability anyway. The semi's and finals should be able to draw on their own competitive strength. So if you have a good match-up, try to slot it for the quarters where you can get an extra crowd.

I was dead right. The interest in Rosewall-Sedgman was sky high. The fans didn't care whether it was amateur or pro. They wanted to see the best players play, and this was good old-fashioned head-to-head king-of-the-mountain. The fans stormed the tennis grounds, and there were still thousands of them milling around the ticket windows when they heard the PA announce the match. The people couldn't wait. Suddenly they started pushing and shoving, the ticket takers were swept aside, and about four thousand fans came in for free. It cost me about $9,000, and Sedgman won easily. He owned Rosewall for several years before Kenny finally turned it around.

246

Later in the same year I signed Hoad, and that was when the Aussie tennis establishment really began to turn on me. It wasn't a matter of pride. To replace Hoad and Rosewall, they had Cooper and Anderson on deck, with Fraser, Laver, Emerson and Stolle all waiting for a chance in the dugout. Basically it was the simple matter of money. The Whiz Kids were better draws. In fact, because there were no interesting Americans, the Aussie fans would not have kept coming out to see Hoad and Rosewall beat up on some U.S. also-rans, but all of a sudden the anti-pro feelings displaced any logic. At one point there were suddenly a lot of rumors and scare headlines, claiming that Kramer was trying to sign up the top Australian swimmers and get them out of the 1960 Olympics.

My problems in Australia rose steeply with the controversies surrounding the 1958 Davis Cup which was held in Brisbane. By now one of my few allies left in the USLTA was Perry Jones, my old friend and patron from the Los Angeles Tennis Club. Perry was named U.S. captain that year replacing Billy Talbert, and since I was going to be in Australia, he asked me to help him with the team. I was delighted to do so, and in fact, to support the effort even more I reached into my own pocket and paid for Dinny Pails to be a playing coach.

I was in Australia because I had signed Cooper and Anderson after the Cup. They were Number 1 and 2 in the world now that the Whiz Kids had gone and had won just about every major event in the amateurs. Obviously then, from any crass practical point of view, it would help the pro tour if they swept the U.S., leaving the amateurs in a final blaze of glory. Obviously too, Cooper and Anderson were overwhelming favorites to retain the Cup; and once, off the record in an interview, I acknowledged this unsurprising fact. Unfortunately the remark found its way into print and infuriated Ham Richardson, our Number 1 player, who accused me of wanting to fix the matches to assure a Cooper-Anderson triumph.

The Aussies were bellowing that I was out to take their best players away. They wanted me immediately thrown off the Davis Cup team. Richardson—the American star and a Rhodes Scholar—was accusing me of sabotaging my own team. I was getting it from both sides. The only good thing that happened in here was that a horse of mine named Big Jake (I owned a quarter of him) won a race at Sydney at 9–1. I took Big Jake's victory as a good omen, especially since I cashed a big bet on him.

My problems with Richardson were compounded by the fact that even though he was ranked Number 1 in the U.S., I thought he was only the best of a bad lot and would be a poor choice to take one of the singles spots. Like Talbert, Ham was a diabetic, and I just did not believe that he was strong enough to endure a three-day competition, especially in Brisbane where it was so hot and humid. Richardson had an outstanding backhand, and he was a real fighter, but there were just too many weaknesses in his game to count on him. For one main thing, his second serve had virtually no overspin, and I was certain that both Anderson and Cooper could eat him up with that. He also served entirely too many double faults in big matches. Then to top all that off, Ham took a bad loss from Bob Mark in the third round at New South Wales and took off from the Victorian championships to rest. I advised Perry that we play Buchholz and MacKay in the singles, and team Olmedo and Richardson in the doubles. They had won the Nationals at Longwood together and were a good team. Richardson would be fresh for the one day's play in doubles. Buchholz and MacKay both had good serves. On a hot day on the turf, there was the chance they could spring an upset.

Jones—and Pails too—both agreed with me about Richardson, but Perry was high on Olmedo, who played in Los Angeles when he was at USC. Buchholz had beaten Anderson at Sydney recently and clearly had the most potential of any American kid in years. This encouraged me to think we should give him the shot; at least he would be gaining experience. But Butch was still in his teens, and as precocious as he was as a player, he was still immature in many ways. He was the first of the racket-throwers. Since both Captain Jones and Pails genuinely liked Olmedo's chances, Perry picked Alex to play the singles with MacKay as well as the doubles with Richardson.

Richardson blew up all the more. He called his own press conference and indicated that I had used my influence with Jones to keep him out of the singles. He suggested that I really didn't want to see Cooper and Anderson beaten since I had them signed to pro contracts, and furthermore that I didn't want to see Richardson play in a Challenge Round since he had no professional plans, and therefore, if he won, the publicity could not be turned into eventual build-up publicity for the pros.

All of this was not only nonsense, it was backwards. First of all Jones had turned down my suggestion to play Buchholz. Perry is the one who had opted for Olmedo over Richardson. Secondly, by hiring Pails and helping the U.S. having a better chance at beating Cooper and Anderson, I was damaging the appeal of my upcoming tour when I was to throw them in against Hoad and Gonzales.

After Ham blew his top, our luck began to turn. It rained like hell in Brisbane. That's almost a tropical town—much closer to the Equator than either Sydney or Melbourne—and the courts stayed soggy. The players had to use spikes. Well, Olmedo, The Chief, had a habit of lifting his foot as he served rather than dragging his toe along the turf (and often as not, into it). The other kids were all catching their toes on service, but the wet ground didn't bother The Chief since he just stepped right over it naturally. He upset Anderson in the opening match in four sets and then took Cooper in four easier sets on the opening match of the final day to give us the Cup.

In between, we won the third point (MacKay lost both his singles) with the help of Pancho Gonzales. Hopman paired Neale Fraser, with his big serve, with Anderson in the doubles, and they won the first two sets 12–10, 6–3. Olmedo was a good doubles player since his weak ground strokes were not such a liability and Richardson was a smart strategist, but it was very unlikely that they could take three straight sets from Anderson and Fraser in Brisbane. Somehow though, they outlasted the Aussies and won the third set 16–14.

This is where Gonzales entered the picture. He and I were both doing radio commentary, but for rival Australian stations. Gorgo knew that I had made an arrangement with my station that if the match went to a third-set break, I could leave the microphone and go down into the American locker room. He came away from his mike long enough to intercept me. "Jack," he said, "tell them to try setting up in the Australian doubles formation. I think that will take care of Fraser's return."

Most people who read this are probably familiar with that formation. It got the name simply because it was first used by some Aussie team. Normally in doubles, when you are serving, the player who is not serving is placed at the net directly across from the player who is receiving serve. In most cases then, the receiver returns cross-court, away from his opponent who is set at the net. In the Australian formation, the man at the net is positioned on the other side, cross-court from the receiver. The server, therefore, has the tougher job of having to dash a few extra steps after he serves to cover the open territory down the line. Obviously, this is the more likely place for the receiver to hit to. If he hits cross-court, as he usually does, the man at the net is there to cut it off and volley back.

The reason then that a team usually switches to this sort of tennis I-formation is to shake up the opposition—if nothing else, make them think differently—and force a player who is returning well cross-court to switch and hit down the line. Fraser was the man in question here. He had a lousy backhand, and for a return of serve in doubles, all he could do was push the ball cross-court. Gonzales was right. Get Fraser out of that groove, make him hit down the line, and we might be in business. I rushed into the locker room at the break and advised Olmedo and Richardson to go into the Australian doubles set-up, and the fact that the advice came from Gonzales made them all the more willing to give it a try. If I remember correctly, on the second point of the fourth set, Fraser lobbed and Ham missed the smash, but thereafter, for the rest of the way, he never won another point except when he was serving. We won the match 6–3, 7–5.

So The Chief was the big hero, not Cooper and Anderson, which certainly didn't help my tour. And the Australians were all the more furious at me because I had been part of the team that took the Davis Cup away (and never mind that Jones deserved all the credit for selecting Olmedo). They began to make it very tough on us. One promoter I had always learned a lot from was Abe Saperstein of the Harlem Globetrotters. There weren't many places in the world where Abe and the Globies hadn't already been. I had always known that he got to play the Australian tennis stadiums for 10 percent rent, while it cost me 25. Okay, we were competitors with the amateurs. Late in 1958 they notified me they were locking pro tennis out of their stadiums altogether.

I had a lot of top players under contract now, and I wanted to start a series of tournaments, so I found alternative sites: bicycle grounds in Melbourne, cricket pitches in the other large cities. But I needed a court. A guy named Ralph Symonds, who was known as the Plywood King of Australia, built me a laminated court for $11,250, but the damn thing took a full working day—eight or nine hours—to set up and another two and a half or three to strike. It came in sections of thirty feet by ten, two-and-a-half inches thick, and it was extraordinarily heavy. Luckily I got another top Australian businessman to transport the thing for me. His name was Reg Ansett, and he ran an airline that competed successfully against the national line. "I'll help you because I think you're getting a dirty deal from the LTA," he said, and he supplied the trucks and rigs to move the court around the country.

The tennis federation would not give an inch. One time we wanted to put on a benefit for Jack Crawford, the old Aussie star who had come within a set in 1933 of being the first grand slammer. In Australia these kinds of testimonials are tax free for the recipient, and Jack stood to make a bundle. In fact, he did make $32,000, but even for a Crawford benefit, the LTA wouldn't let the pros play in White City. So we found another site, Olympic Park, and drew almost fifteen thousand, the largest non-Davis Cup crowd ever to watch tennis in Australia. Anderson and Cooper made their pro debut, and Gonzales, Hoad, Rosewall, Sedgman, Segura and Trabert also donated their services.

But I couldn't get in the black. We had some good tournaments and topped our gate records in Melbourne, but the logistics and the extraordinary expenses—it would cost me $5,000 just to set up seats—became prohibitive. Once when I got rained out in Brisbane, I found out that I made more money in rain insurance than I could have possibly made at the gate. It was obvious that the pros were being frozen out of one of their very best world markets and the home country of many of them.

The United States was declining as a market because there were no new American attractions. Cooper and Anderson were hardly my first choices for 1959. On tour neither one beat Gonzales a single time. I wanted to lead the tour with Althea Gibson and Maureen Connally, but Maureen just could not come back from her injuries. So we went again with Hoad and Gonzales, adding the two new Aussies to the undercard. But the interest was simply not there anymore. The next year I added Buchholz and MacKay, but like Cooper and Anderson, they came on after losing the Davis Cup. I didn't have a choice any longer.

I don't think I would have signed Buchholz and MacKay except both hated amateur tennis so and wanted out. I did believe too that Butch especially had the potential to become a star. But he had two technical weaknesses—he couldn't hit a low volley or a good second serve—and he had too much of a bad temper. That was odd too, because he's such a fine guy off

252

the court. MacKay too. They also wanted to join me because by this time, December, 1959, pressure was seriously building for open tennis.

Curiously, the main agitation was coming from England, which had, in Wimbledon, the only successful tennis tournament left in the world. Things were so bad everywhere else that tennis officials had to consider changes of some sort. The U.S. came up with some incredible concept of segregated open tournaments, whereby amateurs and pros would be placed in separate quarters, and thus could not face each other until the semi's—really two separate tournaments played as one. The French threw out the concept of the "authorized player," which was no more than a professional who would be permitted to play Davis Cup, that is: one not signed by Kramer. As the summer meeting of the International Lawn Tennis Federation approached, I met with amateur tennis officials and promised to do what I could to help bring in open tennis.

The spirit of open tennis was in the air. The night before the vote in Paris, I can remember sitting down with Jean Borotra, the head of the French Federation, and having a long conversation about how open tennis would work and what my own role would be in this new arrangement. We spoke with th full understanding that open tennis had been approved. After all, it was not hard to count the votes, and open tennis had the two-thirds margin necessary.

The next day the vote fell five short. Open tennis needed 139 votes out of 209, and it only got 134. A switch of five votes, and open tennis would have come in in 1960 instead of 1968. It was an absolute fix; one man who had committed to open tennis went to the bathroom when the vote was called. The Big Four all voted for the measure, but it was the United States that brought about its defeat. The USLTA voted one way and lobbied another.

I was shattered. The feelings against me ran so high in the amateurs that federations would vote against me even if that also meant voting against their own best interests. There was madness in the sport. I decided to try one last tack. If I could sign up several top players from all over the world, I could possibly make the pros seem more universal.

I had been thinking about heading in this new direction for some time. It is interesting to note that the really passionate feelings against Kramer began to swell in Europe only when it seemed that I might look to Europe for talent. As long as I only signed Aussies and Yanks the European tennis people mostly liked me. It was only when I wanted to pay their players that it became clear how evil I was. When I went to Wimbledon in 1958, here was the beginning of a story that ran in the *Daily Sketch*, complete with a screaming six-column headline:

KEEP AWAY FROM OUR KIDS, KRAMER
WE DIDN'T GROOM THEM FOR YOU!

Wimbledon starts today. Sitting in the stands will be immaculately dressed, suave, plausible Jack Kramer— Public Enemy No. 1 to amateur lawn tennis.

In ten years his Hollywood smile and million-dollar cheque book has skimmed the cream off the amateur game.

Now the man who was born in money-mad Las Vegas again brings Wall Street to Wimbledon.

We can't keep him out. It wouldn't make much difference if we could, for money talks and Jack's a whale of a talker.

He has weakened the American and Australian game and is now after new blood! For his circus must have a yearly transfusion. BUT KEEP OFF OUR KIDS, KRAMER!

Etc.

Even for an old Dracula like me, the British kids weren't all that appealing. When I did sign my European troupe after the vote against open tennis in 1960, the only Englishman I signed was Mike Davies whose greatest claim to fame was that he once reached the semi's of the Wimbledon doubles. I also took on

Kurt Neilsen of Denmark, Robert Haillet of France, Andres Gimeno of Spain and Nicki Pietrangeli of Italy. Pietrangeli was the best known of this lot (although Gimeno went on to be much the best player). Tony Trabert was working for me in Europe then, and he had Pietrangeli's name on a contract—it was official and legal—but then the Italian tennis federation matched my pro offer and kept him playing as an amateur for Italy. Every other tennis federation in the world knew that too, but they made no effort to censure the Italians or ban Pietrangeli. That was the kind of hypocrisy I had to deal with.

By now, with all the new players, I was a year-round operation with three distinct branches around the world. My headquarters in Los Angeles was staffed with a couple of secretaries plus myself and two other associates. In Australia we had a promoter, Bob Barnes, and a fulltime secretary. In Europe, Trabert had a secretary and an assistant. Altogether, by 1960 I had twelve fulltime people working for me plus what PR and promotional support we had to pick up.

We really had a fabulous tennis group too. Olen Parks had been the operations chief of the tour and had been head of tennis promotion for Wilson. Barnes, in Australia, later put together a large bowling syndicate. John Gardiner, who became so well-known for his tennis ranches, was on my team. So was Vic Braden, who's become the most famous tennis coach-comedian-psychologist-TV star in creation. Myron McNamara, who later put together two top tennis clubs in Southern California and is the coach at U.C. Irvine, was another on the staff. Schroeder was with us on and off, and my secretary, Cile Kreisberg, kept everything together and became the house mother of pro tennis. We were a widespread, major-league organization, a far cry from throwing a couple of station wagons and a truck on the road. We were playing three distinct seasons: one in Australia, one in the States, one in Europe—plus occasionally we'd ship a group through Asia or down into South Africa. And the amateurs showed me no mercy. Whereas we had missed open tennis by a hair in 1960, when

the International Lawn Tennis Federation held its next meeting the following summer in Stockholm, only England pushed
for open play and the British could not even get the issue to a
vote.

Feelings against me intensified. As I mentioned earlier, no
one in tennis had ever been kinder to me than Allison Danzig
of the *Times*. In 1947, as I turned pro, he wrote: "Forest Hills,
in all probability, will not see him again as an amateur, and it
will not soon look upon his like, as a player of the very first
class with all the virtues that are esteemed in sporting competition. . . . Kramer has nothing but well-wishers, and not an
enemy or critic anywhere on the entire tennis circuit."

By 1960 Al wrote of me: "A change has come over Kramer.
The quiet, modest young man who was always in good spirits
and on the friendliest terms with nearly everyone now carries a
chip on his shoulder. He continually attacks the game to which
he owes so much, and he seems bent on wrecking it. . . . Not
only is Kramer weakening amateur tennis . . . he also is
ridiculing the game with the same old drivel about amateurs
taking money under the table."

I was spread too thin to succeed without general support. I
could never establish a pro circuit of real tournaments. The
people in tennis who ran tournaments preferred having
amateur tournaments because the amateurs were then obliged
to be social gigolos, to come to the parties, to stay in people's
houses, to play games with the committee members' children.
If they didn't perform these social services, they were not
invited back. By and large, the tennis people didn't want the
pros, because the pros were grown men who did not want
great obligations beyond playing. (That's not to say that most
of us weren't gracious and polite.) Looking back I know now
that I should have tried to succeed outside of the normal tennis
channels. I should have tried to get the American Cancer
Society, the Heart Association or somebody to help me put on
a tournament at Forest Hills. But tennis had become so narrow
that it never even occurred to me to try to get support from
other sources.

The game was dull, and Gonzales, our champion, remained as dominant and uncooperative as ever. Once he walked out on me in Europe. Rosewall was not old enough to be a beloved legend and not good enough to be a drawing card. Laver was a drab personality, and in fact, when he turned pro in 1963 after winning the Grand Slam, the interest in tennis had fallen so low that there was hardly any fanfare. By '63 I was out as promoter.

Trabert and Sedgman had gone, Hoad's back had done him in, Buchholz never developed. By the mid-'60s, Gimeno was one of the two or three best players in the world, but who knew? Santana, his countryman but nowhere near as good a player, was much better known for winning amateur tournaments. In the pros, Santana wouldn't have been seeded. Except perhaps at Wimbledon, the crowds everywhere continued to drop even though more and more people were playing the game.

Old Segoo was with me to the end. When I started my own tennis club in Pales Verdes, outside of L.A., I named the courts after players. The first one I dedicated to Segoo. He had never been a top banana, of course, but he always gave the pros everything and he did make a good living at it. Whatever resentments he had, he let them out only twice. (Both times he had a couple of drinks in him too.)

The first occasion was in Johannesburg. I had refused to play in South Africa the first couple years I had good deals down there because they wouldn't give Segoo the same visa as the white-skinned players. Maybe that's why I remember it so clearly when we did go there. He said: "Your system is unfair, Jack. You never really believe in the pro game. You only believe in the star system."

"You're wrong, Segoo. We tried everything," I said. "The fans made it that way. They only wanted to see the stars. If they wanted a tournament, they'd go see the amateurs. It wasn't the way I wanted it, kid, it was just the only choice I had."

Then in 1962 I decided to get out. Philippe Chatrier of

France was the one who convinced me that the amateur federations would never deal with me but that they might deal with the players. So on November 1, I volunteered to leave the sport, to free pro tennis of Jack Kramer so that amateur tennis couldn't hold me up as the bogeyman anymore. Segura came at me again one night. "You're running out on us, Jack," he said, and there was a bitter edge to his voice. He meant it.

"No, I'm not, kid," I replied, but wearily. I didn't want to argue anymore. The fight had gone out. "Look, I tried everything and nothing ever worked." I *had* tried everything: star tours, round-robins, traditional tournaments, different rules, different scoring, different serves. "There's nothing more I can do. I've got to get out or we'll never see an open game."

I was right too, but unfortunately open tennis was still six years away.

18

Beyond $24 a Day

Shamateur tennis was finished one afternoon during the Wimbledon of 1966 (which Santana, a clay-court player, won) when Herman David and several other members of the Wimbledon committee dropped by the BBC tent. They spoke with me and with Bryan Cowgill, the BBC executive who was in charge of tennis. At first David and the Wimbledon people spoke tentatively; then they grew bolder. In essence, what David finally said was: look, we're tired of putting on second-class tennis as "the championships" and we want a true champion. But if we go open after all these years of fighting the pros, will the public continue to support us?

I was sure the fans would take to the pros and so was Cowgill. While attendance at Wimbledon never really flagged during the sixties—it is as much a British cultural event as it is a sporting occasion—the TV ratings had begun to decline. It also probably worked to open tennis' advantage that 1966 was a soccer World Cup year, especially since that time it was played in England. Wimbledon looked pale by comparison, and obviously it was clear that nobody cared that the soccer heroes earned a living at their game.

In any event, the upshot of this meeting was that Wimbledon agreed to accept Bryan Cowgill's suggestion that an eight-man trial professional event be staged at Wimbledon the next summer, late August of 1967. The BBC agreed to put up the singles purse of $35,000 and Wimbledon sprang for the doubles money of $10,000. This total made the tournament the largest purse-money event in history. My assignment was to line up players and I certainly had no trouble.

The eight were Gonzales, Laver, Rosewall, Segura, Gimeno, Buchholz, Sedgman and Hoad. It was an absolute smash. The matches sold out every day and the BBC ratings were high— and all this less than two months after the amateur Wimbledon had been played. Laver beat Rosewall in the pro final, while in "The Championships," the young John Newcombe, a 16–1 shot, beat a German named Wilhelm Bungert—who rarely even played tournaments any longer—in three dull sets. The only saving grace of that tournament had been a hundred-pound bet I had made on Newk, which permitted me to buy a little MG for my son Bobby, who was there with me.

A few weeks later, shortly after Forest Hills in the autumn of '67, a promoter from New Orleans named Dave Dixon moved into professional tennis. With Lamar Hunt as a silent partner (at that time), Dixon began signing up what meager talent was still left in the amateurs. He did this because George McCall, the former U.S. Davis Cup captain, already had most of the pro stars locked up. So Dixon—throwing Hunt's name around—picked off Newcombe and Roche of Australia, Drysdale of South Africa, Pilic of Yugoslavia and Taylor of Great Britain. To these five pro rookies, he added Dennis Ralston, whom he took away from McCall, plus Butch Buchholz and Pierre Barthes of France, who were out in the cold because McCall didn't want them. Dixon named his organization World Championship Tennis and called his troupe "The Handsome

Eight." He then scheduled them for a tour of two tournaments a week beginning early in 1968.

As it turned out Dixon was right in anticipating the tennis boom but wrong in how to score off it. WCT was a disaster from opening night on; Dixon lost a bundle of his own money; and within weeks he had to drop out, leaving his assistant, Bob Briner (now the ATP chief executive) to run WCT and Hunt to finance it. By the time all this transpired in February of 1968, however, WCT's finances and stability were moot. All that mattered was that it had caused five more top amateurs—including the Number 1 Newcombe—to turn pro.

Still it has always been my view that Wimbledon would have become an open in 1968 whether or not The Handsome Eight ever existed. I believe the decision had been assured with the creation of the eight-man pro tournament in 1967. Probably, though, the creation of WCT forced the other federations to give in and go along with Wimbledon more quickly. By February of 1968, the U.S. had joined up with the British, and on March 30, 1968 at the Automobile Club at the Place de la Concorde in Paris, the ILTF approved a dozen open tournaments for 1968 (and thirty for 1969) without a dissenting vote. The irony of the whole damn thing is that all along we thought we had to convince the whole tennis world, but when Herman David decided that open tennis would be good for Wimbledon, the country and the world followed in step.

I had been out of pro tennis since 1962, but I had never been far away. Along with Madison Square Garden, I had promoted the richest tournament ever—$25,000!—in 1966. So now, open tennis was born, I jumped back in and helped the BBC organize the first open tournament, which began on April 22, 1968 at the West Hunts Club in Bournemouth, a seashore resort. McCall definitely had better players and bigger names than did World Championship Tennis. Gonzales was still the biggest attraction in the pros, even though he had reached forty. Laver and Rosewall were the two best players, plus McCall also had Emerson and Stolle, recent amateur names, Gimeno, and a few others. I knew open tennis would be better off if it could start out with the McCall troupe involved, and so I worked out a deal with McCall.

To get his group of stars to come to Bournemouth, I agreed to also line up an indoor event the week after in Paris and then to personally put on another tournament the week following at Wembley. McCall had to meet guarantees of $16,000 a week, and so—with transportation costs—he could not afford to come to Europe for a single tournament.

Ironically, while George had the best players, Hunt had the money and the organization. For the relatively few tournaments that WCT promotes, it keeps a larger staff than the USTA. At the time, however, its main attraction on the courts was Newcombe vs. Ralston—and that never lived up to its billing because while Newcombe progressed as a player, Dennis remained in a holding pattern. Ralston's a homebody, and he was always more interested in calling his wife to find out what was going on back home with the kids than he was in playing matches.

So by coincidence, at the time open tennis finally came into being, a competitive promoter system was in force for the first time in the pros. An amateur who wished to turn professional could not just announce his decision and then begin to compete for prize money. Instead, he had to choose between Hunt and McCall and play that circuit.

None of this is illegal, but it sure is unhealthy. It dulls incentive of the players, it restricts the game keeping out independent tournament promoters, and ultimately, it creates suspicious fans. Why should a kid try to win if he's already under a guarantee? Maybe this works in pro team sports, but not in an individual game, like tennis. Nonetheless, I really didn't perceive these dangers clearly until I directed the $50,000 Pacific Southwest championships in 1969. At the time, that was the highest amount ever offered, and our association promised to raise it to $75,000 the following year. But after the doubles presentations, Fred Stolle laid it all out for me. "Jack," he said, "it doesn't make a damn bit of difference whether you put up $75,000 or $750,000 because we're all under contract and we can only play where we're allowed to."

Suddenly I understand how completely did two men—Hunt and McCall—control the whole game. If Wimbledon or any tournament didn't want to pay their price, then all the top players could be held out of Wimbledon. And soon enough, this is exactly what happened.

At that point Lamar really had tennis over a barrel, and I feel fairly certain that he could have gained control of the game of tennis today if it had not been for Arthur Ashe.

Ashe started 1968 as an interesting drawing card because he was the first male black player from any nation and because he was exciting to watch. He was the skinny kid with the lightning first serve, always going for broke. However, as soon as he won the first U.S. Open, that September, he became the pivotal figure in tennis—and even more commanding when he then led Captain Donald Dell's U.S. Davis Cup team to our first victory in five years. He was the first big American gate attraction since Gonzales (McKinley and Trabert had never caught on, and they had only won as amateurs anyhow). And unlike Gonzales, Ashe was attractive as a person as well as a personality. After years of American tennis brats, he was an absolute gentleman on and off the court. He was intelligent, he had a good sense of humor, and the press adored him. Remember too, this was 1968: Martin Luther King had been assassinated earlier in the year, there were race riots, whole cities were burning, George Wallace was running for president. And in the midst of all this turmoil, appeared this dignified young black man who seemed to stand for all the good in tennis and America alike. What greater symbol for open tennis could there be than a black hero, signifying that the closed days of country-club tennis were over?

And finally, especially after Arthur swept through the amateurs in the summer and then triumphed at Forest Hills, he loomed as a great player with a decade or more of big victories ahead. Everybody wanted him to be a great champion. But frankly—and it kills me to say this—Arthur has never been that good. Ashe and Newcombe (another attractive person- ality) are the two modern players with reputations that most exceed their abilities. To put them in perspective, for example, I feel that Schroeder and Segura could have beaten them both under most conditions. Newcombe was better than Ashe. He was more consistent, a smarter percentage player, with the great second serve and a much more reliable net game. But Arthur won a Forest Hills. He won a Wimbledon. He won them both against all comers. He won WCT one year. He was at or near the top of the world for a decade; he's probably in the top fifteen for all time. Please understand: I'm not saying Ashe is a bad player, just that the kid had better PR than his record.

What does it matter exactly how good I think he's been, anyhow? He is probably the classiest fellow I've ever known. He has integrity, loyalty, plus he's always honorable and always good company. Arthur Ashe doesn't do anything wrong except maybe speak out too loud. And Arthur loves tennis too. All the things he could be, and the reason he came back to the tour after his heel operation is because he can't get the game out of his system. The circuit needed him too. He'll make a perfect Davis Cup captain for the U.S. As much as he cares for tennis and as capable as he is, I just hope to hell tennis isn't dumb enough to let him get away when he's through playing. The day Arthur quits, the USTA or somebody should walk up to him and say, now will you please help run tennis in the U.S. for the rest of the twentieth century?

I don't want to gloss over Ashe as a player just because he is such a fine human being. When he was younger, Ashe's serve was extraordinary. I mean it was right up there with Vines'. It had the top speed plus deception and control. Then Arthur suffered a shoulder injury early in the 1970s, and for a few years after that it wasn't the same serve. He brought the arm around more in a circle, more like a cricket bowler's motion.

But then, just about the time he had his great year, 1975, he got his old service motion back. By then he had lost a little velocity to the injury and age, but he had the big crack back.

As smart as Ashe is, he was never a shrewd or tough competitor. Because he was a nice kid to start with, and because he was a southern black growing up in a white country-club game, he was taught to be extra polite on the court. That gave him the peace and composure to survive, but it also robbed him of the real passion to win. Just as he was coming to greatness, the money came into the game and he cashed in. (Newcombe, in contrast, didn't become a conglomerate until several years later, after he had won more big titles.) I'm not criticizing Dell for making Ashe a millionaire or Arthur for accepting that fate, but it's obvious that all the deals cut Ashe too fine. From the minute Dell made him the $400,000-plus deal with Head, Ashe was in conflict with himself because I think he began to feel guilty. He couldn't give Head, Catalina and blacks the time and energy he thought he owed them. And he couldn't give himself a square deal on the court either.

All that aside, he never could have become a really great player because he never seemed to learn the odds. He'd overplay too many points. There are a lot of points—possibly a majority—in any set that you play only for survival. Let the other player take the risks and make the errors. Everybody knows that at every level of play there are far more points lost than won. But not Arthur. He'd go for the winner on the chalk at thirty-forty. It was fun to watch, but it didn't win consistently. The greatest two sets of tennis I ever saw in my life were the first two that Ashe and Laver played in the Wimbledon semi's of 1969. Unlike Ashe, Laver had learned how and when to play it safe, but he also could rise to the most brilliant heights, and he believed that the way to achieve the top of your game was to keep hitting out until it all came together. In this match they both started out shooting the works, and you never saw anything like it. Every point was brilliant, and there were two, three, four placements a game. Arthur blew Rod out the first set, and Laver turned it around in the second, but in both sets, either man could have whipped anybody else who ever lived. It couldn't keep up indefinitely, and it didn't: Arthur lapsed in the third set, and Laver, who was at the height of his powers then, won in four sets. But those first two sets were beyond belief.

That was the kind of player Ashe was in the late sixties. And he was American, and he was the one star not owned by Hunt or McCall. They both knew he was the key. McCall didn't have a fortune, but his operation was costing him around $12,000 a week in overhead plus the players' fees. He had added four women to his group—Billie Jean, Rosie Casals, Francoise Durr, and Ann Hayden Jones—but they hadn't helped the gate. George McCall was a class guy. When I put on that Wembley tournament a couple weeks after the first open in 1968, it bombed, and I took a bath. When he realized what had happened to me, he agreed to bring his guys back later in the year—waiving all transportation costs—to join with WCT's players for another tournament. (I lost a pile on that one too.)

But increasingly McCall had budget problems, and he began to realize that Ashe was his last chance. He bid for him and went as high as $400,000. Hunt moved into the same territory. These were astronomical figures for tennis in those days, and all the more incredible for Ashe, who had never had any money and who had played most of 1968 for $24 *per diem*.

When Arthur asked me which of the two he should sign with, I suggested Hunt. Obviously, WCT had the financial staying power, and beyond that, it had begun to start signing up more good young players, such as Marty Riessen and Tom Okker.

Lamar himself had come to me the year before when Dixon had gone bottom up. At that point Hunt had to decide whether to take a tax loss and clear out or stay in for the long haul. I advised him to get out, but he obviously considered the matter carefully, and once he made up his mind to stay in tennis I knew that he was committed. So I told Arthur that WCT appeared to be his best bet.

Ashe himself had nothing against either Hunt or McCall. If anything, he probably felt some kind of obligation to George because Arthur's worst experience in tennis had come in 1967 when he lost both his singles matches against Ecuador to get us knocked out of the Davis Cup and George out of his captain's job. Increasingly, Ashe began to wonder why it was that he had to sign with *anybody*. Where was it inscribed that an individual tennis player couldn't be an independent contractor? As soon as Ashe began to suggest these thoughts, Hunt should have bought Ashe at any price. That he didn't was the single biggest mistake of Hunt's sports career. Ever since he's been playing catch-up ball, and I can't ever see him catching up.

McCall, with limited resources, was in deep trouble as soon as he lost Ashe. I had suggested to Hunt that he give his players to George with the hope of a delayed payoff, but by 1971, McCall was completely discouraged and Hunt had virtually all the old pros under his banner. Bob Briner had left tennis, and WCT was being managed by Mike Davies, who I had originally signed as a pro player, and then a few years later, when Mike was a teaching pro in Jamaica, I had helped him obtain the visa that got him into the U.S. I always liked Mike and so does Lamar. In fact, sometimes I think that the only conceivable reason for Lamar to keep WCT afloat is to make sure that Mike Davies has a good job.

But Hunt and Davies let Ashe get away when they could have sewed up tennis with him. In failing to sign Ashe they permitted Ashe to create another power. That was his friend, The Lip, Donald Dell.

As I've said, I've known Donald since he was a kid back in 1954 on the junior Davis Cup squad that I coached. He was on the team with a chubby kid from Brooklyn, Ron Holmberg, Mike Franks, Mike Green, and Barry MacKay. Dell worked as hard as anybody, but the kid could never hit a good second serve. And then I'd see him in tennis through the years that followed. He was a Davis Cup player after Olmedo, Buchholz and MacKay turned. After he graduated from Yale and Virginia Law I remember seeing him in L.A. one time in 1967 when he was looking for a job. Dell was really at loose ends in 1968 when Bob Kelleher—now Judge Kelleher, then the head of the USLTA—gave Dell the Davis Cup job after a couple of other kids turned it down. In fact, Donald had almost taken a position with George McCall and was in touch with Mark McCormack, who was not in tennis yet. But then he got the captaincy, he won the Cup, and he fell into the Ashe situation. That changed everything for The Lip and for the game. Dell signed Ashe to commercial contracts which gave Arthur as much or more money than he could have gotten from Hunt or McCall, and yet he retained his independence and the leverage that goes with that. Then Stan Smith, their mutual friend, came to prominence on Arthur's heels, and Dell had a one-two punch that catapulted him to preeminence in the sport.

In the decade since, Donald and I have been through a lot together. Nothing brings you closer to a person than when the two of you are being sued, as we were when Bill Riordan got Connors to go after us. I know how smart and capable Dell is, and I'm not just saying that because he's my friend. (The four people in tennis with the best ideas have been Dell, Chatrier, Riordan and Gladys Heldman, and two of them are definitely not my friends.)

I frankly doubt that tennis ever could have a commissioner in the way that American team sports have one man at the top. You can't even get an effective commissioner of American tennis just by itself. Possibly tennis could be run by some kind of troika, with the various geographical and political elements all getting representation. If we ever get to that, the one man who should definitely be at the top of the list would be Dell. Maybe if the kid would make enough money to relax, then he could get out of that end of things and really serve the game.

While I'm on the subject, let me say this too: that tennis cannot possibly ever be run by somebody neutral from outside the sport. Tennis is not so neat as pro basketball, which could bring in a Larry O'Brien, introduce him to the owners and the players and the television networks, and then tell him to take over. Tennis is entirely too complicated, so it must be run by the ones who have been involved in it and know how it works. The obvious trouble with that situation is that the people in authority in tennis are bound to have some conflicts of interest. I don't know how that situation can be avoided.

I've always felt that tennis tends to attract officials who are selfish. Until very recently most of the people prominent in the sport came in because they liked playing the game. Whenever I went to a USLTA meeting, all the delegates brought their rackets, and they were obviously more interested in playing a game than in improving the game. We've always had the wrong motives—if for no other reason than that the basic profit motive was considered evil.

This is why I'm so pleased with the influx of new boosters who have come to the sport since it went open. They've come from more normally run sports—baseball, football, basketball—where the officials are more interested in making things work and making a buck than they are in playing the sport themselves and having cocktails with the players.

Bob Briner and I have a joke remark we use pretty regularly. In referring to a guy in the game, one of us will say: "Well, he'll be buying tickets soon." You see, the first perk you get when you become a tennis official is a badge which lets you into a good seat for free. Luckily for tennis, a lot of people who have been wearing badges for years are now having to start to buy tickets.

My pal Dell is not going to have to start buying tickets soon but sometimes I wish we could lock him and all the other agents out. Donald isn't going to be surprised by that remark. He knows how I feel on that subject. There are two distinct Dells—the one who puts his whole heart into tennis and the other who signs contracts for his clients. Donald always maintains that there is no such thing as a conflict of interest so

long as all the interests are out in the open—and that if you
don't have a conflict, you can't be very bright. I tend to agree
more with Philippe Chatrier, who is now the president of the
entire ILTF as well as the French federation. Philippe's
argument is that everybody making important decisions in
tennis should be completely free of any personal financial
interest in the sport. Sometimes Philippe even lumps me with
Donald, inasmuch as I have a contract with Wilson. To him
we're all pros, pure and simple. Philippe is adamant that
Donald should disqualify himself from all decisions where any
possible financial conflict may be involved.

The trouble with The Lip, with Mark McCormack and all
the other agents is that they take 10 or 15 percent—even
more—of the money out of the game. I want to see tennis
money stay in tennis, and go toward helping the development
of the game. All our ATP deals—and Donald was the ATP
counsel, and his law partner, Frank Craighill, is now—are
structured that way. The bigger and stronger an agent gets,
the higher his overhead, the more he needs to take out of
tennis to balance his books. An owner in a team sport may be
making a living off the game, but he has an investment to live
with; he has bought a franchise and has got to keep plowing
back to protect that investment. Agents can take the money
and run. It doesn't run smoothly, so in the down periods an
agent may have to scramble to keep the engine going the way it
was in the good times. Take Donald. As powerful as he is, he
hasn't come up with one of the top young male stars. Of all his
clients, only Ashe has won a major title since 1972—and that
was some years ago. (Of course, now that he has Tracy Austin,
his fortunes may be turning.)

In these down periods an agent starts to hustle his players.
He sees a little hole in his star's schedule, so he books back-to-
back exhibitions in Vancouver and New Orleans. The player
needed rest—and he gets wiped out in the first round the next
week—but the agent had bills to pay. Luckily, tennis has
continued to boom, so lately the pressure has not been so tight.

Something like forty-five new brand-name rackets have been manufactured in the past few years, and most of these rackets are made by companies that have previously had no connection with tennis. So some vice-president screams "get me a name," and a kid like Stan Smith can lose his big Wilson contract but walk right into another racket deal.

There are so many new rackets floating around that the best players sign to use different rackets in different parts of the world. And sometimes one racket isn't so good. There have been cases where players have camouflaged rackets to look like the ones they are supposed to be using.

And of course it's not just rackets. It's clothes and shoes plus anything even remotely connected with tennis off the court. A player like Borg, who makes way in excess of $1 million a year in endorsements, looks like one of those guys who used to walk around town with sandwich boards. He receives something like $50,000 a year to wear a handband advertising Tuborg beer, $25,000 to wear a shoulder patch advertising Scandinavian Airlines. He gets $200,000 for wearing Fila tennis clothes, $50,000 for Tretorn shoes, $20,000 for showing his rackets are strung with VS gut. Then he plays with one racket in the U.S. for $100,000 and another for about the same price in Europe. (Not to mention what he picks up on the side promoting cars, cereals, games, bed linen, blue jeans, towels, even comic books.)

I'm not suggesting everybody is making out like that. But a guy like Solomon, who has little drawing power, gets $50,000 to wear Fila clothes. To keep Gottfried, another solid but unspectacular player, Wilson more than doubled a $40,000 guarantee and still lost him to a racket named Snauwert. (A kid who is ranked around seventy-five to a hundred in the world and who is *not* Number 1 or 2 in his country probably only picks up a thousand or two from a racket company and then gets free shoes and clothes.) Sometimes there is so much money around in tennis that I think it might put people off. Television is never very modest, but when CBS guaranteed $500,000 to Connors to play one match the money seemed so obscene that the network refused to divulge the high figure. Gloria Connors once turned down an assured $200,000 for a weekend for Jimmy (and he could have made $500,000) demanding a minimum of $450,000. Japanese promoters put up $200,000 for Borg, Connors, Vilas and Orantes for a weekend, so of course all their agents took that instead of having them play in a regular week-long $175,000 Grand Prix tournament. Believe it or not, we had a meeting of the Council not long ago to discuss a proposed $1 million tournament for the Astrodome. We turned it down. It was too much. It could upset the whole structure of the game.

Before I leave the subject, I do want to add that I am not against players making big money on the side. Since they're human beings, it probably lulls most of them into complacency on the court. But you can't moan about that. Actually, endorsements are only fair because tennis is one of the few forms of entertainment where the stars are not compensated properly at the gate. In a team sport, the drawing cards can demand salaries far in excess of what they deserve as players. Reggie Jackson is paid foremost because he puts people in the seats, and second because he is a pretty good player. Robert Redford never wins any acting awards, but he gets paid more than much better actors. But Connors doesn't get what he deserves as a genuine gate attraction, and so in a sense, the lesser players are living off his reputation—and off Borg and Nastase and Ashe and the other prime draws.

You can't have appearance money set aside for the stars. Guaranteed contracts are bad for the game. Tennis is a tournament sport, and everything must be done to build up competition. Nobody knows that better than I: if you pay your stars wages, if you give the top money to players instead of making them battle for it, you put them above the competition, and pretty soon the competition is ignored. And then, guess what?—soon enough there isn't even money around for the stars.

The agents, more powerful all the time, keep stirring the

nontournament pot, where they can make more money. At the best, an agent can get four different payoffs from an exhibition deal. First and most obvious, he gets his cut—10, 12½, 15 percent, whatever—for delivering the players to the promoter. If he can then bring in TV, he gets a slice there. And if the promotion involves a large company, the agent might also wangle a consultant's fee. Finally, he can get a percentage of the players' purse. I sometimes wonder if the players realize how they are being so profitably used by agents. I can't believe that some of the best of them would tolerate what is going on if they really understood how they were being exploited.

I also have a special concern about how powerful McCormack and Dell have become. Throw out Connors and Evert, who keep it all in the family, and virtually all the top talent in men's and women's tennis alike is controlled by Dell or McCormack. Part of the reason is, that both organizations do a topnotch job—remember, I advised the Austins to have Tracy sign with Donald—but they do so well for the players that they are becoming too powerful. I'm scared that these two giants will be so concerned about competing against each other that tennis will get trampled in the process. Already they are engaged in great recruiting battles. I've heard that McCormack will guarantee a kid a certain amount in exhibition money (somebody has to play *against* Borg, after all) if he will sign a standard management contract. The result is that the two big firms will sign more and more stars and schedule more and more exhibitions to the detriment of tournaments and the whole game.

What we need in tennis is a hero with the integrity and concern that Jack Nicklaus has for golf. Nicklaus broke with McCormack years ago because he wanted to handle his own destiny. He's still making plenty of money from the game, but never at the expense of the game. A few years ago, when Jimmy Connors' tennis challenge matches were doing well on TV and Johnny Miller was looming as the new challenger to

Nicklaus, Jack was offered a million-dollar winner-take-all TV challenge against Miller. He turned it down, because he thought it would harm golf. Sometimes I let myself dream that this sort of thing might happen in tennis too.

19

Beyond the Handsome Eight

When I began to fully understand what a stranglehold Hunt and McCall had on the game, I became convinced that we had to have an alternative. And so, early in 1969, I conceived the Grand Prix—a series of tournaments with a money bonus pool that would be split up on the basis of a cumulative point system. This would encourage the best players to compete regularly in the series, so that they could share in the bonus at the end and qualify for a special championship tournament that would climax the year.

I proposed my plan to Alistair Martin, the president of the USLTA, he was excited by it, and he even sent along Dell, the Davis Cup captain, as his special emissary to accompany me to London. I was going to present the idea to the Committee of Management of the International Lawn Tennis Federation there. First, I tried the idea out on Herman David of Wimbledon, and he approved of it. David even endorsed it before the ILTF had formally seen the plan.

Unfortunately, Hunt and McCall headed me off at the pass. They got wind of my scheme and rushed to London themselves. They informed the major tournaments that if they went along with the Kramer Grand Prix formula they would lose the contract players. In fact, Hunt and McCall even suggested that they would schedule their own events against the major tournaments if they joined the Grand Prix. Since Hunt and McCall had the players my plan was voted down.

But the next year, 1970, few of the contract players bothered to show up for the French championships. In the first two years of open tennis, Laver and Rosewall had split French finals with each other, but in 1970 the final was Jan Kodes over Zelko Franulovic, hardly a classic. It made the national championship people on the ILTF realize they had a deal with Hunt and McCall that was very shakey indeed because they could not necessarily deliver the players that the tournaments wanted.

I was called to Paris while the tournament was still on and asked if I could get the Grand Prix going immediately. I thought it was possible and rushed back to New York where I met with Andy Pearson, the president of Pepsico and a helluva nice guy and tennis fan. He agreed to put $75,000 into the men's bonus pool (and some for the women too), and with that we were able to announce the creation of the Pepsi Grand Prix a couple weeks later, just before Wimbledon.

At the end of the season in Tokyo, there was a six-man round-robin championship played by the top point-getters for the year. Cliff Richey had amassed the most Grand Prix points, but he defaulted to a mysterious malady when he found the surface in Japan too fast for his taste and Stan Smith won the first Grand Prix Masters. In 1971 Pepsi was again the sponsor, and we played the Masters in Paris, again as a round-robin. Beginning in 1972, when the Commercial Union Assurance Company took over the backing and we played the Masters in Barcelona, we qualified the top eight and broke them into two four-man round-robins, with the top two in each division then succeeding to a straight four-man knockout draw. Originally our plan was to keep moving the Masters around the world, but in 1978 we settled it in Madison Square Garden and moved it from just before Christmas to early January, a good TV time. We also shifted the Australian Open the other way, from finishing early in January where it was the first of the Grand Slam, to December when it becomes the finale.

Today the Grand Prix bonus pool, with Colgate as the sponsor, exceeds $1,500,000, with more than $300,000 to the winner. The Grand Prix provides a year-round structure to the game. It incorporates all the traditional major tournaments, while attaching the struggling new ones to the sport's existing framework. In a far-flung, worldwide sport, the Grand Prix gives continuity and identity. Only Hunt and Bill Riordan have fought against it. Both of them have used, or threatened to use, antitrust action. As much as I regret to say it, that is a potent weapon in the United States. It cost the ATP $170,000 in legal fees to fight the Riordan/Connors cases—and who is going to pay that kind of money if a similar suit pops up again? What do you win even if you do win? Neither the men's or women's golf tours or the women's tennis have ever been hit by antitrust actions. We have a sword over our heads.

Actually Hunt's WCT tour was brought under the Grand Prix umbrella in 1978, but it was more of a shotgun marriage than it was the proper end of a long romance. From its creation, the Grand Prix was a thorn in WCT's side. It forced Hunt to regularly change his own tournament formula, and it forced him to open up the ante in purse money or guarantees. I think he might have thrown in the towel as early as 1970 if my friend Mr. Dell hadn't put on his agent's hat and come to the rescue.

WCT was really beginning to struggle then. It had all the top players, but the Grand Prix was beginning to look more attractive. There were rumors going around that even some of the original Handsome Eight, whose contracts were running out, were planning to switch over and play the Grand Prix or on Bill Riordan's new independent circuit. Hunt needed a shot

277

in the arm, so he started courting Arthur Ashe and his friends again as a last resort.

By now though, Ashe was in an even stronger bargaining position. By failing to sign Arthur two years before, Hunt had left him to Donald Dell and in effect, created his own monster. Arthur still liked the concept of remaining an independent, but he has always been a very pragmatic guy, and he felt that unless the amateur associations started to get more professional in their way of doing business, then maybe it would be best for all concerned to let Hunt become the absolute ruler of the game. Ashe wanted people like Bob Kelleher and myself to play more important roles, not only in the U.S. but in making full international decisions. But the USTA and the ILTF wouldn't or couldn't understand what Arthur was trying to tell them, and they specifically refused to put Kelleher on the International Committee of Management. So finally, Arthur said to hell with it and told Dell to start negotiating seriously with Hunt.

The end result was that not only did Dell sell Ashe to WCT, but he also made deals with Hunt for Charley Pasarell and Bob Lutz plus some lesser clients—and for Stan Smith when he got out of the army. Just as important to Hunt, this stopped several other players from leaving WCT, and by the time 1971 started, Hunt had almost every top professional in the world under contract. Only Nastase, who was just coming to prominence and who played for Riordan, and Smith, who was in the army, were not included. The WCT schedule lasted virtually the whole year long, from early in February until late in November.

After Hunt's players were locked out of Wimbledon in 1972, he and the ILTF made some peace. His tournament schedule was restricted to the first five months of the year, and he was limited to twenty-two regular tournaments and four specials. (Before I raised hell, they were going to let him schedule forty tournaments.) By 1974, WCT was using ninety-six professionals, but the talent was split too thin, three ways, and Hunt began to cut back. By 1977 he was down to twenty-three players, using no more than sixteen a week, which meant that the great bulk of the playing professionals would be out of work for much of the year. So the Grand Prix came into the WCT time period, and with its $1,000,000-bonus pool it appeared to be a much more attractive circuit.

Hunt could compete only by going back to his old policy of paying contracts. It cost him, it seems, as much as $700,000 to get Connors for one season; Nastase cost about $1,500,000 for three. Moreover, the agents of the lesser players heard about these windfall payments and began to try and get more money for their boys. WCT was really taking its lumps, and there didn't appear to be any way out of the bind. That's when Lamar decided that he would like to become part of the Grand Prix. He is, as his history shows, just a bully on the block with no concern for the game, and there was no reason to accommodate him. But he got a very lucky break and ended up as the single largest force in the Grand Prix.

Here's how it happened. Derek Hardwicke, the brother of the former British champion, Mary Hardwick Hare, is the British representative to the Council, and at the time when Hunt asked into the Grand Prix, he was also the president of the International Tennis Federation. Derek was afraid that if the dispute between WCT and the Grand Prix continued, history would repeat itself. Hunt would start signing up the big names to exclusive contracts and then oblige Wimbledon and the other major tournaments to hand over fees to help him pay the freight. So Derek, who is a very clever strategist, persuaded the Council to let him explore the waters with Hunt.

I am afraid that he then went further than the Council members wanted him to, and in the process he made a grave mistake, a legal *faux pas*. In a letter to WCT, Hardwicke indicated that WCT would be welcome on the Grand Prix circuit *if* WCT would get out of certain television projects that it had undertaken. The phrasing smelled of conspiracy, and Hunt had a weapon to show in court. He used the letter to the utmost, making no bones that if WCT wasn't accepted into the Grand Prix for 1978, then there would surely be a lot of legal complications for everybody.

As a consequence, Hunt was not only let into the Grand Prix, but on the most generous of terms. He was handed the rights to eight of our twenty-eight major tournaments—what we call "supers," those worth a minimum of $175,000. Thus Hunt has by far the largest portion of the tour. Not only that, but he has retained the rights to WCT as a whole, so he is a tour within a tour with a lucrative championship at the conclusion of his eight events. He can attract more of the better players more regularly because he offers them an extra incentive. He also has two TV specials—with $600,000 in prize money—and a phoney so-called doubles "championship." This is a terribly unfair advantage that never should have been given WCT. I was on the council at the time, but after the decision I started phasing myself out of the political picture and I resigned from the council shortly after.

In response to the Grand Prix's kindness, this is how Hunt pays his colleagues back: he has created two TV tournaments, and he televises these matches so that the tapes often run in opposition to live Grand Prix tournaments. Perhaps just as important, he gluts TV with tennis so that the real Grand Prix tournaments cannot obtain TV contracts. Hunt knows that with his overhead it is impossible for him to make money at the gate or with live TV, so he packages his events for television just to keep the name of WCT up front, to help its ancillary deals. In the process, of course, it greatly harms other Grand Prix events. (I also think he might be using his TV experience as a stepping stone to setting up his own sports network.)

WCT has become primarily a marketing device. Hunt uses his own endorsement ball (made by Spalding) in his tournaments and requires his players to wear WCT-endorsed clothes in his matches, in both cases overriding ATP contracts.

Although he is a large part of the Grand Prix, Hunt does very little to help it or its sponsor, Colgate. In fact, he barely owns up to the Grand Prix's existence. In the eighty-four-page WCT press guide, there are two passing references to the Grand Prix.

Isn't this a fine fellow to have as your partner in the Grand Prix? But of course he gets his way because everybody else in tennis is scared of his money and law suits. As Hunt wrote me in 1976, he had been "advised that the reach of the United States antitrust laws extends beyond the United States itself. . . . United States courts could fashion orders, as they have in other contexts, prohibiting foreign or international bodies from conducting programs not sanctioned by Federal laws and preventing United States residents from participating in such programs, in this country or elsewhere."

As Hunt knows full well, everybody in tennis is especially vulnerable to his threats because we all have so many conflicts. When I was pleading with the Grand Prix not to let Hunt in for 1978, even Dell buckled. "We've got to, Jack," he said. "We're all involved in tournaments of some sort ourselves." Dell's organization runs two in Washington, and a law associate, Ray Benton, puts on one in Denver, and his organization runs the Maskers and the Volvo Games. Donald knew that if his tournaments were included in the Grand Prix but Hunt's weren't, the antitrust implications would be even more obvious and the lawyers' meters would start running.

Hunt is even better off because Riordan did all the dirty work in setting a precedent. The players lost too much money defending in the Connors' suit, so they won't support lawyers again unless they absolutely must. All Hunt has to do is to include the ATP in any suit, and he's got the kids over a barrel. I've proposed that those who care about the game get together and chip in $300,000 so that we have a legal fund to fight these kind of petty suits. I've volunteered to chip in $10,000 myself, but so far, aside from the French, nobody else wants to go along.

Riordan, of course, learned to use the antitrust club before Hunt. Connors has left Riordan; Bill has no tournaments to run and no players to represent. He has to buy tickets now, but the damage he did to the game a few years ago survives him. You got to hand it to Riordan: with far less resources he sort of neutralized the ATP and hurt tennis much more than Hunt has been able to.

Also, Riordan is more difficult to deal with because his motives are never quite so clear. Hunt is a bottom-line guy. Riordan is obsessed. I just never could understand how Bill could be so vindictive. Whatever is going on inside Riordan's head, he is usually a very entertaining fellow. This is hard to believe, but in the middle of his lawsuit against me when the thing had been running for a year or more, when the suit was holding up everything I was trying to accomplish in tennis—in the midst of all this, Bill spots me and a couple of my sons standing in the lobby of the Hotel Commodore in New York during Forest Hills. Bill came over, started chatting pleasantly as if we were the dearest old friends in the world, and then he invited himself to come along to dinner, where he dominated the entire evening's conversation with jokes and stories—and then, of course, he let me pick up the check.

Now how can you fathom a guy like this?

Bill and I originally got along very well. I genuinely admired him as a promoter because he had made a tremendous success of the National Indoors in Salisbury, Maryland, where he ran a dress shop. In the mid-'60s I went down there one year to do the network commentary for the tournament, and Bill asked me to speak to a men's club. He hit me up for a donation, which I gladly gave. I got along fabulously with Riordan. Like me, he was a great racetrack fan too.

In 1970 at the start of the first full year of the Grand Prix, I put together a $50,000 tournament in Los Angeles. Building from the National Indoors, Riordan had begun to put together a small winter circuit, and I attached my L.A. tournament onto this wheel. Bill was a very shrewd guy. He made contact with the Europeans—Nastase would be the prime example—before anyone else in America, and he kept an early eye out for the best new U.S. kids. This led to his association with Connors. Hunt had the big established names, but Riordan could compete against him with the foreigners and the kids. I would have thought he would have been grateful for my support. Soon enough, though, he conspired to fight me.

Sometime after the tournament, he sent me a bill asking me to pay $50 a player—a fee for his "player's association," which was never more than a paper organization. I didn't know what he was talking about; there had never been any such agreement. But Bill called me up, and he was genuinely furious. "Jack, you're welshing on me," he said. From then on it was only a matter of one dispute after another.

The first great argument arose in 1972 when Dell and I worked out the agreement between the ILTF and Hunt, when Lamar gave up his contracts and was granted the first five months of the year to run WCT tournaments. To make this peace, I had to give up my own tournament in L.A. But Riordan assumed the whole deal was aimed just to get him. He could never understand that anybody would do anything for the game itself. He wanted to run his own winter tour, and he wanted to run it absolutely his way. Especially, he wanted to select who would play. We were fighting to make it so that only the best qualified played (and by the way, we have that today).

Then Connors began to move to the top of the sport and Riordan, as his manager, gained leverage. Jimmy, like Bill, also started off as a friend. As a matter of fact, I knew Jimmy's mother, Gloria, before he was born. She was a run-of-the-mill player on the women's amateur circuit. Then when she and her mother brought Jimmy out to Los Angeles from East St. Louis in the late 1960s, I was one of the first people Gloria called. She had gotten a job as a hostess at a place called Nibler's Restaurant, and she urged me to come around and meet her boy and watch him play.

In any event, when all the suits started I never really blamed Jimmy. He was just a kid. I always figured that Riordan was just using him to fight his crusade. Sometimes I wondered if the kid even knew what was going on. All the turmoil seemed to help him get up for matches, anyhow. Previously, the only guy I ever saw play better mad was Gonzales—and he was mad all the time.

Basically the suits revolved around the fact that World Team Tennis had started in 1974, and the French and Italian Opens, which were played during the same time period, barred WTT contract players from their tournaments. The ATP, Dell and I personally and Commercial Union, the Grand Prix sponsor, were brought in the side door as co-defendants. Jimmy had signed to play with a WTT club known as the Baltimore Banners, but he was only required to play a limited number of matches, so he was free to compete in the French. When he was locked out, the litigation began. The fact that he later won Wimbledon and Forest Hills, as he had already won the Australian, certainly gave emotional impetus to his case because it meant that he had been denied his fair chance to win the Grand Slam.

And I'll admit it now: the French and the Italian were wrong to bar Jimmy and all the other WTT players. If the French and Italian wanted to fight WTT, fine—but they should not have used the players as weapons. My whole life, I've fought to open up the game for players, and this one time I got caught on the side that was trying to keep players out. As much as I dislike contract players, they were the lesser of two evils in this case. It was the tournaments that violated the spirit of the Grand Prix.

But I really had nothing to do with the decision, and I don't suppose it matters anyway. Bill was in a suing mood. Whether or not the French and Italian issue existed, he would have found a way to make Donald Dell and me and the ATP support some lawyers in fine style.

The matter was finally settled out of court in August of 1975 after I had countersued Riordan, Connors, and their lawyer for $3,000,000. Connors was going crazy signing depositions, and at last he told Riordan to count him out. The settlement was negligible. The whole thing did nothing but hurt everybody who got involved (except the lawyers, of course). By now the ATP has gotten stronger than ever, and Riordan is suing Connors. And one day, not too long ago, Gloria Connors called me up from St. Louis and asked me to please give her the name of a good antitrust lawyer.

20

Dirt

While the first decade of open tennis has been politically unsettling, it will surely be remembered as an even stranger period upon the courts. Tennis was lawn tennis for most of its history, and for the future it is going to be a hard-surface game. But for this brief period just ending, events conspired to make tennis a slow-clay game.

Traditionally, the sport's three premier events were played upon grass: Wimbledon, Forest Hills and (virtually every year) the Davis Cup Challenge Round. The domination of the U.S.-British-Australian axis was broken by the Musketeers only after all four of them—Lacoste, Cochet, Borotra and Brugnon—set out purposely to learn to play on grass and made a campaign of the effort. Thereafter, and notwithstanding that tennis is the most international of all sports, the game was ruled by the grass-court nations and their players—by Australia and the U.S. exclusively after Fred Perry.

Indeed, the surest evidence of how weak the amateur game had become by the 1960s is found in that various clay-court players succeeded on grass. Rafe Osuna of Mexico won a U.S. Amateur and led his nation past the U.S. into the Challenge Round; Manolo Santana won a U.S. and a Wimbledon; and Nicki Pietrangeli won a Challenge Round singles for Italy in Australia. Good grass-court players simply should never have lost to these kids. It is especially ironic, too, because it should be much easier for a fast-court player to adapt to a slow surface than the other way around.

By the 1970s the dirt kids were coming from everywhere: Kodes, Orantes, Nastase, Panatta, Vilas, Ramirez (I never know where to place Borg), plus even a couple of Americans like Solomon and Dibbs. (In the years just before only Cliff Richey, the son of a Texas pro, had been a real clay specialist.) More important, the focus of the game itself was turning to clay. The Challenge Round was abolished in 1972 so that the defending champion had to play through the competition just like all the other nations, and with that the Davis Cup was opened up for the dirt players. Immediately, the defending nation had a fifty-fifty chance in any year to play the final on their home courts. Since more nations play on clay, the switch was even more emphatic. Then in 1975, Forest Hills' surface was changed into a slow, synthetic clay—brand-name Har-Tru. Even before this radical final transformation, the U.S. summer grass-court circuit had all but disappeared. Grass had become too difficult and expensive to maintain, and besides, as tennis became more popular, the club members became more reluctant to give up their courts to professionals. Instead, most of the tournaments were shifted to public venues. This was great for opening up the game. Usually though, the courts at these facilities were slow surfaces to accommodate the hackers who used them the rest of the year. So in some respects you could say that tennis' popularity pulled it down to a lower common denominator.

Finally, with open tennis, Europe was able to scramble back into the picture. There was prize money, easy jet travel. It made sense for the clay-court players to stay at home, and there was further encouragement for the U.S. and Australians to fly to Europe and shoot for the big purses. The French and

Italian championships, which had seldom been contested by more than a handful of players from off the Continent, broadened their fields and despite competition from World Team Tennis, they became more prestigious.

So in a very short period, grass went from being the main playing surface to a freak one. At one point on behalf of the ATP, Dell and I had to rush over to England and hustle up another grass tournament as a preliminary to Wimbledon, just so that kids would have at least one week and a couple of matches to prepare for the championship (now there are two Wimbledon prelims). At that, some of the top-ranked players in the world gave up all pretense and stopped appearing in Wimbledon. In 1977 many experts ranked Vilas Number 1 in the world even though he went out in the third round at Wimbledon.

At last, in 1978 the pendulum began to swing away from the dirt. My foreign friends have always moaned that American money is going to take over world tennis. For years I've told them that they didn't have to worry about American money, *but* it is the new American surface that is going to change the game. If you want my personal opinion, kids like Dibbs, Solomon and Orantes—and possibly Vilas too—are through as top-tenners and never again will dirt players attain the eminence that they did in the last decade.

A dirt player like Panatta, who is a fine athlete with hard-court tools (although he is a lackadaisical kid on any surface) can survive in the new order. If he works hard enough, he can adjust his style to the hard surfaces. On the other hand, his countryman, Corrado Barrazutti, who got to the semi's of the last U.S. open on Har-Tru, has little chance off the dirt. I can't make my mind up about Vilas. He won the Grand Prix Masters in 1974 in Melbourne, beating both Nastase and Newcombe on the turf. It was the end of the year, and they were a little jaded by play. He beat Connors in a great match on the indoor carpet at the Garden in the Masters of January, 1978. He won the Australian Open in December of 1978. Maybe if he cares enough, he can make it. I am convinced that he will genuinely try and change his style of play.

What I'm positive will happen is that the change of the U.S. Open to a hard surface—brand name Deco Turf II—is going to make clay the minority surface once again. It is not just a matter of our national championship being a hard court. A whole summer circuit of Deco Turf II (or something similar) is bound to spring up. When Forest Hills was grass, so were the lead-in tournaments; when it went to clay, so did the rest of the circuit. It is natural to expect these preliminary tournaments to change again. If not, they're not going to get the players. The U.S. Pro at Longwood proved that in 1978. Prior to that, it was the perfect clay-court prep for the Open. Connors and Borg regularly won it. When the Open surface changed, Longwood didn't, and Connors, Borg and most of the other big names didn't even enter. They took the week off and worked on a fast surface. Gerulitis even put one in his own backyard.

So the whole summer circuit in the U.S. is going to be firm-footed surface play. The grass will remain at Wimbledon and its preliminaries, at least for now. The turf is traditional there, very nearly sacred, but keep in mind that Wimbledon is open to change. It was Wimbledon which forced open tennis on the rest of the world. As early as two or three years before the U.S. Open shifted to Flushing Meadows and concrete, the British told me that they were already examining that possibility for Wimbledon.

Tactically speaking, grass is most similar to concrete, so that is not an overriding issue. Since the indoor surfaces also tend to be fast, the emphasis would be upon fast-surface play almost year-round. Foreign players would begin to pass up the French and Italian, since they would find it ridiculous to learn a whole different style for just a few weeks of play. At that point I think it is quite likely that the Continental nations will give up the ghost and join the rest of the world by constructing hard courts.

There are two other pressures against the clay. First, the

smart women know that it is bad for them (whether or not they are playing Chrissie Evert). As slow as the women's game is on a hard surface, it is a tedious disaster on clay. Nobody wanted to get the U.S. Open out of Forest Hills more than the women. Secondly, clay is a more grueling game. I said earlier that Wimbledon is the easiest major title for a champion to win. Well, without question the French is the most difficult. Every match from the third round on is best-of-five, but with long points. Your stamina as well as your concentration is taxed. The balls are heavy too. Unless you grow up on the dirt and can only win there, no good player and no interested spectator could possibly favor clay courts. For all these reasons, I think it's quite conceivable that by the beginning of the twenty-first century, all major championships in the world will be contested on a fairly uniform hard, concrete-type surface.

I learned to play on a fast court and from early on, I hated the dirt. In a way I feared it too, because while I did not believe that any player should beat me, as soon as I went onto a clay court I often assumed the opposite—that some lesser player could handle me. And this is a ridiculous attitude. I finally learned the right approach, as I did in so many matters, by playing Bobby Riggs.

On our tour we almost always played indoors, but occasionally down South we'd move outdoors on clay. The first two times we met on dirt, he beat me. Certainly I knew by now that I had to change my style on clay: stay back, lob more, wait the other guy out, all that. And that was an easy accommodation. What I couldn't maintain on clay was my patience. I would get mentally tired rallying with some kid I knew I could blow out love and one on grass, so I'd try something, he'd float one past me. I'd be down love–15, I'd try harder, slip and slide some more, love–30, and so on. The frustrating thing about clay courts is not that the surface is slow but that it is so damn slippery. That's what really gets to you if you let it.

The third time I played Riggs on dirt—I believe it was in Montgomery, Alabama—I told myself in advance that I was going to play him at his own game. I was confident by then,

beating him regularly indoors, and I was in good shape.
Besides, I knew he'd been out all night with a dame, too. So I
pushed back at him what he dumped at me. It must have been
hell to watch. it was 2–all after the first forty minutes, and
neither one of us had even tried for a hard shot, much less
made one. Then Bobby got tired of just playing back to a
mirror. First he gave up his steady game and started trying to
come in—no dice. Then he started drop-shotting to try and
bring me in. He ended up here lobbing to my smash—one of
my strongest points. Again, no dice. So then he tried only
hitting extra-soft soft. I just kept my concentration, he threw in
the towel, and I ran through the rest of the two sets in nothing
flat. By the end of my playing career, had you given me a
choice as to where I could play the most important match of
my life, I would have picked the dirt.

It's largely a matter of a leap of faith. Once you make up
your mind that one of these pitty-pat little kids cannot hurt
you, then all that he has going for you is your impatience.
Control that, and the fast-court player will win, because the
fast-court player has more tools. It always burned me up that
grass players were dismissed as serve-and-volley. A clay specialist is a much more limited type. He can only hit defensive
groundstrokes.

The most inexcusable defeat I ever saw—possibly in the
whole history of tennis—came in the Forest Hills final of 1975,
when Connors let Orantes beat him (and in straight sets). This
is when I really began to question Connors' tactical ability.
Sure, Orantes is a clay-court specialist, but even under the best
of circumstances, there is no way he can hurt a kid like
Connors on that surface unless Jimmy beats himself. Moreover, in this case Orantes had two strikes against him. He had
played his amazing comeback semifinal the night before
against Vilas—five sets, lasting well past midnight, and then he
had stayed up till the early hours when he had plumbing
problems in his hotel bathroom. Connors was under the
impression that Orantes hadn't even bothered to leave the
West Side Club. All Jimmy had to do was to keep Orantes

around and wear him out. Hit the ball to him, keep it in play. Instead Connors attacks, he tries difficult shots. He overplays himself right out of the title.

There is no reason why Connors should ever lose on clay because his two major weaknesses—his serve and low volley—are not so crucial on the slower surface. The serve, as Borg showed so conclusively in the '78 Wimbledon, must be improved if Jimmy is going to become a great player on all surfaces. He also needs work on his volley; with balls that come in low, he tends to swing at them, hit them too flat. His forehand approach shot is his greatest liability—he tries to make too many difficult placements off it, and that can hurt him on any surface. I'm still not convinced he has stamina. But he is so talented, he has the best equipment of any player I've ever seen. Jimmy hits the ball as pure as Budge ever did—low to high, with overspin, but with only a small amount of wrist. He obtains power from his whole body, thrusting with his thighs so that he does not put great stress on one single part of his body.

If I played Connors on a fast surface, I would start off with the realization that he had dulled one great strength of mine: I could not serve and come in with abandon. Like Budge, Kovacs, Bromwich, two or three others from my era, Jimmy returns too well. Above all, that is his greatness.

On the other hand, he plays best in a groove. Just as he would force me to change my serve-and-volley pattern, so would I mix up his patterns. I would constantly change the pace of the action, throw in a lot of soft stuff (he tends to overhit, trying to generate his own power when you don't give him speed), try to sucker him into approaching with his forehand, then make him hit low volleys.

On his service return, as great as he hits it, he has a habit of standing too far back—particularly in the forehand court—so I would give him a lot of slice first serves (like Ashe did, when he beat Connors at Wimbledon in '75). In contrast, I would try to serve him tight into his body at other times. Connors likes to work best around the middle of the baseline where he can disguise his shots, which he does well. I'd make the kid hit more angles. I'd try to make him go into the corners. And ultimately, I feel I could beat him on a fast surface because, as great as his service return is, his serve is so average that I could crack it more times than he could break me.

A few years ago, I could have made the same remarks about Borg and his serve. But unlike Connors, Bjorn worked on his serve, and even before his big '78 Wimbledon victory, I could see the improvement. In the year or two before, Borg had begun to develop an altogether new serve for grass, one that is quite different from what he spins in on clay. On grass, he pops his serve, sneaky fast. The same thing is true with his groundstrokes. As formidable as both his forehand and backhand on clay, when he moves to Wimbledon or any hard surface, he cuts his loop, shortens his backswing and follows through with much more extension. Borg has become a different player on grass. He adjusts with the surfaces. He is not afraid to learn and change, and he has earned my complete admiration.

However, despite his three straight Wimbledons and all his other titles, I'm still not sold on the kid for the top rank of all time. I continue to believe that a good serve-and-volley player—say Laver or Newcombe, of a few years ago—could handle him at Centre Court. His volley is improving, but it is still a considerable weakness to be exploited. Budge could have hit with Borg from the backcourt (somewhat like Connors), but Don could have also given him too much on the serve. Players like Sedgman or Gonzales, or myself—we would have poured in on the kid, never let up. Though Borg does continue to adapt, I still believe that he plays too defensively for a fast surface.

There are other factors about Borg that still confuse me. His shots fall so short that I have to believe that his topspin, the ball bouncing so high, must be more difficult to deal with than I ever had to. Of all the players I saw before Borg, from Tilden on, only Rod Laver used excessive topspin, and Borg has much more of an exaggerated loop stroke. I can imagine that Borg's topspin would give me special trouble, bouncing high to my backhand and then at the net, where it would dip low and force me to hit more volleys up. But I never played against a shot quite like Borg's, so I have to reserve that judgment.

Another hard thing to fathom about Borg is that a loss apparently doesn't hurt him. Some champions cry whenever they get beat, but sometimes Borg doesn't even appear to be trying. My own feeling is that part of the problem is that he became a real phenomenon when he was only fifteen. For about three years he played too much tennis, and when he wasn't feeling particularly up to it he just folded up, taking the attitude of what the hell, it's a small event; who cares?

Sometimes I think his agents still overplay him. For example, consider his schedule in September of 1978. Through the tenth he played at Flushing, losing the final to Connors. Then off to Hungary for a Davis Cup match on the fifteenth, sixteenth and seventeenth; a trip to Argentina for a four-man exhibition the twenty-second, twenty-third and twenty-fourth; on to San Francisco for the Trans-America tournament that was scheduled to end on Monday, October 2, just in time to fly to Sweden to play Davis Cup against the United States starting October 6.

I was having dinner in San Francisco early in the tournament. Somebody who knew tennis very well offered to bet Barry MacKay, who was promoting the tournament, that Borg would be out of the tournament by the weekend. Sure enough, Borg lost on Friday night to Andy Pattison in what was proclaimed as a major upset. Was it really?

Borg is hard to figure out. His rackets are incredible. He and Lennart Bergelin, his coach, swear that they are strung at eighty pounds of pressure (an average tension is around sixty pounds), but I just can't believe that any wooden racket would survive against more than seventy pounds. The only other top player I ever knew who was so concerned with a tight stringing was Hoad (and Riggs indoors). Lew wanted freshly strung rackets every morning. Why this one thing took his interest, I'll never know. Myself, I never cared that much about how precisely my racket was strung except if it were strung board tight; I couldn't take that. What I cared about was having the right grip. Laver was a sculptor at that, shaving millimeters here and there off his grip. Kovacs was the other extreme. Sometimes he'd play with a large grip, sometimes very small. With grips and tension, it's probably mostly a case of what you think must be important. You learn that by trial and error.

In any event, if Borg gains acceptance as a great player for all time, he will surely not be remembered for any one particular shot but for his topspin. Some of the best players are known primarily for a style—Cochet hit everything "on the rise," I had the "big game"—but most players are remembered specifically for their one outstanding shot. In nearly a half-century of watching and playing the best, here is how I would rank the best shots:

FIRST SERVE—Vines had the finest serve I ever saw, but Gonzales, the great competitor, was more consistent with his in the tightest spots. Tilden, too, must be ranked, for speed and deception.

SECOND SERVE—Newcombe by far. Then Vines, von Cramm and Gonzales.

FOREHAND—Segura was best, then Perry, followed by Tilden and Vines (although I never saw Big Bill's till he was in his forties). Of the moderns, Nastase's forehand is a superb one, especially on the run.

BACKHAND—Budge was best, with Kovacs, Rosewall and Connors in the next rank (although, as I've said, Connors' "backhand" is really a two-handed forehand). Just in passing, the strangest competitive stroke was the backhand that belonged to Budge Patty. It was a weak shot, a little chip. But suddenly on match point, Patty had a fine, firm backhand. He was a helluva match player.

RETURNS OF SERVE—Budge first, then Connors; Bromwich for doubles.

FOREHAND VOLLEY—Wilmer Allison of Texas, who won

295

the 1935 Forest Hills, had the best I ever saw as a kid, and I've never seen anyone since hit one better. Budge Patty came closest, then Newcombe.

BACKHAND VOLLEY—Close among Budge, Sedgman and Rosewall, with Sedgman getting the edge probably because of his quickness. Schroeder and Trabert were almost as outstanding.

OVERHEAD—Schroeder just tops here, ahead of Vines, Rosewall and Newcombe.

LOB—Riggs, of course. But Segura, Bitsy Grant and Rosewall were almost as effective. Connors is coming on strong.

HALF-VOLLEY—Gonzales and Rosewall. Kenny had to learn to hit a half-volley because his serve was so weak that he had to pick up shots at his feet as he came to the net. With his great serve, I don't know why Gorgo had to hit so many half-volleys, but he sure learned how.

21

Superstars and Socialists

If tennis could survive decades under the tyranny of the amateur officials, it should now be able to succeed despite the greed of the players. I fought all my life for players; I was one, and I hate to say anything against them. But they're the ones with the whiphand now, and sometimes I think they act every bit as irresponsibly toward the game as the old amateur officials used to.

The trouble with the players is that they're pulling in two directions. The big stars and their agents want to free-lance like movie stars, and the average players want socialism, a welfare tennis state. Neither bunch seems to care much for the game that is caught in the middle.

We blew it that time a few years ago when we had the brightest kids—Ashe, Smith, Drysdale, Newcombe—not only at the top of the sport but leading the players as well. If the national organizations could have worked with us then, instead of fighting us as they did in the Pilic-Wimbledon mess, we could have worked out a lasting fair deal for everybody. But we missed taking advantage of that moment. Now unfortunately, most of the biggest names in the game don't give a damn for anything but top dollar for themselves.

The star players have more power than ever, but they only use it for their own benefit. This costs the ATP leverage. Right now, I would say there are only two male super-stars, Borg and Connors. Despite the fact that Borg has won three straight Wimbledons, Jimmy probably remains the top draw because he is so controversial and unpredictable. Ashe and Newcombe retain a certain appeal; they're attractive and becoming sort of nostalgic, like Rosewall. All three can help a gate, but none are reliable enough as players to really promote. Nastase has slumped as a player since he passed thirty and started losing some of his quickness, and he's now much less a drawing card. The same can be said of Vilas since he stopped dominating tournaments on the dirt; Stan Smith was a great draw who lost his attraction. Vitas Gerulitis gets a lot of off-court publicity, but he doesn't sell many tickets, and that secondary American group of Stockton, Gottfried, Tanner, Solomon, Dibbs, and Mayer have no individual drawing power. Except perhaps in their own country, neither do kids like Orantes, Ramirez, Panatta or Fibak. John McEnroe is the one kid who does look like he will make it soon.

The point is, no matter how much sports become show biz, people want to see winners. Chris Evert may be dull as a player, but she's the best, and she is still the one woman fans will pay to see—though Tracy Austin and Pam Shriver may soon be genuine gate attractions. Men's tennis has a lot of stars, but the power belongs to Connors and Borg. If they cared as much for their game as Palmer or Nicklaus do for golf, it wouldn't take long to put tennis' house in order. But so far the top guys have shown no such interest or obligation. Connors has never joined the ATP, and I think this example made it easier for Vilas to drop out (when Tiriac took him over) and for Gerulitis also to refuse to join. Now McEnroe has turned pro and failed to sign up. Except for a handful of players from the hard-line Communist countries who are forbidden to join, ATP has virtually every tournament player in the world except for the ones mentioned above. Borg has always been a member, but he is generally apathetic to tennis issues beyond those that can be settled on the court. Sometimes we forget how young he is, and perhaps he will exert himself as he grows older.

One thing you can say for Borg is that, young as he is, he appears to exercise control over his own independence in ways that Connors and Vilas do not. Jimmy has always been so dependent upon his mother, and Vilas does precisely what Tiriac tells him to do. Lennert Bergelin, Borg's coach, appears to be more of a father figure to Bjorn. He coaches him, he handles detail, he provides company. But he doesn't order the kid about. Of course, Bud Stanner of the McCormack organization gives him a heavy exhibition schedule.

For now then, all the top players do pretty much as they please. For example, Connors often defaults, claiming injuries at the last minute. In the last few years he has pulled out of more than a dozen tournaments. He passed up playing in the Grand Prix masters three years, once choosing to play a mixed-doubles event instead. When Vilas and Borg realized that a round-robin defeat in the '77 Masters could not keep them out of the semifinals, they both feigned injury and pulled out, leaving 18,000 fans cheated. That was obscene. Of course they were both healed the next day, in time for matches that counted. Let me tell you: a guy like Gonzales took a lot of heat through the years for generally not cooperating. He sure wasn't any prince. But if he were committed to play, Gorgo would play. He'd scream at me until he was due on court, but then he'd go out there and play his guts out. He knew that a professional's first obligation is to the public that buys the tickets and pays his bills. But our modern hot-shots don't believe in those priorities.

At the other extreme are the kids who are just making it in the game. They've become a strong lobby. Let's face it, there must be a whole lot more losers than winners. In a thirty-two-man draw, only 25 percent of the players make it to the quarter finals; in a major championship, barely 6 percent. And it helps a sport to have good depth. The women have suffered because the early rounds have been so lopsided. But that is no reason for pro tennis to subsidize losers, and that is exactly what has been developing.

The players—the losers—are trying to dilute the sport. They want more tournaments scheduled and more money allotted to the losers. In golf, a player can work for two days—half the tournament—miss the cut by a stroke, and he doesn't make a penny. Then he's got to hustle to the next tournament site, practice and qualify. In tennis every first-round loser is guaranteed a payoff. This keeps a bunch of has-beens hanging on, denying fresh faces a chance to get into the draws. I'm not saying that all the prize money should go to the winner or the four semifinalists. All you would have to do is take away first-round loser money and give that to the second-round losers. Make a guy win one match before he gets paid. Just that and it would clear out a lot of flotsam, retire some guys early.

Originally the agitation to reward losers came largely from the European players, who had been brought up in a more socialized environment. Now in the U.S., with athletes in all sports demanding no-cut contracts, this feeling is more widespread.

Golf has one major advantage over tennis in that it can accommodate more players at a single venue. Tennis can't possibly play more than sixty-four at any one site in a week, and so it is only fair to add an extra, smaller tournament to the circuit every week. But two a week is enough. If all the losers in the ATP had their way, we'd have a dozen tournaments every week so everybody would be seeded somewhere. The trouble is, the big names make your gate, and there are only so many of them. If a promoter is putting on a $175,000 Grand Prix event, and he finds out that four members of the top ten are taking the week off, two more are playing exhibitions, three others have been spread around to smaller tournaments, all of a sudden he's left with one top-tenner in his tournament—he feels cheated and he's right. His crowds will be down, he can't get TV coverage, the sponsor is disappointed, and the next

300

year he pulls out and the players have lost a tournament.

And who's the big loser? Connors, Borg? Hell no, they can pick up a week's worth of exhibitions for twice what they could make working their tails off to win a real tournament. The ones who get hurt are the losers whose short-sightedness diluted the tournament fields in the first place.

In tournament golf there is a concept known as the designated tournament. Every player must play in these tournaments or suffer major consequences. In 1978, for example, a tournament at Philadelphia was designated the week after the British Open, and Jack Nicklaus had to fly back after winning at St. Andrews to play in Philadelphia in the middle of the summer. Of course it isn't what Nicklaus wanted, but it was great for golf. We had always been afraid to consider a designated-type rule in tennis, because Riordan had put us on the antitrust defensive and we were afraid that one of our great stars might sue.

However, in the fall of 1978, meeting in Tokyo the nine-man International Council—three players, three tournament directors, three national federation representatives—decided to go ahead and take the chance. Beginning with 1979, each player who wants to participate in Grand Prix tournaments must agree to play six designated tournaments. Every effort will be made to give the player the tournaments that he would prefer and that fit into his schedule, but invariably sometimes the pro is going to have to play at a time and place he doesn't care to. But if he doesn't accept designation, then the Grand Prix won't accept him into their tournaments—most particularly meaning Wimbledon and Forest Hills. Maybe a star will refuse to go along and will sue the Council. Okay, tennis believes that this new system meets the legal tests of fair play and is ready to stand up for it. I think it's a terrific advance for the game.

My view has always been that tennis does not owe a player a living. We ought to be able to ask for something back, and if a kid's not in the top fifty or sixty in the world, then he's lucky just to be around and certainly doesn't deserve a voice in running things. The trouble is that the people running the

ATP, which is so powerful in the sport today, are forced to think like politicians. They're supporting policies that please the most members rather than fans. In a sport that must have more losers than winners, it pays to go after loser votes with loser policy.

One weekly ideal format that I've suggested (without any success so far) would be to play two equal tournaments each week, each with forty-eight players. (Generally, what we have now is one major tournament with a sixty-four draw, and one or two additional thirty-two draw tournaments.) With my forty-eight plan, sixteen players would be seeded and given a bye in the first round.

This system would make playing tournaments more appealing to the best players, the gate attractions. When they play a sixty-four draw tournament today, that means six matches for any player who makes the finals—plus possibly another three or four in doubles. With a bye, the stars would get an extra day off and play one less match.

This system also has advantages for the lesser players because it means they are guaranteed not to meet a seeded player in the first round. Not bad. Everybody has a better chance. But the socialists in the ATP scream that it isn't fair for the best players to have a bye. Why? Didn't they earn that bye by winning in the past? Isn't it better for all the players to encourage the big names to play more tournaments? And then, if we threw out first-round losers' prize money, we would really increase incentive.

A second plan for the tennis year appeals to me even more. With this system about thirty-six or thirty-seven weeks would be set aside for the circuit, leaving fifteen or sixteen weeks free for Davis Cup, exhibitions (unfortunately, they're still with us) and other specials. Then the circuit would be divided into three tiers.

The top level would play for weekly prize money of $150,000 to $250,000. It would have a thirty-two-man draw and come from the top forty on the computer. Each week, two spots in this first level would be saved for the finalists of the

302

week before on the second-level circuit. There, prize money would be in the $50,000-$100,000 range, with players coming from about forty-one to eighty-five on the computer. A third plateau tournament would offer prize money from $35,000 up—with the finalists moving up to the second level just as the second echelon finalists move up to the top rank.

The great advantage of this system is that the top money would get the top players; and at all levels, players would be competing against opponents of their caliber. A kid number ninety-seven on the computer would not have to worry about drawing a top-tenner and getting eliminated in the first round. The worst he could expect, playing the third plateau, would be number eighty-six. The player truly capable of improving his game would have the chance to do that since he would be playing against opponents of relative ability.

A prospect like McEnroe would, to be sure, have to start in the third group, but it would not take him long to work his way to the top. On the other hand, an older player who started to slip and who suddenly found himself bumped out of the "majors," the top echelon, would have to decide whether he wanted to go down to the second level and play for lesser purses or whether he should find a permanent job off the tour.

I would love to see this system tried.

In any event the players better soon start approving the changes that the tournaments and officials want, or the kids are going to wake up one morning and find they've lost all control. Right now the tournament directors particularly have had it. Philippe Chatrier feels that the national associations must be given back much of the power that was taken from them with open tennis, but I'm afraid that I just don't think that's feasible. First of all, there remains too much ill feeling from the past. When the national associations were running things, all of the players and most of the tournament directors hated them. Memories are not that short. Secondly, I can't imagine how the national associations could establish jurisdiction over the players today.

The players have the control they always wanted, and the

303

only simple alternative is chaos. The kids have got to be more responsible themselves. They all bitch about the Davis Cup, about how the schedule is too protracted, the officials too arbitrary. So in 1975 I worked my tail off to come up with another international competition known as the Nations Cup. It was just what they had been screaming for—only the best nations qualified off the ATP computer to play each other at one site in a short period of time. Moreover, if the Nations Cup worked, it would apply pressure upon the Davis Cup to change its format. So what happened? The players talked about supporting the ATP's team competition, but when the time came most went and played exhibitions instead. As usual a few guys showed class and loyalty—Ashe, Tanner, Ramirez, Fillol. Of the seven teams that qualified by virtue of their perfor-mance (we permitted a "home team" wild card from the Caribbean as the eighth), only two—the U.S. and Australia—even showed. We had to go down the list to the number seventeen country before we could even come up with seven teams to play.

Stories like this are legion. These guys have dumped on too many sponsors and too many good fans. What really worries me is that the older generation of players—Ashe, Rosewall, Laver, Smith, that crowd—the ones who knew what bad times really were, will soon be gone from the game. Without their influence, the attitude may grow worse. It is the younger players, the ones who never knew what it was like to hustle for "expenses," who have been the most selfish. I also sound too chauvinistic to say this, but I can't help it: basically the foreign players have not shouldered the burden the way the American kids have. There have been exceptions, like Drysdale and Newcombe (though I have my reservations about some of their motives), and Fillol (the current ATP president, who has played such a large role in encouraging the non-English speaking players to get involved in player affairs). But most of the foreigners have been very reluctant to exert themselves.

But just as Americans have stood up most in tennis, so have we hurt the game the most with the antics of people like

Riordan and Hunt. And one of our great strengths is that we are such an international sport. People in golf make such a fuss over Gary Player, who plays a worldwide schedule. Tennis has fifty Gary Players.

We should divide the tennis year up in a geographical way that is more sensible, and that builds on our international quality. I think there should be about ten or twelve segments, with a super event concluding each one. To take an obvious existing case, Wimbledon would be the super event following Wimbledon Circuit events at Queens and Nottingham. Or there might be a super event in Tokyo following three weeks of qualifying events in Hong Kong, Manila and Osaka. To get into the super, a kid would have to score a certain number of qualifying points in the preliminaries.

Players should be obliged to enter these circuits two or three months in advance, which would give the promoters the ample time they don't have now to find out what big names they'll have and to promote them. (Now a player needs give only forty-two days notice, which is not enough). I also think that players should be required to play a minimum of twenty tournament weeks a year.

But don't misunderstand me. Despite all my criticism, I'm excited about the future of tennis. We have worldwide appeal, our stars are international celebrities, the players have a major voice in the game, we grow every year. Talk about soccer or any other sport—tennis is *the* world game because people everywhere of both sexes and all ages play it. I'm very anxious to see it become an Olympic sport again too. No doubt if that happens, the "amateurs" of the Communist countries will have the best chance at the medals, but even despite this exploitation, I'm for Olympic tennis on balance.

There are a lot of countries which will not designate federal funds for sports that are not in the Olympics. Even a nation like East Germany, which emphasizes sports as much as any in the world, puts virtually nothing into tennis. I'm convinced that the instant tennis becomes an Olympic sport, tennis will be emphasized even more—and in those few places still left in the world where it obtains the least attention. No doubt the U.S. will have to field a squad of college kids against mature East European subsidized players, but we'll still do okay. If collegians had an Olympics to point to every four years, it might serve to keep a few of them in college a year or too longer, and that could only help NCAA tennis. It might also help some of these kids who turn pro too soon for their own good.

I also have a selfish reason for wanting Olympic tennis. My one great personal dream is to see a magnificent tennis center built in Los Angeles. Here is the richest part of the world—in money and in sport—and it is ridiculous that we've never had any sort of public tennis facility. If tennis is included on the agenda of the Los Angeles Olympics in 1984, I'm sure we will have the thrust to get this center constructed.

The standardization of tennis' surface to the concrete type, which I'm sure will come to pass in the next decade or so, is bound to have a profound favorable effect upon the game. Variety is good for a sport but the range of difference in tennis has been too great. I always knew something was intrinsically wrong with the game when I could beat some kid from the Continent love, love and one at Wimbledon—but realize that if we same two guys played the next day a hundred miles away across the channel, I'd be fighting him tooth and nail and would be fifty-fifty to lose. That's too big a swing. When Orantes beat Connors on the dirt at Forest Hills in '75 and then signed to play a TV rematch on the fast carpet at Caesar's Palace in Las Vegas, it bordered on fraud, because most of the public assumed that Orantes and Connors would both have legitimate chances. But the differences in the two surfaces were such that—as anybody in the game knew—Orantes was being paid a quarter of a million dollars to lose. That was a greater deceit than all the winner-take-all semantics.

The Deco Turf II surface that was employed at the new tennis center in Flushing Meadows in 1978 came under a lot of predictable criticism from slow-court specialists who called it too fast. (A standard surface would stop players from always complaining about surfaces.) In fact, the Flushing surface wasn't even as fast as the California concrete I learned on. Flushing has more bite to it, which is good, because it neutralizes the slick bounces and forces a player to be adept at both offense and defense. This is one thing both Connors and Borg have already done for the game, too. One may be controversial and the other bland, but both have shown young players that you must be accomplished at both ends of the court to win today.

The new surface will emphasize this even more. Sure it'll be much faster than the dirt guys would like, but it won't be nearly as fast as grass. Never again will a kid like Johnny Doeg or Neale Fraser be able to win a major tournament with a big serve and little else. On grass, the best shot to attack with is an underslice that skids, but on the concrete that kind of ball sits up much more and offers a better return. By the same token, concrete will provide the firmest footing of any surface and that will encourage players to take more chances. The problem with clay is not just that it is slow but that it is slippery, so this inhibits a player mentally; grass can be too slick. But concrete is solid, an athlete doesn't have to worry about falling, and so he can go all out more. Concrete is going to make for a more exciting all-court game. Watch.

With the big money and a single prime surface, tennis is going to attract those better athletes we used to lose to other sports. And you might as well get used to the two-hand shots, because more and more kids are going to start playing the game young when they need both hands on the racket to manipulate it. I'm afraid that the majority of public recreation officials in the country haven't caught on to the value of tennis as exercise and its growing popularity. That will come; more and more municipal tennis facilities are going to be built.

People are always asking Arthur Ashe why there aren't more blacks in tennis. Go to a black neighborhood and see how many tennis courts there are, and you can answer the question for yourself. It is more a question of why there aren't more inner-city kids of any race in tennis. Tennis remains largely a middle-class game.

But the democratization of tennis has come a long way in a short time. Build the courts, and the process will be complete. Basketball and tennis are very much alike. They require a relatively small space to play on, and the players' movements in the two games is quite similar—emphasizing quickness and change of direction.

And speaking of basketball, I'm sure you can expect to see taller tennis players excelling in the future. With all the slipping on the dirt, the big man was disadvantaged. But tennis has traditionally been a sport for six-footers: Maurice McLaughlin, Big Bill, Vines, Budge, myself, Gonzales, Trabert. Concrete will encourage the big man's power and leverage as much as the little guy's stability. Tennis is a sport for all-sized people, so there will always be some good little kids, but I'll know tennis has really made it to the very top when we develop a champion from the inner city who's six-foot-five and moves like Rosewall with a serve like Vines.

The next fifty years is really going to be something. I'll buy tickets to get in.

Index